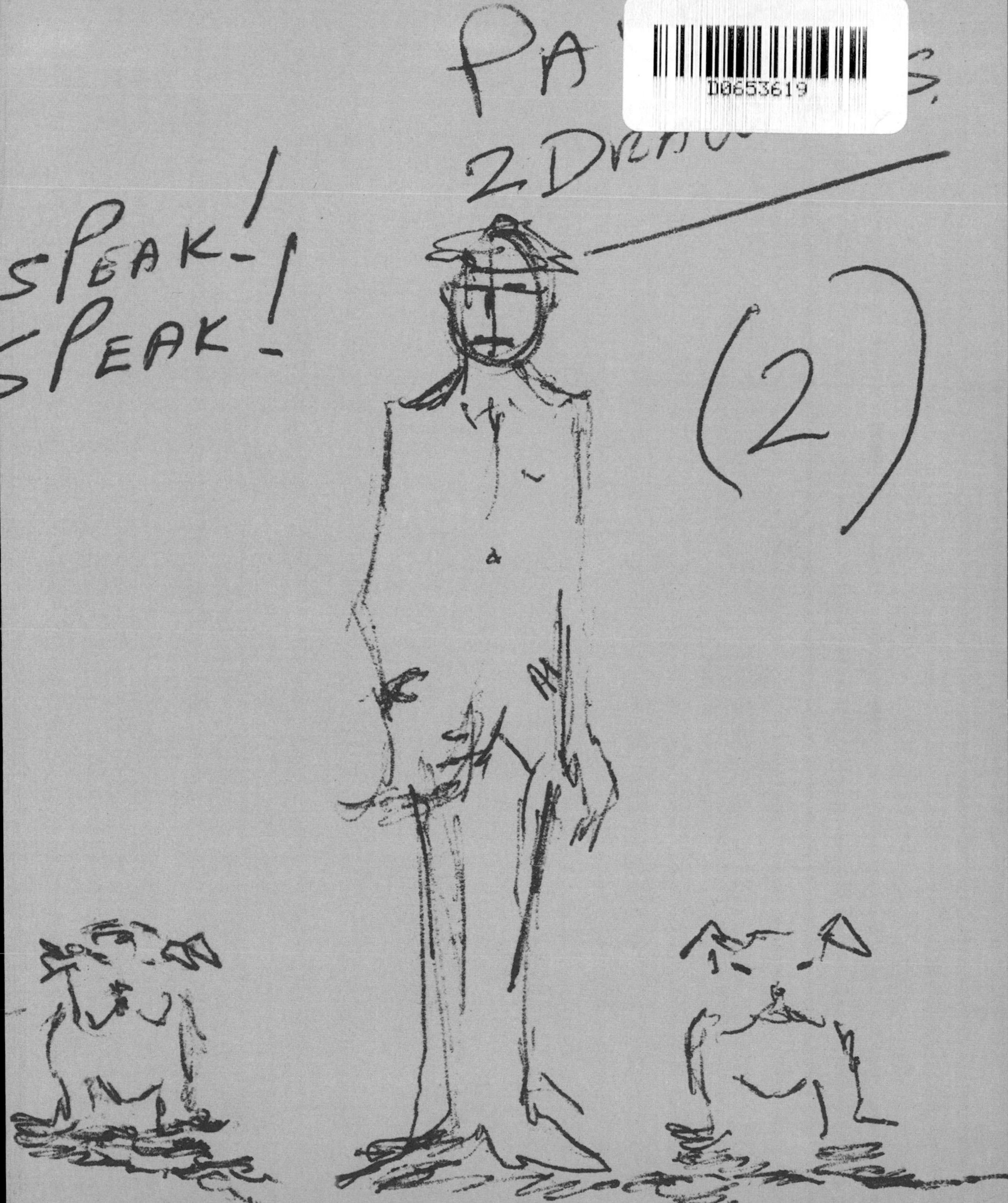
SPEAK!
SPEAK!
(2)

"Just Daft"

THE CHIC MURRAY STORY

"Just Daft"

THE CHIC MURRAY STORY

Robbie Grigor

Foreword by Billy Connolly

BIRLINN

First published in 2008 by
Birlinn Limited
West Newington House
10 Newington Road
Edinburgh
EH9 1QS

www.birlinn.co.uk

2

ISBN13: 978 1 84158 755 4
ISBN10: 1 84158 755 9

British Library Cataloguing-in-Publication Data
A catalogue record for this book is available
from the British Library

Designed and typeset by Mark Blackadder

The endpapers show Chic Murray's original
outline for The Battersea Dog (see 'The Door', p. 136)

Printed and bound by MPG Books Ltd, Cornwall

CONTENTS

AUTHOR'S NOTE

It's naughty to start with a negative; nonetheless, this book does not set out to cover the artiste's life in blow-by-blow detail. Nor does it wish to highlight the undoubted moments of sadness that every great clown confronts in his life. Its principal purpose is to pay tribute to the memory of an outstanding and original comedic craftsman and to remind us of a remarkable man who left a legacy of gold-embossed memories of helpless laughter and intense happiness. His stunning sense of humour, his immaculate sense of timing, his originality, his delivery and so much more, led to communal hilarity where every eye cast salty water. This book, then, with the help of Chic's family, sets out – wherever possible – to be a happy one!

There is a profound irony that, towards the end of Chic's life, he brilliantly represented the larger-than-life Liverpool legend, Bill Shankly, onstage in *You'll Never Walk Alone*. (The family still possess 'Shanks's' training jersey given to Chic by his widow.) Those who hadn't noticed his presence on a surprise visit to the changing rooms at Liverpool FC, on hearing his voice, believed that 'Shanks' was back from the dead – testimony to his underestimated dramatic capabilities. Herein lies the irony. Chic was elevated to the same status as the man he so convincingly purported to be. It had undeniably come to pass, wheeling out an overused and abused cliché, that Chic, too, was a legend in his own lifetime.

Imitation, the saying goes, is the sincerest form of flattery. Chic should have been flattened by flattery then, because no one was imitated more than himself! No one. And today, nearly a quarter of a century on since his passing, they still do. Think of the countless friends you know who have attempted a Chic Murray impression. Count on the fingers of one hand, those

who have not! Even Billy Connolly, now an icon himself, is 'so comfortable onstage that he will even interrupt the end of a very strong – but very long – anecdote about visiting his father in a stroke ward to tell a slew of old Chic Murray jokes that have just sprung to mind.' (A review of Billy Connolly at the Symphony Hall, Birmingham, *The Times*, 11 September 2007.)

And as an illustration of the above comments, there is a sketch in the *Pink Panther* series, where Clouseau obsequiously approaches a stranger to inquire: 'Does your doggie bite?'

'No,' comes the reply under heavy-lidded eyes.

Clouseau then pats the dog's head as it turns on him, snapping, yapping. 'But you said your doggie doesn't bite!' Clouseau whines, clutching his freshly bitten hand.

'But that's not my doggie!' comes the indifferent reply.

This sketch was purloined from Chic's repertoire, devised over fifteen years earlier. It's all there in his notes.

The invaluable contributions and the boundless enthusiasm and energy of Chic's family, his former wife, the irrepressible Maidie – 'aren't you glad you met me?' – and their two children, Douglas and Annabelle, make this compilation unique. They were appointed sole executors of their father's estate, including the intellectual property of his life's work contained in notebooks, exercise books, wee scraps of paper of laugh-out-loud comic material, and even witty caricatures and cartoon illustrations all in his own hand. (His calligraphy sometimes would have challenged those who cracked the Enigma code but, in fairness, they were for his use, not intended for publication.) With the first publication of many of his creative musings, it follows, then, in the unique gift that was Chic Murray, that this book becomes unique too.

A final word on Billy Connolly who, with his characteristic generosity of spirit, agreed to write the foreword. Everyone associated with this book owes him a huge debt of gratitude and I hope he finds new inspiration from its pages. But Chic's family remember Billy for other reasons. He was a rock at Chic's funeral, where he offered to pay his own unique tribute to a lost friend and, one year on, he demonstrated his kindness yet again when he interrupted a busy schedule to escort Chic's daughter Annabelle up the aisle on the occasion of her marriage. Nice one, Billy, and thanks.

To all
Chic Murray aficionados,
past present and future

The author gratefully acknowledges
the unrestricted access to Chic's
papers, jottings, musings and
'funnyosities' granted by his family:
Maidie, Douglas and Annabelle.
Their invaluable assistance made
this book a reality.

FOREWORD

I have a photograph at home of Chic Murray standing at the gates of Annfield Stadium in Liverpool. It was taken while he was playing the part of Bill Shankly, the legendary Scots manager of Liverpool, in a play about his life. For me, the greatest thing about the picture is the fancy ironwork lettering above the gate spelling out the Liverpool legend, 'You'll Never Walk Alone'. The reason that I place such importance on it is that in this case it is a complete fabrication. If ever a man walked alone, that man was Chic Murray.

I first came across him when I was a teenager in Glasgow. I had heard him from time to time on the radio, although his appearances were quite rare; broadcasters seemed to be a bit wary of him, he wasn't like the others, his style was different, his timing was different, his subject matter was different, his appearance, his demeanour was different; 'He yodels for God's sake!' He walked alone.

I remember so well, sitting in the house of my friend, Billy McKinnell, watching Chic on television. It was one of the very few times that I actually fell down with laughter, although in my case I think I actually fell up and then down, due to the arm of the couch, as I completely lost control of myself in blissful ecstasy. I was sitting on Billy's mother's beautiful new couch, pressed up against the arm, as Chic went into a routine about two friends who were emigrating, I think to Canada, but it doesn't really matter. The guy's surnames were Semmit and Drawers (Undervest and Underpants). I can't remember if they had Christian names or not, that has all been abandoned to the fog of the past. What I do remember though is laughing heartily through the sketch with Billy and his mother, until close to the end of the piece, where Mr Drawers is giving his son, young

Drawers, some stalwart advice which is supposed to stand him in good stead in the colonies as he sets off on his intrepid journey overseas. The part that nailed me, and had me over the arm of the couch onto the floor in a helpless heap, was when old Drawers, in as sincere a tone as he can manage, says to young Drawers, 'Never let the Drawers down!' That was where I took off like a rocket, over the furniture and onto the floor. Billy was laughing, his mother was laughing, and I was trying to breathe. I had just been blessed by the elegant touch of a true comedy genius.

As the years rolled by I became a comedian myself, but saw little of Chic as we worked in different fields. He seemed to concentrate on films and corporate-style entertainment, while I was doing the clubs and concert halls. Inevitably, our paths crossed in Glasgow, at the BBC club, where we were introduced by a mutual friend, Robin Hall, the folk singer. Chic proceeded straight away to tell me about a trip he had taken to see his favourite football team, Morton FC of Greenock, who weren't doing very well at the time. The game was played in the midddle of a drizzle storm, if there is such a thing. It was really just a series of observations of people at the match, beautiful observations, unequalled by anyone I had seen or heard. The whole hilarious thing ended with a description of a miserable sodden supporter, holding a crying, soiled and somewhat ugly child in his arms. The miserable snot-covered child is bawling in the man's ear, the drizzle is cascading down his neck, and he is recalling the nagging of his wife, which happened just before the game, and resulted in him being bullied into taking the child with him (all of these parts acted out by Chic) when the opposition break away yet again and score a seventh goal against a hapless and mud-covered Morton, whereupon the poor soul raises his weary head and comes out with the legend, 'Come on, Morton, stop the kidding.' I was completely poleaxed, the exact feeling of that night on Billy's mother's couch.

I was lucky enough to be able to regard myself as his friend, although he never stopped being my hero. Like a lot of funny men, he was blessed with a funny appearance: broad at the top, narrow at the bottom. He had a peculiar and funny walk, with his hands almost parallel with the floor, and a face, a beautiful, jovial, round Halloween-cake face, which never failed to make

me smile. I find myself talking about him on stage sometimes, recalling his stories and feeling great as people laugh again at his genius. His popularity shows no sign of diminishing, whether he is alive or not. I have never known a more loved figure, the mere mention of whose name makes people smile, laugh, or glaze over in reminiscence of great and happy times.

For a man who walked alone, my hero sure attracted a crowd.

Billy Connolly

CHAPTER 1
GREENOCKIANS

Greenock is not a 'new town' in the conventional sense but it is a township of comparatively modern origins. Made a burgh in 1635, its foremost natural advantage was its bay. This brought modest prosperity through the herring industry, though even by 1701 the population was still a measly 746. Some years on, boat building, for an expanding fishing trade, became a significant marker that was to lay the foundation for the growth of shipbuilding and associated industries in the area. More than a hundred years on, in the nineteenth century, there was a sad exodus from the Highlands of Scotland, a drift to the south, or over the Atlantic, or to Australia and beyond. They clutched each other for warmth and reassurance in their sad, white-sailed boats which they knew would never return. Meanwhile London toffs in their recently acquired tartans danced Highland reels and strathspeys in the hunting lodges that had mushroomed across the Highlands, unmindful and uncaring of those who had husbanded the land for generations before the sheep or the stag-stalker. Many of those who chose to stay within their national boundaries headed to the west coast, including Greenock, in search of work as labourers, fishermen and sailors. Indeed, even by 1801, when Greenock's population had escalated to 17,450, it was estimated that three-quarters of the town's population were native-born Highlanders – and the great majority from Argyll. So there is a strong likelihood that, with his parents bearing the names of Murray and McKinnon, Chic's roots lay in a northerly direction from his place of birth. Greenock's prosperity grew with sugar refining, shipbuilding, potteries, tanneries, paper mills and more besides. But this dynamic had its downside in overcrowding, substandard housing and a record of poor health amongst the citizenry. And the first limited efforts at

And here's an important newsflash that's just been handed to me for people who live in and around Port Glasgow. It reads, 'Hard luck!'

When I was a baby, my mother would pop me in the bath to make sure it was cool enough for her elbow.

slum clearance and the construction of housing by the local authority in 1919 coincided with another event that year – the birth of Chic Murray.

Although born in Stranraer, William Irvine Murray, Chic's father, was a 'Greenockian' for most of his life (a curious mouthful, pronounced to rhyme with 'see Jock again'!). Before the First World War, William was foreman with the Glasgow & South Western Railway. He was, by all accounts, a thoroughly decent, well-respected man who was about to confront two major life-changing events. Along with the majority of his brave comrades who enlisted on the outbreak of war, he believed that hostilities would cease within the year. However, before he was sent to the Western Front, he had fallen in love and had become engaged to a bonnie, exceptionally gifted woman named Isabella McKinnon. Soon after, at the bloodbath Battle of the Somme in 1916, he was hellishly badly gassed and the consequent damage to his lungs was to leave him partially disabled, poor soul, for the rest of his shortened life.

The wedding of Chic's parents, William Murray (top right) and Isabella McKinnon (bottom right), 19 April 1917

He returned home, but it was a year after he had made a limited recovery before he could recommence his employment and, more importantly, marry his sweetheart. During these days of hardship he was, in relative terms, more comfortable than most, having his own apartment in Bank Street and a job to return to; this was a time in Greenock of disillusion, depression and privation. It was during these leaden-skied days, when there was still no realistic hope of economic recovery, that William and Isabella had their first and only son, Charles Thomas McKinnon Murray. Born on 6 November 1919, Chic always maintained that the town's annual so-called Guy Fawkes celebrations were in fact instituted to commemorate his birth and that the Greenockian registrar of births and deaths had been drunk and had mistakenly entered his date of birth as the 6th instead of the 5th. 'They've just dreamed up these blethers about Guy Fawkes,' he would say. 'Pah! Blowing up Parliament, indeed! What will they think of next?'

Despite his infirmity, William became involved in evangelism, helping to form and establish the Burning Bush Society in his home town. With his own war-inflicted disability and having witnessed dreadful suffering and human carnage at the Front, perhaps this was an understandable step to take and Chic (an abbreviation of Charles and McKinnon, coined by his mother), at the tender age of seven, was asked by his dad to play the organ at the Society's meetings. From his earliest years, this boy was a gifted musician and his sense of timing and of rhythm was to contribute hugely in times to come, as he honed his exceptional skills as a comedian. But that was still a long way off. These modest gospel meetings were something of a watershed for Chic because they marked his very first perform-ances in public, revealing a born-natural entertainer. He would bang out a medley of gospel songs, but only after a rendition of 'We are the members of the Burning Bush Society'. At every meeting, of course, there was a collection during which Chic would play 'John Brown's Body' but with a twist to the lyrics: they reprised, 'When the plate is passed around / Don't forget your half a crown!'– a considerable sum in those days. Naughty members who attempted by whatever subterfuge to donate less than the prescribed amount were met with increased volume from organist and assembly members alike so that the tight-

The new house had no chimney, so they had to carry the smoke out in a bucket.

fisted miseries were shamed into upping their Christian charity. And, all the while, wee Chic was running up and down the keyboard like a 'lintie'. That's showbiz, folks!

One of the more bizarre features of the Society occurred once the session had prayerfully come to an end. It involved the Society members participating in extra-curricular incendiary activities. They would venture forth, and, in three-dimensional reality, would proceed to set fire to and/or burn down some unsuspecting bush or shrub. Obviously, this was not good news for the bush, but neither was it for the somewhat displeased bush owner because, often enough, he had to brace himself for a double whammy, as he would then be called upon to pay for the services of the Greenock Fire Brigade. Unfortunately, that was the way things were done in those days gone by. Maybe these roaring fires were the real reason for the phrase 'The Roaring Twenties'? Perhaps not, but who can say?

In 1920, when Chic was still just a 'babbity', a married man's wage was a shilling an hour, seven pence for a singleton. But, by the mid 1920s, the two pre-eminent yards in Greenock, Scott's and Kincaid's, had flickered back into life in a modest revival due to a demand for motorboats. Times, though, as the decade wore on, were still bloody hard. The dreaded Means Test had been introduced whereby benefit was calculated on the total income of the household, not on the individual honest journeyman desperate to work, even for a subsistence wage. This led to the break-up of close-knit families and to the protests of thousands on the streets of Greenock, deputations laying siege to their council, more in a gesture of frustration than a meaningful appeal to impotent functionaries for employment and self-respect.

Mercifully, despite his poor health, William, Chic's dad, continued to keep his managerial position with the railway company through the Stygian darkness of the 1920s in Greenock. And he was blessed by the loving support of his wife, Isabella. Simply expressed (and there are many, still alive, who can recall her infectious bonhomie), she was an educated, serene woman, who treated her spouse with great tenderness and evinced total tolerance to his Burning Bush Society. Bill Jenkinson, one of Chic's school buddies, spoke in warmest terms of Isabella's astonishing kindness and her style: 'Just a cut above,' he said.

Money was no object. So they didn't give me anything!

And his old friend Big Neilie, of whom there's more to tell, said of her, 'She was the best-respected, nicest and cleverest woman in Greenock.'

High praise indeed. Isabella knew her husband and she knew, also, that he loved his beliefs and his fellow evangelical 'happy-clappies' with their shouts of 'Praise the Lord!' and 'Hallelujah!' Those beliefs, in reality, were light years from her origins and her upbringing, inducted from her earliest days into the Free Church of Scotland, but such was her devotion and commitment to her husband. And Chic reasoned that he had the best of both worlds, accompanying his father to the Burning Bush meetings and, on the Sabbath, attending church with his mother.

Chic's children treasure their grandmother's memory as they do their father's. Isabella was a statuesque woman of equal height to her husband (both were six feet tall) and blessed with a lifelong love of books. She read widely but liked in particular astronomy, the works of Robert Burns and any historical novel. Banks of

My mother was so house proud that when my father got up for a sleepwalk, she had the bed made by the time he got back

Chic with his grandmother (centre) and two aunts in Dundee in 1925

Yes, he's got talent. Brains, too.
Two of them, actually.

bookshelves lined the walls of their house in Bank Street and this clearly was to have a lasting impact on Chic, the master story-teller. William would often take his son into the country, sometimes on fishing expeditions where they would discuss a wide range of topics from politics to ornithology. In addition, in the evenings, Isabella would read to her family as she acted out the leading parts in her latest novel whilst Chic's imagination soared in rapt attention. It was no surprise, therefore, that such stimuli were to markedly benefit his results at the school desk.

Sadly, Isabella could not fail to see the deterioration in her husband's health. 'My poor bonnie laddie,' she would say, tenderly. And in due course, William had to forsake his dearest cause, the Burning Bush Society. It broke his heart (and Isabella's, for different reasons), and William, now in deep depression, began to hit the bottle to ease the pain of his respiratory illness. It is all the more poignant that, up to that time, he had led the life of a total abstainer. Even under the influence, by all accounts, he remained a loving husband and parent. It probably did not come unexpectedly, but it was still traumatic for Chic, now a teenager, to learn that his dad had to enter hospital and that his illness was nothing short of terminal. There was no long-term hope. William continued to write to Chic throughout, encouraging him in his studies, recounting stories from his life and offering advice to his son for the future. Chic treasured those letters all his life.

On his fourteenth birthday, 6 November 1933, Isabella had arranged a wee 'do' for him, having invited his pals to come round to Bank Street and celebrate the occasion in the evening. But that very morning she was summoned to the hospital where her husband was dying. Chic accompanied his mother in time to say their farewells. He was naturally in shock. As they stood in stunned silence Chic repeatedly whispered, 'Dad's gone . . .' Eventually they returned home to find a postcard lying on the hall carpet. It was addressed to 'Master C. Murray'. Isabella picked it up and gently handed it to her son.

My Dear Chic,

Fourteen years today, you came into the world and made a great big noise. You have not been a bad boy thro' all these years. I wish you every good wish and hope you have a jolly party tonight.

Daddy

Chic lost his self-control as tears tumbled from his distraught features onto the comforting arms of his mother.

Tom, Isabella's brother, was not among the 1,500 men from Greenock who never returned from the Great War. He had been taken prisoner at Salonika, spent two years banged up, then succeeded in escaping and heading home. He had lost a great deal of weight and had gained introspection, moroseness and an inner anger in a profound personality change. Out of compassion and shortly before William died, Isabella had invited him to stay for an indeterminate period. Tom managed to be reappointed to his old job on the railway, but otherwise had become a virtual recluse. Chic did his level best to make allowances for uncle's sullen behaviour but that was to alter markedly after William's death, as Tom assumed a new role as the head of the house. To aggravate matters further, he and Chic had a spat over William's gold watch, with Tom claiming it as his own. That put the lid on Chic's antipathy and resentment towards him.

But life went on, and Chic, actively encouraged by his mother, continued to play the organ under the tutelage of a Miss Brown. Chic loved her – she could do no wrong in his eyes. 'We didn't have a piano at home then,' he said, 'just this enormous American organ, so the dear lady started me off on that instead. My party piece was Handel's "Largo" which I played so often, I even began to like it! I practised for hours. It took me out of myself although I won't say where it took me!' (Was this remark the green shoots of a future comedic career?) Anyway, Chic found a piano too, at a pal's house. Isabella insisted he play the organ for an hour after school every day before joining his mates for football. Whether she knew or not is hard to say but, by now, Chic was getting to grips with a guitar, a banjo and even a mandolin. It remains something of a mystery, apart from his pitch-perfect yodelling, that he didn't exploit his abundant musical talent later in life.

He's a hopeless producer. He once put an acrobatic team on radio.

CHAPTER 2
THE BUDDING PERFORMER

Boys will be boys and Chic was a leader in the midst of them. Unsurprisingly, his favourite leisure activity was 'footie' in the street. Trouble was, though, football in any street in Greenock at the time was deemed an offence (not so much by law as by bye-law). Bill Jenkinson, one of his pals, remembered both of them being fined half a crown the first time they got nabbed. So, on another occasion (Chic in goal), the boys in blue reappeared. The outcome, however, was somewhat different. Bill was fined five bob as a repeat offender while the resourceful Chic had spotted the 'bizzies' arriving. Casually, hands thrust in pockets, he ambled from the makeshift goal-mouth to join a passing lady shopper, and then got in step with her. The police clearly had failed to observe the wifie's bemusement at being accosted by this strange youth, blethering a load of meaningless gibberish as they progressed from the scene of the crime! So football, even when playing keepie-uppie on your own, clearly was still an offence in Greenock!

Another school chum that Chic vividly recalled was one Sammy Cruickshanks. When the teacher took the class through an early 'get to know you' session, Sammy was asked what his father and mother did. 'Please Miss,' Sammy replied, 'I dinnae ha'e either!'

'Oh dear!' said the teacher, 'Are you an orphan, then?'

'No!' Sammy retorted, 'I'm my auntie's bairn by one of the lodgers!'

And then there was Gooey . . . on one occasion the teacher remonstrated with him, 'I'm sorry, Gooey, but I really must have your real name. A nickname is not acceptable.' Gooey insisted that it was his one and only real name. The teacher, then, with a heavy sigh, asked him to write his name down on a piece of paper. From this she was informed Gooey's real name was Guy

*'How can you
ever say such a thing?'
'I just opened my mouth
and out it popped!'*

9

THE CHIC MURRAY STORY

'I've sprained my ankle.
What should I do?'
'Limp.'

I wouldn't say I was a slow
developer, but our teacher was quite
pleased to have someone her own
age in the class.

but her triumph was short-lived. It transpired that Gooey's mum had found the name in a novella and liked it, but, for whatever reason thought Guy was pronounced 'Gooey'. So Gooey it had been and Gooey it remained!

What characterised Chic's school days, first, was that he was a growing laddie. Not so long after he had left school, he measured six feet three inches tall. (Mind you, to match his height, he had a prodigious appetite!) Second, he was developing a reputation as an idiosyncratic timekeeper with the excuses for late arrival such as, 'Sorry I'm late. I got press-ganged by a bunch of landscape gardeners,' becoming steadily more convoluted much to the suppressed merriment of the teaching staff as they looked forward to the next off-the-wall defence submission! But it was obvious, way back then, that he had developed the art of the straight face because in this department, other than Jack Benny perhaps, he had no equal onstage. It would be wrong (even at his height!) to say that he was head and shoulders above his classmates but he did well in all subjects save one – arithmetic. It's funny that, because most of his friends in his later life can confirm that Chic was more than capable of counting the pennies with acuity! Och! Maybe he was just a late developer!

As a schoolboy, he was wont to rush like hell down the stone stairs that led to their apartment on his way to play football (for heaven's sake, *not* to school!) and, on one occasion, he overdid the rushing, chipping bones in his left ankle in a nasty fall. This led to Chic's unique style of walking, toe first, then gingerly to the heel which was another hallmark of his presence onstage. The sight of his silhouetted profile entering stage left with his particular manner of walking was enough for his legion of fans to look forward to a dose of helpless laughter.

Shortly before leaving school, Chic applied for an apprenticeship in marine engineering at Kincaid's. It was a good time to take the action he did, because by 1934 unemployment was waning and, at long last, the Clyde basin was getting a decent 'kick at the ba'. Orders for new ships for the Royal Navy confirmed that the British fleet had to be augmented and the country's forces rearmed partly on account of Churchill's pleadings from 'the wilderness'. Kincaid's was working overtime, and flat out besides, to produce engines and boilers for Scott's, the next-door yard.

10

On acceptance, Chic's wages were minuscule, under ten shillings a week, but they did help to make ends meet for Isabella who, by now, was living on her husband's railway pension. Chic had two great incentives. The company gave him the prospect of travelling abroad (he was obsessive about travel) and, as long as he endured the frugality of his apprenticeship, there would be a dramatic change in his earnings when he'd 'done his time' at the workbench. But meantime, Chic asked himself, how do I get by during my five-year apprenticeship? How can I turn a shilling over the period? In all probability, two considerations influenced him. First, he regularly attended the Central Picture House in West Blackhall Street, known locally as 'The Ranch' because of the preponderance of Westerns shown there. Chic was cowboy daft and would readily distract his mother as she drove, taking imaginary pot-shots at injuns and baddies alike. And then there was Big Neilie McNeil, an old school pal who was a useful banjo player and, handily, a near neighbour. Together they formed a hillbilly group and christened themselves the Whinhillbillies after an area, Whinhill, near the Greenock golf course. 'That'll fox them!' Chic remarked. Their act began to develop. They stuck

My boss is so narrow-minded that when he has an idea, it comes out folded.

Kincaid and Co., marine engineers and boiler-makers

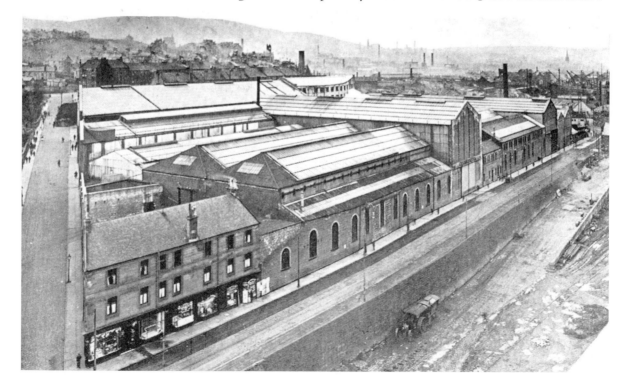

on a couple of scraggy false beards, wore checked lumberjack shirts and swaddled themselves in brown bibs and braces, Chic on organ, doing the vocals, and Big Neilie strumming away on his banjo, his regular shouts of 'Yeeehah!' something of an entertaining addition to the routine.

But no, no . . . this wasn't enough for the bold Chic! He acquired a fair-sized toy horse on wheels and proceeded to lead it onstage by a rope at the start of their act, and, of course, couldn't resist a bit of play-acting. Feigning the horse's stubbornness, he would struggle with its halter before eventually wrapping the rope round a piano leg, centre stage. This went down so well with the assembled Greenockians that matters were taken further. After leaving the audience to generous applause, towing his 'gee-gee' behind him, he would reappear with a brush and shovel and proceed to collect mythical horse droppings. Then, with the empty shovel, he would advance to the front of the stage and fling the imaginary contents over the front rows of the theatre. Incredibly, some of the locals actually used to duck, but the crowd loved it anyway until . . . oh dear! . . . until, one night, with Big Neilie totally unaware of Chic's intentions and having already left the stage, Chic took the act that little bit further and replaced the would-be horse manure on the end of his shovel with small, gnarled old potatoes. On jettisoning the shovel's contents, pandemonium and uproar ensued, with several shrieking wifies in the front rows shoogling faux fur coats which had been touched by wizened tatties. In this particular instance, the star of the show opted for Plan B which involved speedy withdrawal (rather than taking a bow), and fast-forwarding to the emergency exit offstage, still bearded, with a bemused Big Neilie in hot pursuit demanding to know, 'Chic! For Christ's sake! What the fuck's happened?'

As mentioned, Chic was a woefully bad timekeeper, regularly arriving late and regularly overrunning his act. As the theatre's profitability depended on its bar sales, this often resulted in real aggro with the manager: 'What are you playing at? You've buggered my bars, you lanky bastard!'

But such onslaughts made not one a whit of difference to Chic's sangfroid. 'Sod him!' he would remark to Big Neilie, 'Who does that idiot think we are? We're entertainers, for God's sake, not bloody licensed grocers!'

I once tried smoking hash.
I couldn't get corned beef
anywhere.

He was just as erratic at his work but, once there, he would apply himself conscientiously. Nonetheless, Isabella fretted, worrying about this bad habit.

And then, the Second World War broke out which did not concern Big Neilie unduly. As a bus driver, he was automatically exempted. Not so for Chic, and the dreaded day arrived when his call-up papers dropped onto the hall carpet. But his apprehensions soon dissipated as he failed his medical because of flat feet. 'Doesn't everyone?' Chic postulated. 'Anyway, I wouldn't want bumpy ones!'

His mother, though, was still concerned about Chic's indifference to timekeeping and put out feelers which led to Chic being sent south to Fairey Aviation in Middlesex where he stayed with his mother's sister, Tizzie (she came, after all, from a family of fourteen!). It was to be no cushy number, and during the six months he spent in the south, he had the front of his jacket blown clean off by an enemy dive-bomber which temporarily but seriously affected his eyesight. 'There's not much call for a

*'I didn't know
you were left of centre.'
'I'm not really. It's just the way
my tailor styles my trousers.'*

Chic writes home.
A postcard from Middlesex

blind marine engineer,' he said quietly, but without self-pity. The outcome, however, was to be a happy one. He recovered fully but just the same was sent homewards back across the border.

The ensuing years of conflict were no picnic for Greenock as it became a strategic target for German bombing. Air-raid shelters were hastily constructed, barricades erected and civil-defence centres, for wardens and first-aid volunteers, mushroomed whilst tram lines and railings were ripped up for the war effort. And Isabella, being the leading citizen that she was, was appointed welfare officer for the town. To begin with, it was the sight of bomb- or torpedo-damaged ships limping into the harbour which shocked the populace into the grave reality of war. But, by May 1941, when the air raids had begun in earnest, the people of Greenock knew at first hand the might and terror of the enemy. The first attack comprised about fifty aircraft; they returned the following night with a fleet of 300. There was terrible devastation and suffering: 280 people lay dead, 1,300 injured. Good fortune spared Bank Street from the blitzkrieg but Chic never forgot the two nights he spent in an air-raid shelter with his mother, uncle and neighbours. These were his own recollections: 'There was mountains of rubble everywhere, whole houses wrecked, walls scorched. Rows of bodies were laid out in the streets covered with white sheets and tarpaulin. I spent the rest of that night and most of the following day helping the exhausted firemen – the last blaze was put out in early afternoon but it was days before the town lost its scorched smell.'

But it's an ill wind that blows no good and the hostilities, if anything, seemed to have increased demand for performances by Chic and his pals. The Whinhillbillies had by now metamor-phosed into a skiffle group, periodically called Chic and the Chicks. Jimmie, another neighbour, played bass guitar with Gooey, a gifted instrumentalist, on the washboard. Gooey, however, incurred Chic's displeasure by suggesting they should include some slower numbers like 'Someday My Prince Will Come'.

'Don't be daft, Gooey, that would just slow down the pace of the act. Besides, that song should be sung by a lassie! Since when did you become a music critic?'

'Well,' said Gooey curmudgeonly, 'it would be better than some of the garbage you spew up!'

Chic in Greenock just
before he met Maidie

A few nights later at a gig, Chic was giving it laldie with one of his favourites, 'I'm alone because I love you', when the audience burst into laughter. 'Shit!' Chic thought, 'Are my breeks coming down?' No. 'Maybe my flies are open?' No. Then he glanced behind him. There was Jimmy and Big Neilie, both powerless to intervene, as Gooey, holding his beak with one hand was pulling on an imaginary lavatory chain. Gooey froze in the headlights of Chic's stare, but the audience just laughed all the more. After the show, Gooey vamoosed double-quick but followed very soon after by Chic and the anxious remainder of the flock. 'Who's a right little smartie-arse then?' bawled Chic.

'But I didn't mean any harm,' Gooey replied timidly, as if rolling over on his back to have his tummy stroked in an act of submission.

Chic, in both senses being the big man that he was, replied, 'You're right, Gooey. It didn't do any harm. As a matter of fact the audience loved it. So we'll just keep it in as part of the act!'

CHAPTER 3
MAIDIE

One day in 1943 an event occurred which would change Chic's life. It was mid evening and the rain was bucketing down outside. Chic and Big Neilie were seated in the parlour when there was a knock on their door. 'Mother,' Chic bawled, 'could you answer that, please? Neilie and I are busy rehearsing.' Isabella duly went and opened the door to find two young, drookit, exhausted girls in front of her. They quickly explained that they were booked to appear in a variety show at the Empire Theatre in Greenock for an eight-week season and that they were advised to contact her, as welfare officer, to recommend suitable digs in the area.

'Come in out of the cold, dears, while I make you a nice hot cup of tea,' Isabella said. She took an instant liking to them and sympathised that they'd had to drag their luggage up the steep incline of Bank Street. The smaller of the two in particular had lugged along her suitcase in addition to a heavy-looking encased accordion. Isabella also felt sorry about their plight as young women with no fixed accommodation, and she was reluctant to send them out again into the gathering darkness on rainswept streets. No, she decided they would stay put with her. She left the girls and went to let Chic know her decision.

'Mother! Did I not tell you Neilie and I are having a serious practice session?' Chic protested.

In her own serene way, Isabella could handle Chic with consummate ease, her voice and intonation never wavering. 'Now Charles,' she said (when she sussed a mini-tantrum on the horizon, perhaps the suggestion of a foot-stamp or a pouty lip, she was wont to address her son as the more sober 'Charles'), 'that's how you'll be getting high blood pressure! Please listen! Two wee dears arrived at the door when you were concentrating

'Do you believe in love at first sight?' *'Yeah! And it saves you time and money!'*

*'I can lick any heavyweight
with just one hand!'
'Aye, but be fair! There's not
many one-handed heavyweights
going the rounds these days.'*

on other matters. I've decided they will stay here in the spare room.'

'But, you can't do that! Och! For goodness sake, what about all my railway stuff?' Chic huffed indignantly.

'You're far too old for model railways,' Isabella replied curtly. 'You're a big grown man now and you're going to stop this choo-choo nonsense! I'm going to prepare the girls a late supper and in the meantime, you go through, please, and pack your last trains to San Fernando!'

Grudgingly, he obeyed his mother, packed up his beloved train sets close to a tantrum, and sloped off out with Neilie.

An hour or so later, the girls were tucking into a hearty supper, despite the privations of the ration book. And then, the front door flung wide and noisily open. Chic had returned with his pals (having completely forgotten that Isabella had guests), Big Neilie, Gooey, Jimmy and Bill Jenkinson. Clumpity clump, they wandered in on the diners. Then Chic's eyes fell on one of the girls and he mused in wonderment, 'Who's that gorgeous wee bird?'

Isabella had no time to draw breath, never mind introduce everybody, before Chic and this little dreamboat began swapping furtive glances and modest smiles. Isabella could see the chemistry between them developing. She discreetly left the young ones to talk together. When they were introduced, below his newly cultivated pencil moustache, a smile broke out on Chic's handsome features as, in a somewhat twee, refined accent, he said, 'Pleased to meet you,' to the admiring recipient of his handshake. Chic's unyielding gaze had fallen upon a diminutive, very pretty, precociously talented brunette. Her name was Maidie Dickson.

'Dainty Maidie', 'The Scottish marvel', and sometimes billed as 'The girl that has something everyone wants', unlike Chic who bestraddled amateurism and professionalism, was, every inch of her five feet in height, a seasoned professional on the stage. Seventeen years of it, to be precise, and she was just twenty-one! She was born on Tron Square in the beating heart of Edinburgh's Old Town, her father originally from the High Street of Edinburgh and her mother a Dundonian, and her first engagement, aged four, was at the Capitol Theatre in Leith. It was also in Leith that her gran had successfully prevailed upon

Maidie as a child performer

Alec Burns's mother to persuade her son to teach Maidie 'buck' dancing, later to be known as tap-dancing, save only that her 'buck' dance shoes had ebonite rather than metal to register the rhythm. (He had point-blank refused to teach her because she was so young.) But, here's the point! The audience back then just adored her and they were doubly enchanted by this wee mite because she sang 'Walking My Baby Back Home' with a lisp. Imagine! Four years old! She was to receive 7s 6d per night for two performances. Child stars today might baulk at such modest rewards.

By the time she reached the grand old age of six, she had added to her versatility by playing the accordion, which must have half drowned her, with Will Fyffe (of 'Twelve and a Tanner a Bottle' fame – a lament at the exorbitant price of whisky!) in a revue in Burntisland. At the end of their stay, to show his appreciation, Will Fyffe gave her a ten-bob note inscribed, 'To a very clever wee lassie. Yours aye, Will Fyffe.' Aged twelve, Maidie was booked for an eight-week stint at the Prom Palace in Portobello alongside an up-and-coming singer, one Donald Peers. (It was around this time that Maidie's dad was fined 10s for breaching the restrictions on children's performances by the Edinburgh magistrates.) Two years on, Maidie was principal girl in pantomime in Newcastle and, although able to hold down a

'I don't wish to be unkind,
but you must appreciate he was,
ahem, something of a freak.'
'Why?'
'Well, he did have three legs
and four arms. I suppose you could
say, he was a man of many parts.'

The young Maidie in
front of a microphone

leading role by night, to conform with regulations to curb child exploitation her days were spent in the strange surroundings of a Geordie school. Over the years Maidie was to share billboards with hosts of stars, including, notably, Dickie Henderson, and she brought a wealth of experience with her by the time she was booked to appear at the Empire, Greenock.

When Maidie, on the first night they met, explained to Chic that her life, from earliest recollections, was in show business, Chic, the smoothie, the proverbial cool cat, was reluctant to be upstaged. 'Yeah, same for me, I guess,' he said, examining his fingernails casually, 'of course, although it certainly was before, showbiz has been non-stop for me since I left school – I'm surrounded by comedians in the yard!' There is some truth in that as Billy Connolly can bear witness.

The following night, Chic attended both houses at the Empire Theatre, meeting Maidie at the stage exit. 'You were just terrific, Maidie! The best in the show!' he chirped, as they walked home. And, as luck would have it, Chic and the Chicks were asked to do their bit at a Royal Navy dance the very next night. He arranged for her to attend the minute she was offstage. As thrilled as Chic was by her appearance in a lovely gold dress, so, too, was Maidie well impressed by her new escort's routine. When it was their turn to go back onstage, Maidie suggested she could help out on a couple of numbers, 'I'm Gonna Drink My Coffee From An Old Tin Can' and 'Steam Boat Bill', but, on this special occasion, without Gooey up to his lavatorial antics! They were a huge success and the dancers on the floor cheered and cheered again. Chic and Maidie had a goodnight kiss before bedtime but before she could snuggle up and prepare for sleep, she was roused by a far-too-loud American organ with Chic bawling out meaningless gibberish:

Two lovers went strolling down a coal mine,
The girl had been a female from her birth,
Give me back the ring I never gave you,
For this has been your second time on earth.
Ten weary years have passed in fifteen minutes,
So wipe the cobwebs from your ears,
And always think of m-o-t-h-e-r,
And the Dublin Fusiliers!

Maidie (in the white hat, left) with
fellow performers, 1937

Maidie laughed herself to sleep and asked Isabella in the morning
about the origin of Chic's oratorio. 'Och,' she said, 'that's just one
of his daft party pieces. What a blinking racket last night and we
were all forced to listen! He's been at it for years and, of course,
despite his exertions, it still neither scans nor makes one bit of
sense. There's far wiser in padded cells, you know!'

The weeks whizzed by during which she had had brief
sightings of The Ghost (Uncle Tom) and she asked Chic if there
were any other tenants lurking around. 'Oh yes,' he replied,
'there's Woolchester Copperthwaite and Mrs Pollack.'

'Oh, where do you keep her? In the broom cupboard,
perhaps?' Maidie asked mischievously.

'You'll be hearing plenty about her, m'lady,' Chic intoned.

Most weeks, after the last show on a Saturday, Maidie would
rush back for an early kip to rise first thing to catch the train
back to her mother's, returning on Monday morning. Chic, on
one occasion, offered to escort her to the station but his usual
wonky timekeeping meant they arrived at the station by near
enough 11 a.m. Maidie never suspected that his offer to humph
her luggage to the station would involve his company all the way
to Edinburgh and she was highly delighted and touched by
Chic's gesture. Yet she parted with him at her house, figuring it
was maybe too soon to announce their romance. Nonetheless, it
was only a matter of a few weeks before Chic met Anne,
Maidie's mum, and the two got on famously. (Hugh, Maidie's
father, was at sea as usual, serving in the Royal Navy).

Chic visited Maidie at Millport, her next venue, then when she moved on to perform in Hawick she was thrilled to receive her first letter from him, which ended:

Nothing doing in the afternoon so I gave the organ big licks until Mum came to get me for tea. I wasn't hungry and could only manage two platefuls of cottage pie; I must be unwell. As usual the pie was a stotter. Mrs Pollack had evidently dropped in for a chat, but I had missed her. By the by, Mum has won some sort of national newspaper competition for the best review of Gone With The Wind. *I hope it doesn't go to her head, me being so modest and that, but I always did say there was talent in this family. She sends her warmest regards. Take good care of yourself. Here's a kiss and love from Chic.*
P.S. Write soon

Maidie loved the letter except the mention of this ruddy 'Mrs Pollack'! She'd never met the woman and so Chic's references to her made Maidie somewhat apprehensive. Some weeks on, Maidie was appearing at the Victory Theatre, Paisley. At the first opportunity, she rushed from the venue and hopped on a bus to Greenock. She rang the bell which produced no response so, seeing the door off the latch, she gingerly entered to see her boyfriend, hands waving above his head, yelling dementedly, 'Send for Mrs Pollack! Send for Mrs Pollack!'

Behind Chic, his mother was in close attendance. 'Please, Chic, calm down! You'll just be having the high blood pressure again!'

To add to the consternation, The Ghost, making one of his rare guest appearances, opened his bedroom door. He spotted Maidie looking somewhat puzzled by events. 'This place is a bloody madhouse!' he bawled at her, as if it was somehow her fault, before slamming his door shut, the substantial building shuddering under the impact.

'Hello, Maidie,' Chic had quietened down, 'you're not Mrs Pollack, but you more than make up for her.'

This provoked a further shout of hateful derision from The Ghost's room – '*Fuck Mrs Pollack!*'

After a minute or two, the dust began to settle. 'Who is this lady, Mrs Pollack, anyway?' Maidie enquired, concerned.

'I haven't a clue, dear,' Isabella answered. 'I guess she's some sort of cleaning woman that Chic's dreamt up. If he finds the place untidy, I get this blinking Pollack woman hurled back in my face!'

Chic, as was his way, was completely relaxed over this scene of family uproar and never mentioned it again. Still, it was unexpected, to say the least, when that same night, with Isabella reading in her favourite armchair and Chic and Maidie holding hands across the table, Chic broke the silence with a life-changing proposal: 'Maidie, let's tie the knot.'

'Oh Chic,' Maidie replied, 'are you sure?'

'He's sure alright,' Isabella said. She marked the page in her book, crossed over the floor, gave Maidie a hug, and whispered, 'I couldn't be more pleased – you're just a wee cracker.'

'Now, just a minute, here,' Chic boomed, 'the wee cracker's never said "yes" yet!'

'Yes I have, you big galoot,' Maidie riposted.

Chic was all smiles but then switched to the role and gravitas of an elder statesman, 'Of course, there is the outstanding matter, still to be settled, *ahem*, of the dowry.'

'Oh! Chic, can't you be serious just for once in your life?' Isabella asked her son, as she lovingly embraced him too. Anne, Maidie's mum, was equally chuffed, managing to smile every time Chic raised 'the small, but still outstanding matter of the dowry . . .'

She used to milk a cow until her eyesight got worse. Then she made a mistake and this bull kicked her teeth clean out.

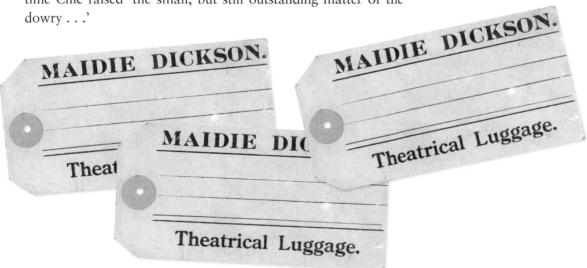

CHAPTER 4
A MATCH MADE IN HEAVEN

There was the small matter, next, of purchasing the engagement ring, a relatively straightforward exercise. (It would be reasonable to assume that, anyway.) Maidie was let loose to shop around within the limitations of their budget and, in Edinburgh, found a lovely sapphire and diamond antique ring below the agreed maximum price threshold. Nonetheless, when informed of the cost, Chic's eyes rolled heavenwards and the colour drained from his cheeks as he spluttered and gagged for a bite of oxygen. He loved the drama of these little cameos so much that Maidie, taken in by his affected state of trauma and shock, became genuinely concerned for his well-being (and, of course, it was just the naughty, wonderful Chic at his play-acting best – but you're not supposed to know that!). 'But, it's second-hand, Maidie,' he moaned, wringing his hands, 'it wouldn't have been quite so bad if it had been a *new* ring!' Anyway, in due course, Chic having made a full recovery, off they both set for Edinburgh to conclude the purchase.

However, before embarking on the train eastwards, there was an obvious need to obtain the necessary funds from Chic's bank in Greenock. 'You will come in with me, Maidie, won't you?' Chic asked outside the bank.

'No, you'll be fine. I'll wait for you here,' she replied.

'No! *No!*' Chic pleaded. 'Banks make me nervous. What if I pass out? I might well collapse, you know – you must be there to bring me round! It's funny, though, it only seems to happen when I'm withdrawing cash!'

Maidie relented, thinking it a fuss about nothing.

In they went together, joining a queue for the teller. In the fullness of time, the bank assistant asked Chic how he could help. Chic froze, he seemed mesmerised. Then two gruff clear-

I used to write her love letters in the sand. But it was an incredible hassle trying to get the sand into the pillar box.

THE CHIC MURRAY STORY

ances of the throat seemed to resolve his hesitancy as he said curtly, 'I'd like to withdraw some money from my account.' He looked about nervously, as if expecting some gunslinger to crash in and hold him and the bank up.

'Your name, please, sir?' the teller asked. 'Ummm, ah yes, my name . . .' Chic paused, 'well, on point of fact, I'd rather not say.'

'Look, I'm sorry, sir. No name. No money. It's just that simple!' came the reply.

Chic looked behind him. Nothing untoward there. Then he stared vacantly at poor Maidie who, by this time, was somewhat agitato herself, wondering what the hell was going on. Then, inexplicably, he blurted out, 'Oh, all right then! It's Tighthole. Timothy Tighthole!'

Both his fiancée and the teller were lost for words in their astonishment (not to mention the shock/horror of the other bank patrons). 'That's why I'm reluctant to say it!' he continued, having now moderated the decibel level of his voice. 'But I'm thinking of changing my name in any case.' He asked the teller politely, 'What do you think of 'Charlie Tighthole?' In the nick of time, the bank manager appeared. 'Is it a withdrawal, Mr Murray?' he enquired solicitously, his head tilted forward to indicate concern.

'Well,' Chic remarked with a nervy chuckle, 'if it isn't, I've certainly got all the symptoms!' So they withdrew with their withdrawal, but it had been a tough assignment in the passing.

Anne Dickson wanted the wedding of her daughter to be solemnised in style in the Moray Aisle of St Giles' Cathedral, named in honour of the patron saint of Edinburgh, long before John Knox came on the scene! The service was to be conducted by Dr Charles Warr, a king's chaplain in his distinguished red robes and also a war hero. (He was a friend of Isabella's from his days as a parish minister in Greenock, just after the Great War.) The night before, Chic and his mates went off to get 'unco fou' as tradition dictated, though in reality they behaved with Greenockian decorum! Isabella stayed with her future daughter-in-law. 'Chic can be an awful handful at times, Maidie,' she counselled, 'but it's over with Chic as soon as it starts. He doesn't bear grudges and, at the end of the day, he's a kind-hearted soul. Mind you, I won't deny he has his weird ways. That dashed organ is one of them – he seems to lose himself in it, sometimes

'Do you want to come to the disco on Thursday?'
'I can't. I'm getting married on Friday.'
'How about Saturday then?'

26

for hours on end.' (Maidie was to be apprised of that in the immediate future!) 'However,' she continued in a conspiratorial tone, 'although he's had the odd girlfriend – actually some of them *very* odd – he is head over heels in love with you for his first and only time.'

The great day arrived: 28 April 1945. Chic, leaving things to the last minute as usual, needed to sort out a couple of headaches – pyjamas and new shoes. (He used to sleep in the 'altogether' but thought that a trifle risqué for the honeymoon night!) He dashed round to his uncle Alex to borrow a spanking new set of pyjamas and to purloin his uncle's clothing coupons for a new set of burnished shoes.

With the distinguished Dr Warr in charge, there was hardly a blooper or incident worthy of recall during the wedding ceremony. It ran like clockwork. They were a smashing couple: Chic, a handsome dashing hero, his Errol Flynn 'tache sitting astride a huge grin of happiness, and Maidie, the radiant bride, bonnie as a picture, a 'wee cracker' as Isabella was fond to say of her. Except for one thing . . . there was a distracting sound at the commencement of the proceedings from which the bride was fortunately spared. The congregation's eager expectancy was disturbed (generating mirthful comment, discreetly whispered) by squeak, squeak, multiple squeak as Chic, his generously proportioned feet in brand-new shoes, and his best man, Big Neilie, strode solemnly up the main hallowed thoroughfare of the cathedral!

At the reception, Chic mingled with relations and guests alike and he was particularly pleased to see his aunt Tizzie again, up from the south. The only notable absentee was The Ghost, his uncle Tom. Chic figured he wouldn't have enjoyed it anyway, and even if they had asked him he would have refused to attend. Same difference. Auntie Marion, another member of Isabella's large family, vacated her house in Dundee to give the young newly-weds a bolthole for a brief honeymoon. But it was to be no ordinary honeymoon because they had no sooner arrived at the house when Chic discovered a pedal organ in the front room. After supper, Maidie, after all the excitement of the day's events, felt tired. She decided to turn in and snuggle down in bed, dressed in a lovely diaphanous négligée, breathlessly awaiting her Prince Charming. As it happened, she had a helluva wait!

*'I never realised you
had such a yellow streak.'
'Oh yes, my hairdresser says
it's all the rage!'*

Chic, for what appeared to be hours, played 'In The Mood' *fortissimo* on the organ, again and again ad nauseam! Only a foolish man would have ventured to predict any move Chic was about to make – even on his honeymoon night! He was a cool dude . . .

It was sad for them that the weekend seemed so short. Maidie had to jump on a train to an engagement in Stonehaven and Chic headed back to the yards at Kincaid's. Things were made a bit more bearable because they knew they would be reunited the following weekend, a notable time, as hostilities were to cease in Europe and the war, for them, was over.

Some weeks passed with Chic and Maidie snatching weekends when they could see each other. And then Maidie was booked to perform in a charity 'do' in the Usher Hall, Edinburgh. She overheard the producer commenting that they were short of one act, preferably a musical act. She moved into overdrive for Chic, hoping he would resurrect the Whinhillbillies to fill the gap in the billing. He was apprehensive when she first announced this possible break for him and Big Neilie, but no more than that. Big Neilie, in contrast, was rigid with fear. 'Christ! Chic,' Big Neilie whined, 'I'm not cut out for showbiz. A local hop is one thing, but the Usher . . .'

'Och! C'mon, Neilie,' Chic interrupted, 'let's just call it our farewell gig for auld lang syne!' He was eventually won over after severe arm-twisting worthy of the Spanish Inquisition.

'I had terrible heebie-jeebies,' Big Neilie recalled, 'and, to calm my nerves further, his nibs just vanished out of sight. I found the bugger eventually in the lavatory, "doing his hair", he said, and me shouting the bloody place down! We got to the stage entrance just as our act was announced, but I have to admit, it went down well – Chic as cool as a ruddy cucumber just to annoy me further!' The curtain, a heavy brute of a thing that can deliver a knock-out, crashed down as they left the stage to warm applause. Chic, the dodger, took evasive action in time but the unfortunate Big Neilie was less lucky. 'That was my exit from show business,' Big Neilie reminisced, 'rolling around on my arse, legs flailing in the air, but with the audience still clapping! Not such a bad way to go, I suppose.'

Maidie could see Chic's potential. He was professional in all but name and she was full of admiration for him as any young

Chic and Maidie shortly
after their wedding

lover would be. She proposed they form a double act although Chic was far from convinced. 'Look!' she said, 'I'll start. I'll sing and play an opening number, then you can come in and harmonise. Then we'll do a duet. You tell a few gags and we'll finish off with another song or two. What's wrong with that Chic?' He was still uncertain. It was a mammoth step into the unknown – the stage full time or back to the shipyards? A bloody great gamble with no guarantees on the one hand, or the security of a steady wage, but without the 'buzz' on the other. Maidie kept going. She explained that she would appear on the billboards on her own just to begin with. 'It would be easier to get bookings that way,' she added with practicality. 'And if you decide in favour of what I've suggested, we will be partners in every sense. Don't think I just need someone to carry my accordion!'

Chic had arrived at a crossroads and although neither of them was aware of it, Maidie's initiative and Chic's response would hugely affect both their careers. She was the first – or certainly one of the first – to recognise the scope and potential of Chic's talent. And she was prepared to nurture and support her man, even if it meant changes to her own career. So both of them looked to the future with excitement and trepidation in equal measure as Chic decided to take up the gauntlet and address what was a daunting challenge: to establish himself as a successful freelance entertainer. The groundwork, of course, had been carried out long before, but the real countdown and lift-off of Chic's career (which would take him round the world and

Bank robbers, making a hasty exit after a hold-up, ran through freshly poured cement. The police are looking for two hardened criminals.

29

*There's always a crowd
following him – mainly creditors.*

would involve weeks upon weeks performing in the West End of London, film and television appearances, even an invitation to the Royal Comand Performance), in reality, started from this time forward. Some journey lay ahead!

A year of married life went by and, bang on the year after their wedding day, Maidie gave birth to a son, Douglas, By now Chic had left Kincaid's and they were getting by on savings and Maidie's bookings which understandably were in decline during her pregnancy. Two weeks on from Douglas's arrival, Maidie was hired to appear at the Links Pavilion, Carnoustie (or 'Carsnooty', as Chic called it!). Archie McCulloch (his wife, Kathy Kay, was the resident songstress for Billy Cotton, the band leader) and his young assistant, Eric Morley, had wanted an accordionist. They hadn't really counted on a singer, tap-dancer

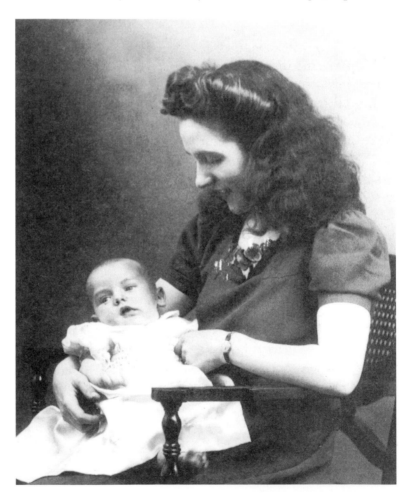

Maidie with Douglas

30

and comedian thrown in as well; this was to be their first showing in public together! Only when they arrived at the venue did Maidie inform the producer that her husband would be an integral part of her act. He was not a happy boy scout! 'I booked a solo act,' Jack Barton protested.

'Now look here! We're not charging for Chic. Remember that! And he'll share my fee. Either he's with me or there's no me either! It's that simple,' she declared. Maidie had made her point. The producer backed off, muttering to himself.

At rehearsals Chic became morose. 'They've heard these jokes before, Maidie. I'm not a jokey, jokey bloke. All I want to do is make people laugh, and there's a world of difference between the two, believe me.'

Maidie did her best to reassure him, 'Chic! Your jokes are tried and tested and, after all, you're only on the stage alone for six minutes.'

But his genuine concerns couldn't be assuaged. She asked him to leave the theatre for a bite to eat, hoping a change of scenery might snap him out of his blues. 'You go, dear, and eat for me! I want to have a right think on my own.'

Maidie yielded. 'Maybe he just needs a bit of space,' she thought, and so left him to himself, a solitary figure on an ill-lit stage. He began to recall his story-telling days at school and at Kincaid's, and his imagination clicked into overdrive. Eventually he left the theatre and ambled across to a nearby hostelry where he grabbed a drink and began scribbling furiously on beer mats and empty fag packets. Chic was striking out on his own and following his gut instincts.

Monday night soon came round, their first professional performance together, here at 'Carsnooty'. Maidie went on first, to be joined by Chic in harmony, then a spot of yodelling (at which he was uncannily adept) and then, Maidie having exited to warm applause, there he was, centre stage, tweed-suited and tartan-bunneted, jacking up the microphone to his height. 'I got up this morning,' he intoned, 'I like to get up in the morning. It gives me the rest of the day to myself!'

'Jesus Christ,' a squirming, freaked-out Maidie exclaimed to herself from the wings 'what the hell is he playing at?' She silently beseeched him, 'Oh, please, *please*, Chic, stick to the jokes we rehearsed together!'

I'm off to France for a spot of exercise with a knife and fork.

But it was too late. Chic was in full flow.

So I dressed, actually I always dress. I like to be different, but I think undressed you're a bit too different. I went down the street, went down the front – oh, you can go down the front, there's no law against it – and I was walking in my usual way, one foot in front of the other, oh yes, that's the best way. I've tried various methods, I suppose. I remember once, I tried a series of jumps. I heard someone say, 'Look at that Australian!' I didn't answer. I just wagged my tail.

Perhaps it was Chic's reflections on absurdities, or the sheer surrealism of his humour to which the audience had never previously been exposed, but for whatever reason, silence prevailed in the audience and Maidie just wanted the agony to finish. He batted on . . .

Then I met someone. [Pause.] I knew him, otherwise I'd never have spoken to him. He was sitting on top of a horse with a briefcase, bowler hat and wellington boots. I said, 'What are you doing on top of that horse?'
He said, 'I thought you'd say that.'
I could have cut my tongue out! I wished I'd never mentioned it. I thought – if I'd only just said 'Hello' and never mentioned he was on a horse – or 'Fanny's your aunt', or anything. I should just have passed him as if it were an everyday occurrence.

At this juncture, the audience began to get a shade frisky, showing their impatience as one or two stamped their feet. This provoked a heckler to bawl out '*Gerroff*! Rubbish! Give us Maidie.' Chic stared in the vague direction of the barracker but swiftly regained his stride; Maidie, by this time, was ash-white and shitting herself. Chic continued,

Then he said, 'As soon as I saw you, I said to myself, he'll say, "What are you doing up on that horse?"'
Of course, I was awfully embarrassed – and to hide my embarrassment, I patted the horse. I said, 'This horse

has a flat head.'
     He said, 'You're facing the wrong way, you guffy!'

Chic pulled a face, muttering,

I did wonder why it had refused a sugar lump!

He had begun to crack it! All over the theatre, ripples of laughter broke out and Maidie's demeanour brightened to some degree. There was no stopping him now!

I gave the horse a thump on the rump and it reared up. He looked down and said: 'If you're coming up beside me, I'm getting off,' as he slid, helplessly, down the horse's neck, landing on his head. Luckily the pavement broke his fall.

More mirth followed with Maidie praying he would get off while still ahead. Not a bit of it!

So I hung about till he recovered. It was the least I could do. After all, I was the last one to talk to him. So when he came to, I said, 'That was a dreadful thing that happened just now.'
     He said, 'Just now! It happened five times this morning already.
     I said, 'What are you doing on that horse in the first place?'
     He said, 'Ah! That's another thing that's infuriating me, I don't know.'
     I said, 'You don't know? How's that?'
     He said, 'I can't get my briefcase open to find out.'
     I said, 'I'll have to go now, half the summer's gone just talking to you.' He led the horse over to a wall so that he could remount the animal. I said, 'Now, now, don't get on your high horse!

This gag was well received. It gave Maidie a chance to cue the conductor as the instrumentalists struck up with 'Painting the Clouds with Sunshine'. Behind clenched teeth Chic vented, 'I

The wife does bird impressions.
She watches me like a hawk.

hadn't bloody finished.'

'Finished! Finished!' Maidie protested behind smiles for the audience, 'You bloody nearly finished me!'

They returned to their dressing room, Chic looking as pleased as Punch. 'Well, Maidie, how did that grab you? The audience loved it, you know,' he said, with more than a touch of hyperbole.

Maidie was still overwrought from the torture session he'd forced her to endure, 'Why on earth did you have to come out with that daft story? Why couldn't you just have stuck to the jokes?'

'Aw, look, Maidie, say what you like, the jokes were bloody awful, just crap. I decided to throw the lot in the bin and then I wrote my wee story in the pub. I didn't like to mention it to you. You'd just have worried all the more. Anyway, it still went okay in the end, didn't it?'

There was no time to reply as the door opened and, unannounced, in came the producer of the show. 'What the hell was all that about, then?' Jack Barton demanded.

'Oh, I was merely serving up what the public wants,' Chic said dismissively. A faint smile flickered and vanished on account of Chic's hauteur.

'Well, try modulating it a bit!' he said, leaving as quickly as he'd arrived with a congratulatory door-slam.

Maidie persuaded Chic to write out his new routine in longhand there and then in the dressing room. Chic obliged but left his script bereft of a single punctuation mark. Studiously, and using a deep well of experience (having listened to some comic 'greats'), she broke up the script by inserting 'Ha-Ha' to indicate pauses where, hopefully, the audience would react with laughter. So how did this singular comedian perform an hour or two later at the second house? Well, he stuck to his script, but with one important addition: 'I like to get up in the morning,' he began, 'it gives me the rest of the day to myself.' Then his shoulders commenced to rise and fall as he scornfully uttered, 'Ha-Ha!'

'Oh my God!' thought poor Maidie, 'don't tell me he's going to repeat every "Ha-Ha" I put in? I just can't believe he could do this to me!'

Chic continued, 'So I dressed. I *always* dress. I like to be different but I think undressed is just *too* different. Ha-Ha.' It

dawned on the wee heroine that her worst fears were about to be realised. But her misgivings, thankfully, were misplaced . . . what she had done with her best intentions, and what Chic, with his oblique look at life, had had the vision to anticipate, was that from there on in, there was to be a riot of laughter. The 'Ha-Ha's gave the audience time to recognise a new form of humour and every 'Ha-Ha' became eagerly awaited by the audience. They triggered the laughter. They multiplied the enjoyment. Pavlov would have been proud of them! In reality, Chic was beginning to master the control of his audience. It was as if he was saying, 'You will laugh when I tell you – Ha-Ha!' Now, with the punters enthralled, Maidie had the good sense and judgement not to interrupt Chic in full flow.

Chic cracked on, cued the orchestra himself and was accompanied by Maidie back on centre stage to ongoing applause. Meanwhile, the theatre manager summoned Jack Barton to his office. 'What the hell's going on here? I booked Maidie. Who's this idiot she's got in tow?'

'I thought he was quite good, actually,' Jack replied, fairly.

'Well I'm getting in touch with Archie McCulloch.' He picked up the phone and dialled. 'Archie, I've got a problem. I booked Maidie Dickson and halfway through her act her husband appears, telling way-out stories, supposed to be funny.'

'Did he get any laughs?' he was asked.

'A few, I dare say.'

'Well keep him in! Use your noddle! We're still getting full value from Maidie and I'm not paying for him. So a little less moaning would be a wee bonus!'

'Christ!' the manager thought resentfully, 'Next time I order an elephant, it looks like I'll have to settle for a duck-billed bloody platypus!'

Meanwhile, back at their flat, Maidie asked Chic where he'd got the idea for a monologue. 'I dunno, Maidie! I just let my imagination go wandering. I've been doing that since schooldays, I suppose.'

'Well, don't forget, Chic, we're booked here for ten weeks and the show is reinvented every Thursday when there's a change of programme, so you'll need to keep the wandering going!'

'Jeepers! Maidie,' Chic exclaimed, blanching, *two* routines a

'It's getting more and more difficult for me to believe you're working late.'
'Why?'
'You're unemployed.'

35

'Oh darling, I love you so much! Can I sit on your lap?'
'If you must.'
'There. What a thrill!'
'Well that makes one of us.'

'For years, I've admired you from afar.'
'Mmm, that's about the right distance.'

Chic and Maidie:
The Tall Droll and the Small Doll

week for ten weeks! – that's a tall order!'

'Ah, but do them right, Chic, and you'll have enough material to take right across the country. It'll be worth it in the long run!'

'Just one other wee thing, Maidie . . . do you remember Gooey being cheeky behind my back? It worked well in the act and . . .'

'Don't tell me, Chic,' Maidie interrupted, 'you want me to be some kind of a fall guy when you start pulling faces behind me, I know what you're after!'

Together their act developed and bedded in, with Chic, as Maidie expected, severely pulling her leg, twice nightly. But what was particularly engaging about their double act was Chic's final address to the audience. It seemed to cement things, anyway, and ended their routine with a laugh. 'You may think I've been a bit unkind to Maidie, y'know, having a wee go at her. But let me tell you this – there's nothing I wouldn't do for that girl.' This always met with five-star audience approval with smiling 'Aws' and 'Ahs'!

'No! *Nothing*! And there's nothing she wouldn't do for me! And that's how we go through life – doing nothing for each other!'

Early press reaction, however, was cautious. While Maidie defended Chic's corner as a potentially great comedian, some of the hacks dismissed Chic as no more than a 'blether'. The show went on with its twice-weekly about-turns and then, two weeks in, Jack Barton handed a document to Chic. 'What is it? Is this my 'Gerroot Gerroff' papers?'

'Not at all!' Jack beamed, 'It's the proposed layout for next week's programme. Read it, for God's sake!' Chic glanced down to note with delight that Maidie featuring as a solo artiste, as of next week, would be a thing of the past. From now on, her act was to be known as 'Chick and Maidie'.

Straight-faced, as usual, Chic said, 'You've misspelt my name!' but inwardly he thought 'They can call me "Chicken Curry" for all I care,' as he shook Jack Barton's hand with warm enthusiasm. Another marker in his career had come to pass.

Just the same, it was not easy for the couple. Theatres weren't over-keen to shell out double wages for double billings, and although their weeks at 'Carsnooty' were well received and,

by and large, well reviewed, they were considered unexposed newcomers by some, implying a risk to the potential takings at the box-office. Their booking agency, fusty offices in Glasgow's Sauchiehall Street, were light years away from those of Bernard Delfont who would ultimately manage Chic. Not a great deal of work was offered in early 1948, but that was in part because Maidie gave birth to a daughter in May of that year. Annabelle first saw the light of day at Chic's family home in Bank Street where her grandmother, Isabella, helped deliver her into the world as a true Greenockian! Her grandmother, thereafter referred to Annabelle as her 'May Blossom'.

Semmit and Drawers, Drapers

Coming in here tonight, I heard someone say, 'Charlie,' and I turned – not too quickly, but I turned just the same. 'Do you remember me?' the bloke asked, sat there like a frog up a pump. He said, 'You're Charlie Drawers, aren't you? I mean that's your own name, isn't it? Charlie Drawers!'

I said, 'Yes it is.'

He said, 'What a funny name that is, Charlie Drawers.'

I said, 'Don't shout it out all over the place!'

'Chic Murray, now,' he thought aloud, 'that's a stage name, I suppose. But are you still *really* Charlie Drawers?'

I said, 'I suppose I am.'

He said, 'That's a funny name that, Drawers.'

So I said, 'What's your name?'

He said, 'Erskine.'

I said, 'Then what are *you* talking about?'

Of course, that's my name, Drawers. It was my father's name – he was Sir Charles Drawers. And it was handed down – the name, not the drawers, of course. And we used to have a shop, it was a draper's shop we had, in partnership with another fellow, a Highland chap from Islay called Semmit. It's an old-fashioned name, I believe. David Semmit – Semmit and Drawers, Drapers.

So it was quite good for business, because people would enter the shop and say 'Mr Semmit, can I have a pair of drawers?'

And we Drawers – let me tell you – we were a *warm* family. There was my brother, my youngest brother, he was Chester. What was that? I missed that! Oh, I see *Chester Drawers*! Oh yes, he was a tall boy. But wooden. He played violin and I played piano and we used to play duets together. If I finished first I'd put the kettle on for a cup of tea.

And I remember on one occasion, my father taking me aside. 'Sit down a minute,' he said, and I knew something was wrong the way the shotgun was pointing at me. 'I think it's about time you went out into the wide world,' he said, 'and made your way.'

'Well, if you think so, Dad,' I replied.

'Well,' he said, 'you've got a good name and a good Scots tongue in you. An excellent name. Always uphold it, my son, and always watch what you're doing.'

'Well, you can rest assured, Father, I'll never let the drawers down!'

CHAPTER 5
THE INLAWS
AND OUTLAWS

In October 1948 things were looking up when they were rebooked to appear at the Roxy Theatre, Falkirk, as 'Chic and Maidie – The Lank and the Lady' (they'd performed there earlier that month). Chic's routines were constantly developing, becoming increasingly more abstruse, certainly more surreal. He also began to realise that the first house (usually with more women) differed from the later house. So he was to meet hostility, from time to time, in the earlier performances, every time he slipped behind Maidie when she was playing, singing, or doing both, to start his Gooey-style facial gyrations. Even though they were riotously funny, some budding feminists were liable to shout, 'Stop making a bluidy fool o' thon nice lassie! Ye're nae that bluidy guid yersel', ya big wallic!' In contrast, the later audiences, probably having recently vacated a licensed hostelry, lapped up Chic's shenanigans and the comedy miming behind Maidie's back simply upped the overall entertainment quotient!

On opening night, Maidie arranged for her parents to come through for the second house to see her double act with Chic for the first time, but as the rehearsals progressed that Monday morning, the producer ostentatiously stood halfway up the theatre aisle with his stopwatch, like some demented amateur athletic timekeeper with a comb-over and an exploding proboscis. Chic was unhappy. 'First, I get a loony with a stopwatch wanting me to be a bartender in Greenock,' he thought, 'and now this geezer's about to shout out "take your marks" on some imaginary set of starting blocks!'

At lunch he told Maidie he was far from happy, but she was too excited about her parents attending to take much notice (after all, her Dad had recently returned after years of service as a petty officer in the navy during the war and had last seen her

'Do you know the piano's resting on my foot?'
'No, but hum it and I'll play it.'

My wife went to the beauty parlour for a mudpack. She looked great for two days until the mud fell off. But she's a classy girl just the same. All her tattoos are spelt right!

Chic's own artwork for the double act

perform when she was still a young teenager). Chic had a pie and a pint and they returned to the theatre where the clock-watcher ordained that the full cast should assemble onstage. 'The show's running for far too long, I'm afraid,' he announced, 'and the bars obviously will suffer accordingly, particularly after the second house. We're running a business here first and foremost and I need those bars hoatching with punters after the show.'

'Gawd,' Chic groaned to himself, 'we're back to being licensed grocers.'

'Now I admit part of the problem I made myself!' he continued. 'I booked too many of you in the first place. It's that simple. So, for the rest of the week, we'll just pare back a bit on all your routines. I can't do that today, though. It's just too late. So one of you can have the night off – Chic and Maidie go and have a nice meal and put your feet up!'

Maidie, dreadfully upset, began to cry. 'Why us?' Chic asked.

'I'm the boss around here and, I'm sorry, Chic, but you're not the lead comic act!'

Maidie regained her composure in their dressing room. Against Chic's advice, Maidie announced, 'I'm going to plead with him. These are special circumstances, my parents and all that . . .' But, sure enough, she reappeared, fifteen minutes on, empty-handed and inconsolable again.

Chic left the theatre and wandered aimlessly around the

town centre and Maidie tried to cheer herself up by having the works done at some fancy hairdresser. Chic was there later to greet Maidie's parents at the station and explain the situation to them. Typically, they never expressed their own disappointment, but gave Maidie a comforting hug when they all met up as arranged. They headed for a hotel where Chic had booked a *table à quatre,* and he had chosen well as they later learnt it was Falkirk's premier hotel. Their table was prominently positioned close to a small dance floor and a baby grand piano where a nice wee mannie was banging out his versions of the light classics. During their meal, Chic kept them all amused and Maidie – bless her! – began to unwind.

They were enjoying their coffee, when the diminutive pianist concluded his programme to generous applause. 'Ladies and gentlemen,' the wee man continued, 'I'd like to extend a warm welcome to two professional entertainers who are having a night off. Maidie Dickson, you've all heard of, well, she's since formed a double act with her husband Chic, and they're here with Maidie's parents. We're very honoured to welcome them all [applause] and I just wondered if they might give us all a thrill by doing a turn?'

Maidie was stunned, 'But, but . . .' she stammered before Chic, the picture of innocence, interrupted her.

'Ah! . . . what price fame?' He led her to the dance floor as the diners began to cheer.

'But I've not got my accordion,' Maidie panicked.

'You have that!' Chic replied, as the pianist carted it in. 'You on the squeezebox and me on this beaten-up joanna! Maidie looked across at the surprised delight on her parents' faces.

'Come here!' she beckoned to Chic as she hugged and kissed him to the thrill of the onlookers. 'Now let's give them the works!'

They did just that – and for far longer than their routine onstage – and those present just loved it! The applause was deafening as they made their way back to their table where Hugh and Anne Dickson hugged them both with heartfelt pride. A waiter arrived. 'Some of the diners would be honoured if you would accept a bottle of champagne from them,' he said.

'Aye,' said Chic, 'we could just about manage that,' and waved happily towards the donors' table. Chic had met with

'Would sir care for an aperitif?'
'Why? Is the steak tough?'

Triumph and Disaster and had treated those two imposters just the same.

Chic and Maidie saw her parents off at Grahamston station on the very last train amidst hand-pumping, back-slapping and smiley faces. 'How on earth did you manage that, Chic?' she asked as they watched the train puff out of Falkirk.

Tongue in cheek, he replied, 'Well, I, too, can arrange bookings, y'know!' (This assertion was utter tosh! Chic never did, nor ever intended to arrange bookings! Tsk! Tsk! That was for lesser mortals to attend to!) He continued, 'Actually, I had nothing to do but waste time when I came across this hotel. "Right!" I thought, "I'll reserve a table to take our minds off things." So I told the lassie we were having a night off from appearing at the Roxy and were willing to do a turn for the punters. At that, she ran to fetch the manager who loved the idea: "Your dinner's on us, sir, whatever you want!"'

'Bloody hell!' Maidie squealed. 'That explains why I never saw you pay the bill! I remember thinking, "Who's a clever boy then?" because, naturally, I assumed you'd made some arrangement. Och! Trust you!' She gave him a playful smack. Chic was becoming frisky as homewards they ventured, closely cuddling each other. It was homewards and to bed . . .

'You've got acute appendicitis. We're going to have to operate as a matter of urgency.'
'Will the scar show?'
'Not if you're careful.'

But times overall were still tough for the couple. They were still not well known on the circuit, so when Maidie heard of a chance to tour Glasgow Corporation's mental institutions, she grabbed it, despite the fact it was not particularly well rewarded. Nellie (yawn) Sutherland, a representative of their agent, drawled in a monotonous voice not unlike Maggie Smith in *The Prime of Miss Jean Brodie*, 'It's not much, Maidie, but it'll suit that man of yours!' A back-handed compliment if ever there was one (Chic never took to her, so she reciprocated in kind!).

Perhaps a little like his sense of humour, Chic saw sanity and madness as next-door neighbours – a proposition he repeated on numerous occasions. 'Shipyard humour,' he reflected after his experience with the inmates, 'is not so far away from mental-home humour, believe me!'

There was one patient in particular who was convinced that Chic and Maidie were doctors in disguise, a theory that won additional credence when the participants were asked by Maidie in jolly mode, to join in the chorus. 'You see now! That's how

these bloody crafty doctors ken which o' us are willing tae co-operate and which willnae! They'll have marked ma caird by noo, wait an' see!' A conjuror, likewise, who made a rabbit disappear, was accused of performing this trick so that the inmates would be held responsible for its disappearance.

But, in general, their visits were a success and Chic sympathised with the prevailing theory of the 'chaps' that the medical staff were 'aff their heids'! (There was a germ of truth in that!) For example, there was a welfare officer (in loose terminology) whose tour of duty involved the extension of his neck round each patient's door and an 'Everything's all right, then? Good! Cheerio!'

One patient turned touchingly to Chic and said, 'Ye ken that would-be welfare officer, Chic? Christ! For fuck's sake! D'ye no think he's mair like a bastarding "farewell" officer?' A delightful, if somewhat overstated, spoonerism!

During this period, Chic and Maidie lived out of suitcases, and the children (who were much loved and cosseted), were mainly looked after by their grandparents. They moved around between Greenock, Maidie's parents in Edinburgh and Isabella's brothers and sisters in Glasgow and Dundee. Where that was not possible, they would batten down the hatches in theatrical digs – never Chic's favoured option, being a canny man who approached personal expenditure with traditional Scottish caution and frugality! They ate simply and well and wherever they landed Maidie would prevail upon whoever necessary to be granted access to the kitchen to prepare Chic's favourite staples: lentil broth, and plenty of it, followed by mince and tatties or bangers and mash, invariably, in Chic's case, with double helpings. 'The Lank' was edging towards 'The Tank'!

Despite everyone's hospitality and generosity, Maidie, often separated from her little ones, began to make nesting noises. 'Chic,' she said, 'I've spotted a flat for sale two floors above my folks in Montague Street. Let's make enquiries, please.' Chic was a little hesitant for no other reason than that they had limited savings to cobble together for a deposit. He needn't have worried. When he returned from his appointment with the building society manager, he looked puzzled rather than crestfallen.

'You'll never believe this, Maidie! We don't qualify for a

'She carries a torch for Big George.'
'Really? She must be in love with him, then?'
'Don't be daft! He's a plumber!'

I love food. It's come to the stage where I won't eat anything else.

'I rang the bell of this bed and breakfast house. A lady appeared from an upstairs window. 'Yes,' she said, 'what do you want?' I said I wanted to stay there. She said, 'Well, stay there, then!' and slammed the window down.

Chic and Maidie – and bunnet.
One of the early routines

mortage. We're classified as "of no fixed abode". Doesn't that apply to everyone trying to buy their first home? Who do these pen-pushers think I am, a gentleman of the road, perhaps?'

'Maybe that's the trouble,' Maidie replied ruefully, 'we're not on the road enough.'

'Well, as a reclassified gypsy, I have the second sight and things are going to get better. Wait and see . . .'

Gradually their prospects brightened, and in 1949 they were signed up for the summer season at the Gaiety in Leith. 'Big City!' Maidie said delightedly.

'Wee theatre!' Chic countered.

In any event there was an air of optimism that didn't exist back in the early 'Carsnooty' days. At that time one of Maidie's fans, Ramsden Craig, was a hack with the *Evening Citizen* who had often written in fulsome terms of Maidie when she performed on her own. But he hadn't taken to Chic at that time. 'You've made a boo-boo here, Maidie. Marrying the man is one thing, sticking him on the stage with you is another! He'll pull you down. Mark my words!'

Maidie countered vehemently. 'There's jokesters galore,' she said. 'Chic will be a great comedian! You wait and see!' He left wholly unconvinced, threatening to eat his hat if he was proved wrong. A year on, during the Gaiety's summer show (where interestingly, Hector Nichol, often unfairly described as the 'poor man's Chic Murray', made his debut onstage as a singer!), this part review appeared in the *Edinburgh Evening News*: 'We all know Maidie and she's always been a favourite. But take a listen to her funny husband Chic. He's not a 'Scots' comic, he doesn't tell jokes in the ordinary sense, but he's starting to tickle audiences with his daft stories, which are cleverer than they sound. Maidie's obviously taking a relative back seat to give her husband's talent a chance to come through. I think this act could go places.'

Bookings began to pick up. The pedestrian Nellie Sutherland landed them a leading role in Motherwell's annual Christmas show and it was now commonplace for Chic and Maidie to appear jointly on the billboards. Then on to the Empress Playhouse in Glasgow, where they were billed as A 'Large and Small Scotch'. Their act, by now, was going great guns with glowing reviews. There was one night in Glasgow, with Isabella, on one of her rare sorties up to Glasgow, in the audience, and before political correctness had removed much of the fun and laughter in vaudeville, when the two of them appeared onstage blacked up as a tribute to Al Jolson. (Any theatregoer of the late forties could confirm Chic was terrific in this role.) Except on this occasion! There they were onstage with their black faces and white-gloved hands. But Chic – Shock! Horror! – had forgotten his gloves! They had entered the stage in fine form with 'Toot Toot Tootsie, Goodbye' only for Chic to spot his state of

'Did I know him? Of course I did. I was in the actual firing squad that shot him.'
'Funny, he didn't mention that.'
'Och, he was a quiet lad really.'

undress! Quick as a flash, he skedaddled offstage, quicker than 'Tootsie' even, leaving poor Maidie to vamp on as best she could in what was essentially a man's song. Charging up to the attic to their dressing room, a begloved Chic eventually reappeared whilst the conductor, who must have been studying his musical score at the *moment critique*, remained totally bemused by the whole affair. But not the crowd, who went daft, roaring their delight as Chic waggled his mitts in the air and grinned widely, milking the audience and the situation for all it was worth! Maidie recalled Chic's re-entry was met with a Hampden roar; Chic could do no wrong. He 'slaughtered' them, as the showbiz expression went.

And then, with the audience resting in the palm of his hand, he said, 'Our last number is singularly appropriate. You'll see what I mean when I tell you my mum's with you in the audience.' This time, if anything, he underplayed the impersonation of Al Jolson, someone he hugely admired, as he sang 'Mammy'. By the end, there wasn't a dry eye in the house and that included Isabella. And thankfully, Chic, on this occasion, stuck to the lyrics and not to his amendments which somewhat spoiled the sentimental nature of the song. They were spared the Chic version!

> *The sun shines east. The sun shines west*
> *The wind's in the north and I'm wearing a vest!*
> *Oh! Mammy! Mammy! I'd walk a thousand miles*
> *For one look at your piles!*
> *That's my Mammy!*

Chic and Maidie spent the summer season at Largs, 'doon the water' from Greenock, where they were billed as 'The Big Yin and the Wee Yin'. These were happy days, the family all together at Granny Murray's for some idyllic months. And they had moved up the billboards from the 'wines and spirits' (showbiz jargon for bottom or near-bottom billing) to third in the pecking order, a sure sign of experience and recognition. Their Christmas season was spent at the Palladium in Edinburgh where, amongst the company, a young Yorkshire dancer made his debut: one Lionel Blair. Of Chic and Maidie, *The Scotsman* said, 'An act to watch. Their appeal baffles me, but they're loaded with it.'

Chic gives Maidie one of his famous looks

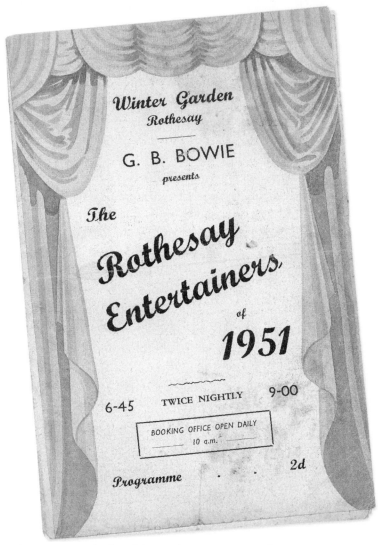

'Have you heard the joke about Rothesay?' 'Yes. It's a Bute.'

Money and bookings began to gather momentum, confirmed by a telegram from their agents: 'Contact us immediately. Chance of summer season at Rothesay. Attractive offer.' The vagrant couple of no fixed abode were now able to raise a mortgage, and with a pal lending them the deposit, they bought the very flat Maidie had set her heart on so long before (as providence would have it, in the interim, it had remained unsold). Visits to theatres in Paisley and Inverness were slotted in, before their arrival in Rothesay in their own motor car, a Standard 10, testimony to their increasing financial well-being. And here, for the first time in Rothesay, they were now announced to the world as 'The Tall Droll with the Small Doll'.

Their stay in Rothesay was eventful by any standard. For example, they met two brothers during rehearsals, the Maiberts

– 'Poetry in Motion', their tag alleged – a dancing duo. On their opening night, their act commenced with one of the 'poets' motionless behind a frame, dressed as an unlikely representation of Rabbie Burns. The other brother was due to mince onto the stage, look up at the tableau and utter the immortal words, 'Oh! It's yersel' Rabbie!' This, then, magically was to bring Rabbie to life, jumping out of the frame to recite 'To a Mouse'. All augured well as he recited the opening couplet, the 'Wee, sleekit, cowrin'' bit before ('whit a shame fer the wee laddie!') the recitation nose-dived. He'd dried up like a dessicated fig. Cue embarrassing silence with the poor wretch 'cowrin'' himself. Chic and Maidie were hanging in the wings, (they were next on), and although Chic tried to prompt the 'poet in motion', it was to no avail. So in he jumped on a rescue mission with the following gibberish:

> *Oh graven o' the graven grouts*
> *Graven o' the grossets*
> *Grossin' o' the graven grouts*
> *An' graven o' the grassets*
> *Oh, grossen groosin graven grouts*
> *An' graven o' the grossets . . .*

The other brother, still stranded onstage, and responsible for Rabbie's inglorious revival, compounded the agony by trying to continue single-handed, but in the face of 'the groundlings, who for the most part are capable of nothing but inexplicable dumb-shows and noise', he reacted wisely to the mob's hoots and whistles of derision, hastily exiting with the hint of a bow.

Over now to Chic who began by issuing a warning, 'If you don't laugh at my act, I'll arrange for that last lot to do an encore!' The audience roared their approval in stark contrast to the manager's wrath at Chic's gaffe – Rule Number One: Never, never criticise a fellow artiste! Chic was to receive a fearful tongue-lashing later, aggravated by his customary inability ever to appear on time for rehearsals, but it was a good result overall because Maidie had visions of a one-night summer season with their HP payments on the car still in their infancy! The earwigging clearly had a profound effect on Chic; he nonchalantly turned to Maidie and said, 'Was that guy a stagehand or what?'

A few weeks later, Chic and Maidie were invited to do a

There was a man standing stationary at a funeral, some 60 yards from the graveside. 'Who's that?' a friend asked a fellow griever. 'I'm not sure. But I think he's a distant relative.'

piece for the BBC in a radio show which was the forerunner of *Worker's Playtime*. Chic was specifically requested in a memo not to have a go at the quality of food in the canteen. It had become tired and worn out as a theme and would he please choose some other subject matter? They should have known better. This was Chic! Maidie squirmed with embarrassment as he ignored, as usual, the rehearsed script.

We're not going to talk about the food in the canteen; after all, it's not worth talking about. Now I won't say the custard's hard enough to dance on, but I saw someone try it. He slipped and broke his ankle. I'll say this, though, about the mince they serve here, it looks just the same coming up as it does going down. Never mind, the tea's excellent. It's the finest paint-stripper I've ever come across. Oh, and they tell me the cook recently came back from a holiday abroad. Amazing! They must have relaxed the quarantine laws.

'I believe the minister's going to give a sermon today on the milk of human kindness.'
'Well, I hope it's condensed.'

The producer, Eddie Fraser, a gentle soul, asked Chic after his 'performance', 'Didn't you get my memo, Mr Murray, about the food?'

'I did,' Chic replied with mock concern and sublime innocence, 'but what I said could never be construed as criticism. The food in this canteen, let me tell you, is in the finest tradition of food in the blackout, where no one can see what they're eating. Credit where it's due, what the Nazis couldn't do in bringing our proud nation to its knees, has been accomplished with terrific panache right here in this canteen! It's some achievement!'

The producer did his best to ignore the gratuitous insults, 'Look, Mr Murray, you only arrived here minutes before the broadcast! In fact I was worried you'd be late. You've never even seen our canteen, never mind eaten in it!'

Quick as a flash, Chic turned in mock shock to Maidie, 'Is this true, Maidie? If it is, heads will roll . . .'

And the moral of the story? They don't lick Chic – not easily, anyway!

Bookings continued to pop through the letter-box regularly,

from the east to the west of Scotland, and from Thurso to all points south. A *Daily Record* reporter caught up with Chic in Dundee and gave both Chic and Maidie a good 'jolly': 'A new trick in the field of comedy is the act of Chic and Maidie. This husband-and-wife team is on the way to a very big reputation, although it's hard to explain why. Onstage, Chic doesn't seem to do anything but blether, while Maidie supports an accordion and looks at him. But these blethers are among the funniest things in the Scottish theatre today.'

And then they had a stroke of good fortune. It was spring 1952, and the couple were back at the Edinburgh Palladium for their Easter show. The Palladium was something of a relic from the music-hall days, cheap and cheerful, in contrast to Edinburgh's Empire which was part of the Stoll Moss conglomerate, invariably attracting the big names from the south. It was the afternoon of their first night, when Chic answered the telephone in their flat. 'Hi! Chic, it's Dan Campbell here.' Dan was the manager of the Palladium. 'I've just had Jimmy Hill from the Empire on the blower and he's bang in trouble. Terry Scott was supposed to top the bill of his *Folies Bergère* show and he's just been informed that he's indisposed, seriously ill. The chances of hiring anyone else at the eleventh hour are on the wrong side of zero. He wants you and Maidie. You're his only hope, honestly! What do you think?'

'Tell me more, Dan.' Chic concentrated on suppressing his growing excitement.

'Right. If you're interested get straight round now to Jimmy! He'll run through what he wants from you and then fire yourselves back to me, pronto. I'll stick you on early. You'll have to taxi back to the Empire to close their first house, and then whizz straight back here again to open my second house. And if that's not enough, then back you go by taxi to finish off their second house. Once you've done that, you're free to pop off home!'

'Thanks a bundle, it all seems pretty straightforward then,' Chic said sarcastically. 'What about money?'

'Double rates, maybe more and obviously he'll cover the taxis,' was the reply. Ten minutes later, after a mini-debriefing with Maidie, they were taxi-bound for the Empire. This was a genuine door-opening opportunity, make no mistake, and Chic

was determined to go for it.

Jimmy Hill (who had visibly aged in the previous few hours), was still in a state when they arrived. Never, with the exception of the Usher Hall, had Chic seen such a massive stage; the Palladium was a matchbox by comparison. But it took more than that to overawe the Tall Droll! They rushed through their routine with the clock against all of them, then hopped back into a taxi to the Palladium as the nightly process got under way. It was an immense challenge in retrospect, but Maidie, consummate professional that she was, handled the demands on her nervous energy and concentration with sublime, unruffled ease. Chic, blessed with unfathomable depths of self-assurance, simply excelled himself. This was in many respects to be one of the greatest triumphs of his career. Let Maidie recall these life-changing events in her own words:

> *To say that Chic rose to the occasion is putting it mildly. He was in his element in the Empire and established a tremendous rapport with the audience. Here he really began to master his comic looks. I'll never forget one night he didn't follow me on – I'd already started 'Nellie' on my own and was wishing the floor would swallow me up, when in he strolled. He got a tremendous hand just for coming in late! He did a little curtsey and stuck his finger under his chin – another bit of business he was to become associated with.*

It was a vicious rumour! The music teacher and I were only trying on our Adam and Eve costumes.

Actually, Chic used the finger-under-the-chin routine to control the stagehands – depending on the positioning of the index, they knew when to crash down the 'tabs' (theatre babble for curtains!).

Their two-week shuttle was an outstanding success and every night at the Empire was a sell-out. A critic in *The Scotsman* wrote, 'As a spectacle the *Folies Bergère* revue would certainly take a lot of beating. In one sphere – that of humour – it has acquired further distinction through the work of Chic and Maidie. Chic is in a class by himself, with an economy of expression and gesture which can be funnier than any demon-strative technique. Their act last night was deservedly received with a storm of applause.'

The Skunks

I have a brother in the zoo in Edinburgh. He's a keeper there. You can tell that by the ring on his finger. I was up the other day, watching him float about in the hippopotamus pool. Then he said to me, 'Do you remember the pregnant skunk I told you about?'

'Yes,' I said.

'Well, she's had a family,' he said.

'Oh, has she?' I don't remember exactly, but there was surprise in my voice so the 'Oh, has she?' was quite high-pitched.

'Yes,' he said, 'she's given birth to two boy skunks. And just to be a wee bit different, instead of calling them the usual Jim or Charlie or Andy, I thought, for a change, why not call them "In" and "Out"? So I did. You'll know them from now on as In and Out or Out and In, depending on which you see first.'

He went on to tell me that some days later, the mother skunk went out and left In and Out in. But, before she left, she said, 'I don't want you going out, In. And you stay in, Out, too.' But she'd only left minutes before when In went out. However, luckily, Out stayed in because when their mother returned, she praised Out for staying in. 'It's nice to see you're in, Out, but where's In?' she asked.

Out said, 'In's gone out, Mum.'

'Well, I know it's not your fault, Out, but you'd better go out and bring In in. So Out went out and found In and marched In in again.

Then their mum said, 'Good boy, Out. How did you find In?'

'Instinkt,' Out replied.

CHAPTER 6
SHOWBIZ

Several engagements followed, including a show at the Metropole, Glasgow, hosted by Renée Houston, a bountifully talented actress/comedienne. It was notable because in the 'wines and spirits' was a young man at the very beginning of a distinguished career, the late, well-loved Andy *'Scottish Soldier'* Stewart. And despite their contretemps over canteen food, BBC producer Eddie Fraser simply loved their act – he was a huge and loyal fan. Wherever they were, sessions for BBC Radio peppered their diary and were very popular.

Tommy Morgan, the resident comedian and compère of the Pavilion Theatre in Glasgow was a mega-star in the west at this time – so much so, the local press often referred to Tommy as 'Mr Glasgow'. He was also a gifted inventor of 'characters' and probably his most memorable was his drag act as 'Big Beenie McBride, The Pride of the Clyde', alternatively known as 'Big Beenie McBride, The G.I. War Bride'. He was one of those lovely, altruistic people without a jealous bone in his body, who loved to help many a budding (sometimes struggling) comic. He gave them their breaks, and he did his damnedest to help shove them up the ladder. He wanted Chic and Maidie with a passion – not that they were in need of an upward push! – but since their double whammy in Edinburgh at the Empire and Pavilion, he had to get in the queue while other previous bookings were honoured. When Chic and Maidie eventually arrived in Tommy's show at the Pavilion, his introduction of the two of them touched Chic deeply. Chic said of him, 'How could you do any less than your very best for a man like that? He's got a heart bigger than his bank account – and that's saying something!'

Tommy introduced his guests in the following prophetic manner: 'There's a couple coming on next who are the funniest

It was so boring, six empty seats got up and walked out.

'Why not do something, for once, for your own country.'
'Okay, what?'
'Emigrate.'

First time in London

57

comedy act I've ever seen. Make the most of them now, for I promise you, we're not going to keep them long here in Scotland. They're going right to the top as big stars. Welcome – Chic and Maidie Murray!' A piquant reminder of their now high-flying status was encapsulated in the long-gone and much-lamented *Bulletin*, a Scottish daily newspaper that was still riding high in the fifties. A cartoon depicted Chic and Maidie carousing with some Glasgow 'haing-oots'. The caption formed a little ditty:

> *It's Christmas day in the workhouse,*
> *In walked a welfare lady,*
> *She asked the inmates what they'd like,*
> *They answered, 'Chic and Maidie!'*

The big break was still some way off and Maidie was sick of criss-crossing Scotland. They even did a series of gigs in Ireland. To make matters worse, Chic was not only a bloody awful driver, he was an even worse front-seat passenger. It was the same rigmarole every time they embarked on a journey – one question after another. The only saving grace was that he varied them, so poor Maidie was kept on her toes. 'Did you bring some food for the journey?' 'Did you remember the keys?' 'Did you leave the gas on?' And, one of his most irritating questions (after his wife, small of stature, had lugged their suitcases into the vehicle), 'Are you sure the car is properly balanced?'

On one occasion, he awoke from a snooze, when Maidie was waiting for a big brute of a lorry to pass by at a road junction. Had she taken Chic's advice, they would both have been goners as wide-eyed, he shouted in panic, 'Drive for your fucking life!'

On another occasion, she handed him the car keys and said, 'Go off and drive. You need to practise.' When he returned, she asked, 'How did you get on?'

'Fine,' he said nonchalantly, 'but I knocked over a policeman outside the post office.' There was little or no discussion thereafter. Clearly 'knocking over a policeman' was just one of these things. Oh, well . . .

On a picnic outing with the children and Nana Dickson, official sandwich-maker, they tootled down the east coast under a cloudless sky in late spring. They were staring up at the

A letter from Chic, which he wrote shortly after joining the AA:

Dear Sirs,

I recently joined your motoring organisation and despite sending my annual fee, I have yet to receive my uniform, van and roadside phone box. Please give this your urgent attention.

Yours faithfully,
Chic Murray

Tommy Morgan

Chic and Maidie with
Duncan Macrae (left) and
Andy Stewart (right)

heavens on their beach-side rug when Chic asked Maidie, 'Do you fancy a proper holiday abroad, dear?'

'That would be nice, Chic, but we've no time, and where's the money coming from?'

'Och! Let's worry about that later, Maidie, what are we working for, for heaven's sake?'

Maidie rose up from the rug and onto her elbows to address him earnestly, 'We're working to make you a star!' Whether she made this remark because she keenly sensed the audience's increasing eagerness to have Chic all to themselves, because the

wear and tear of giving her all in non-stop performances from earliest childhood had taken their inevitable toll, or perhaps because responding to the natural yearnings of a mum hungering for more time with her children , who can say? The likely answer was a bit of all of these things, and, to this very day, Maidie confirms that all these considerations were contributory to a greater or lesser degree. Nevertheless, this was a Road to Damascus moment.

And it was to recur. One evening, a few weeks on, the bairns safely in bed, they were relaxing, feet up, a cheery fire, a drink in hand. Maidie broke the reverie, 'It's time for new thinking, Chic. It's well past time we changed the act. I mean *radically*!'

Initially Chic was taken aback. 'Why change something, just for the sake of change? For goodness sake, it doesn't need fixing. It's going fine just as it is,' he argued defensively.

'Look,' Maidie reasoned, 'the act has been changing, developing, maybe is a better word, since our earliest days, Chic. Wake up and recognise that! I'm willing to be there as back-up, let's say, at the end of your stint. At the start, too, if you insist. I'll support you any way I can, but you have got to be realistic – it's you they've come to see. Come on! . . . I can see that and you'd see that too if you'd just be honest with yourself! I'm a realist and there's nothing wrong with that. All I'm saying is that I'm going to take a much lower profile from now on.' This was not the first time that Maidie had selflessly guided and shaped her husband's career. What was to prove different was that her faith was soon to be rewarded.

Shortly thereafter, they were booked to appear back at the Empire Theatre, Maidie's own patch where they had gone down such a storm back in 1952. Around the same time, Nellie, 'the monotone' Sutherland called them from Glasgow, tipping them off that the Beeb was holding auditions for television and emphasising that doing nothing was not an option. The results of their efforts at BBC Scotland were a long way off, months in fact, so meantime, Chic pulled out the stops and applied himself unstintingly in rehearsals for the show at the Empire. Their efforts were rewarded accordingly. The *Daily Record* said, with justification, 'It's refreshing to find an act that has slogged it round the wee halls of Scotland getting the real breaks at last.' And then, cometh the hour . . .

Looking at the obituary columns, it never fails to amaze me how people die in alphabetical order.

A man entered a pet shop and asked to buy a pet wasp. 'We don't stock pet wasps.' 'Well, how come you've got two in the window?'

Red Riding Hood, originally, had nothing to do with kids' stories. He was an eighteenth-century Russian gangster.

Back in Glasgow at the Pavilion with their number one fan, Tommy Morgan, the piranhas were now circling! Hymie Zahl was first to open the bidding, offering to sign Chic and Maidie for £3,500 a year. They were certainly tempted but wisely played the 'wait and see' game. Hymie was there for their opening night but none of them anticipated that there would be two other agents, also circling for the kill. One was a representative of the Grade brothers, the other, Billy Marsh, was eager to sign them on behalf of Bernard Delfont. (An up-and-coming comedian, part of Billy Marsh's stable, had already visited the Pavilion and had begged, cajoled and arm-twisted Billy Marsh to sign up Chic and Maidie. He was to become a close friend, Frankie Howerd.) They descended on the Murray dressing room after the show. The outcome was that Chic and Maidie opted for Billy Marsh, not only because he offered the most (originally £6,000 a year which Chic, through bloody cheek and brinkmanship, nudged up to £6,500) but because he had plans for their future career far more advanced than the competition. They were set to appear at top venues across the country prior to the 'real action' in London! And their money was to increase annually over three years with fees from radio and television appearances an extra source of income. The contract was signed the following day and

Chic and Maidie sign up with the
Delfont Agency's Billy Marsh

the press were given the treatment. Billy Marsh said, 'Everybody in the business has been after Chic. I think I've made one of the best signings in my career as an agent.' Many years on, Billy reminisced,

I had first seen their double act at the Pavilion much earlier and I remember wondering how Chic would progress. He went down tremendously there, but I wanted to wait. The Pavilion had its own audience, who loved him, so he was comfortable with them, and he kept pushing his style further and further. I wanted to wait until it was distilled to the point he was ready for the circuit, and I knew it wouldn't be long. What the two of them had was incredible. Chic was a genius, but comedy is a peculiar thing. Often the funniest act can disappoint an audience with a weak ending. I saw that with Chic and Maidie this never happened. When Chic was merely good the act was lifted by the slam-bang song and dance-act finale – but when Chic was brilliant the climax paralysed them!

When they had some time to themselves, they headed off to the big smoke; neither had ever been to London before. With the car properly 'balanced', a prerequisite for a journey of any distance for Chic, Maidie, as usual, did the lion's share of the driving. 'It wasn't worth it,' she recalled. 'If I threw a few "zeds", he'd end up some blinking cul-de-sac miles off the beaten track and, of course, it would always be my fault as the navigator. I was better just to drive myself!'

'How the hell did you manage to get this car in my kitchen?'
'Och, that's easy. You just turn left between the first bedroom and the airing cupboard.'

They spent a few days touring the West End, visiting theatreland, and on their return home they were greeted with the news that the Beeb wanted them to make a television appearance in *Garrison Theatre* to be recorded at the City Hall, Perth. Also on the bill was the wonderfully lugubrious 'Wee Cock Sparra' Duncan Macrae, Margo Henderson and Andy Stewart, and hosted by Teddy Johnston who made something of a name for himself in one of the earliest Eurovision Song Contests.

Chic doggedly refused to rehearse before the programme and perhaps it was his spontaneity which won over the critics. For example, Tom Nicholson of the *Sunday Mail* interviewed Chic

Just bought the wife a Jaguar. Great investment – it's just bit her leg off.

who confirmed that he had a rough idea of what he was going to say but the idea of learning a script from back to front was a total non-starter. Nicholson observed that therein lay the secret to Chic's success: 'It explains why he's so good.'

The *Dundee Courier*, commented: 'The outstanding feature of the show was, without doubt, the appearance of Chic Murray, who justified all that was said about him. The success of the show was due to the fact that he gave us something entirely new.' High praise indeed!

Their careers, from this moment onwards, took on a gathering, increasing momentum. One producer who watched their *Garrison Theatre* act, booked them for a series called *Face the Music*, where they appeared on one occasion with Bob Hope. Par for the course, Chic glided through, unfazed by his distinguished colleague. 'Bob who?'

And Bernard Delfont now began to ratchet things in an upward direction. For the rest of the year their diary was bursting with appointments and reappointments, beginning back at the Empire, just to keep their hands in, then off south. They were well known in Geordie-land but the Stoll Moss theatre conglomerate had prestigious flagship theatres from the north to the Midlands and to points south. They appeared in almost all of them.

After a stint in Newcastle to the usual tip-top reviews, inexplicably, Chic became very nervy at the prospect of appearing in Manchester. 'They won't understand my Scots accent. This is too far south!' he grizzled. Maidie did her best to reassure him and it remains something of a mystery that when they arrived in rehearsals in Manchester, Maidie was taken aside by the manager of the theatre.

'Hrrrmph,' he cleared his throat conspiratorially, 'Mrs Murray, I understand your husband doesn't speak English.' (What the hell he was thinking of is anybody's guess – a comedian appearing in a theatre in the heart of the Midlands, unable to speak English?) He continued, 'Would you please explain the running order to him, if I write it down?'

Chic, hanging around within earshot, interrupted, 'It's okay. I do understand English, just a little bit. You can cue me direct.'

The manager was utterly confused, 'My assistant informed me that . . .'

Chic and Maidie in London

I walked into the bedroom. The curtains were drawn but the furniture was real.

Chic broke in, 'You see Maidie, I told you! I'm not easily understood.'

It was no surprise when the press reacted with delight: 'The solemn wonderment with which Chic describes the business of minute-by-minute living is as unearthly as a Goon show.'

In amongst their many engagements, and because of the success of their earlier appearances on telly, they signed a contract with BBC Television to appear in eighteen further shows over two years. One of these shows, entitled *Highland Fling* received the following notice: 'Here's a Scot with a quaint knack of making you laugh, although he tells hardly any jokes at all. Mr Murray has a very individual style which might be worked up into a first-rate comedy act.'

Chic commented, 'Jeez, Maidie, talk about hedging your bets!'

Another, writing in *The Scotsman*, said, 'What can be done with a natural, individual gift for humour, without any straining after-effect, is excellently illustrated by Chic Murray, whose manner towards his partner Maidie, is as comical as ever, and whose story-telling is unique.'

It was now 1956 and it was becoming a habit as success pursued success. The pair appeared in a pantomime in Glasgow entitled *Just Daft* with Duncan Macrae, Dave Willis and Jack Anthony. In one sketch, Chic was dressed as a giant fairy, sporting a huge bendy wand and a ludicrous white tutu. As he shot through the trapdoor to make his magical appearance onstage behind a puff of smoke, the Tall Droll hit his 'napper' on

the ascent journey to the stage. The public collapsed in spasms of laughter, so much so that the poor man had to include this painful exercise from then on, as part of the act! The show was such a hit, it transferred seamlessly to Edinburgh. And hardly had that season run its course when they returned to Glasgow's Empire for another triumphal series of engagements. But then matters took a remarkable twist . . .

Totally unexpectedly, a request to come down south to make a record on the Parlophone label for EMI was made and rapidly accepted. The couple were met by that little hero Norman Wisdom, another of Billy's clients, who had been introduced to them once or twice before. The 'wee man' met them off the train and took them to the recording studios where the musical

The *Just Daft* team
take to the streets

PARLOPHONE RECORDS

Telephone: LANgham 5544   Telegrams: EMIRECORD, WESDO, LONDON.

PARLOPHONE ODEON RECORDS

THE PARLOPHONE COMPANY LIMITED
(Controlled by Electric & Musical Industries Ltd.)

RECORD DIVISION
8-11 GREAT CASTLE STREET, LONDON. W.I.

TRADE MARK   TRADE MARK

GHM/JLS.   March 1st. 1956.

Chic Murray Esq.,
3, Montague Street,
Edinburgh,
Scotland.

Dear Chic,

    I am enclosing herewith cheque for £20. 0. 0., which I mentioned
to you on the telephone, to cover your expenses on your last visit.   I
am also enclosing Letter Agreement covering issue of the two titles which
will now be, "Satisfied Mind" and "Lucky Star".

    Your record will now be released on April 2nd. and I look forward to
seeing you next week.

    Kind regards,

           Sincerely yours,

           George Martin

           G.H. Martin.
       Artistes & Recording Manager.

encl.

George Martin writes to Chic
(in pre-Beatles days)

director, Philip Green and Beatles producer George Martin (later
to be given a dubbing!) were on parade. They made several
recordings including 'Satisfied Mind', 'Red River Valley' and
'Are You Mine?' and left EMI to decide which numbers they
wished to feature. Norman asked them to spend the evening
with him as his guests. He was the star that night of *Sunday
Night at the London Palladium*. They returned to his dressing
room after the performance for a few glasses of bubbly before
heading back on the night train to Scotland. The record was
issued in April 1956 and was received by the public with less
enthusiasm, perhaps, than the couple's musicianship merited,
probably because their nationwide recognition, by this time,
rested firmly on comedy.

    Yet in many ways, just as Chic and Maidie used pathos and
comedy in equal parts, their musical abilities played as important
a role in their act as Chic's comedic gifts and that remained the

'Do you approve of small families?'
'Very much so! My father was the
youngest of seven midgets.'

Chic practises his *Just Daft* ballet
steps with daughter Annabelle

case until Chic went solo years later. Even then, music still contributed to his act. Maidie was a dulcet soprano with great expertise in her favoured instrument, the accordion; her interest was first stimulated, ignited even, on a visit with her father, as a six-year-old, to the Empire in Edinburgh to hear Arthur Tracy, the 'Street Singer', accompanied by his own accordion. She never looked back from that defining moment in her determination to master the instrument. Chic, from the outset, was a gifted musician, organist, pianist, guitarist – a multi-instrumentalist. It is puzzling that he is remembered first and foremost as an outstanding comedian but not for his pitch-perfect baritone voice or his uncanny ability as a yodeller. To have both talents in excess was perhaps the most important contributory factor in the overwhelming standing ovations they received from an adoring public, one minute shedding tears of laughter, the next, a tear or two for sentiment and old fashioned notions of love. Even then, however, Chic sometimes couldn't help himself! 'China Doll' was hugely popular as a closing number, almost a signature tune in reverse! If not, they sang 'Melancholy Baby' but Chic could never play either of them entirely straight! The latter, he referred to as 'My Alcoholic Baby', Maidie would begin singing like a 'lintie':

> Come! Sweetheart mine, don't sit and pine!
> Tell me of the cares that make you feel so blue.
> Answer me, hon, what have I done? . . .

At this point, Chic slips in a quip – 'Nothing much up to now, dear' – which Maidie would elect to ignore, as she continued to tug the heart strings,

> Have I ever said an unkind word to you?

The see-saw of humour and romantic lyricism is a dizzy potion for any audience and, as Billy Marsh commented, it never failed to succeed.

And then there was a lull in activities. Somehow they managed to get a whole week off! 'Nice of Billy to give us a wee break. He must be going soft!' Chic remarked. It was Monday, a local holiday in Edinburgh, and Chic decided to visit

Oh, Nellie! I'm truly sorry you're broke. Let's just go to the pawn shop. I want to get you alone.

The piano part for
Chic and Maidie's greatest hit

Tynecastle. 'Willie Woodburn's asked me to watch Hearts tan the hides of Falkirk. It's a lovely day, Maidie, so I'm offski – see you later!' He was away about twenty minutes when the phone rang.

'Maidie, it's Billy Marsh here. Why aren't the pair of you in Birmingham?' He sounded almost hysterical.

'Why should we be? We've got the week off, haven't we? We've nothing on.' Maidie's anxiety level was escalating.

'Nothing on!' Billy Marsh roared, 'You're due to appear with Ruby Murray in Birmingham in four hours' time! Didn't you get a letter from my office?'

'No, we didn't,' Maidie insisted forlornly, 'and to make matters worse, Chic's at the football!'

'*What*? Look, get a hold of that man immediately and I'll phone you back with travel arrangements.'

Her heart beating ten to the dozen, Maidie scoured the telephone book for the Hearts' number. She got through luckily to a competent official who assured her Chic would be alerted. Across the Tannoy system, as the home side were about to kick off, an announcement: 'Would Chic Murray, the television comedian, please go immediately to the manager's office?'

'Must have left the chip pan on,' Chic mumbled. However, once apprised of the situation, Willie Woodburn drove him straight home, where Maidie was waiting, already packed to go.

Then Billy Marsh came back on the line. 'Get out to Turnhouse right away. I've chartered a plane from Prestwick to pick you up. Get going!'

They took off from the airport at 4.40 p.m. in a tiny three-seater plane. Maidie stretched out. It was good not to have to drive for a change and so Chic's moans and groans would have to be diverted to the pilot instead. And she didn't have to wait long for the 'heid-nipping' to commence. 'I, of course, don't want to tell you your job, but it is Birmingham we're supposed to be heading for, isn't it?' The pilot agreed cautiously. 'Well, why,' Chic replied, 'are you heading for Glasgow? You're going in the wrong direction.' One pissed-off pilot riposted that he was following a standard route and that in general terms, he would prefer the small matter of flying the aircraft to be left solely in his experienced hands. But Chic was having none of that! 'I did some time with Fairey Aviation, you know . . .'

The pilot interrupted him, 'You could have spent time with the fairies, for all I care! Leave the flying to me or get out and walk!' This final rapier thrust had the desired effect as Chic decided to call it quits and to try and enjoy the flight. But two things still bugged him. He remained convinced they were heading in the wrong direction and his humour was not improved by the aircraft, which was freezing.

'That pilot must have sneakily changed direction at some point because we did land in Birmingham at the end of it all.' Chic said later, 'But there's no substitute for a fleecy Biggles coat in an aircraft with no heater!'

On landing, a car was laid on to whisk them to the theatre. Within five minutes of entering the stage door, they were onstage to receive rapturous applause from a packed audience. They obviously had been informed of their efforts not to let their public down. In the interval, Billy Marsh phoned them. 'I've been in the States with Norman Wisdom for the last couple of weeks. And I've got to apologise to you both. I sent instructions to inform you about Birmingham and, on returning to my office, I've seen the letter addressed to you here, still unposted. I'm really sorry. It was not your fault.'

Chic was quite sanguine about the episode and readily accepted Billy's heartfelt apology. 'How did it go, in the States?' enquired Chic.

'It was a case of having a look-see. I won't push Norman over there until everything has been considered and acted on.

I had this terrible dream of a fellow with a knife at my throat. Luckily I woke up and there was this fellow with a knife at my throat which gave the dream terrific reality.

On stage again

Why are you asking, Chic?'

He replied, 'I'd like to have a go over there myself, maybe not now, but in the future.'

'Wait until you've cracked London! Then you can think Stateside.'

'When will that be?' Chic fired back.

'When I say so,' came the reply.

The Nose

You might be wondering why this Eiffel Tower's in my whistle and flute. Well, I put it in for a wedding, just in case you thought it had been thrown by some careless maiden in Stirling. So I went to this wedding – a nice wedding – in Blackpool – nice wedding, well, just the *usual* type of wedding, a man and a woman getting married, that was all. That was all that was in it as far as I could see. Eight times married, I didn't know that, but the fellow sat beside me, he knew that. 'Eight times married,' he said, in a whisper that carried all over the church! And then I realised it myself as soon as I heard the organist. He didn't play 'Here Comes The Bride', he played 'Here We Go Again!'

And an incident happened I didn't want to mention, but it's out now. There was a woman there with the longest nose I've ever seen. Now, I've nothing against long noses. We have them in our family. They *run* in our family. But she had a real beaut – you could have touched it. I didn't, but you could have touched it. And I thought, if things don't liven up, I'll touch her nose! But what attracted me to it – speaking in the neutral gender of course – was the way she used it to turn the pages of the hymn book. [Here Chic demonstrated with flick of the head.] And then she said to me – *sotto voce* – she went sniff sniff and said, 'There's someone cooking cabbage in Manchester!'

So we left the church after the ceremony and we made our way to the hall adjacent to the church, which they must have paid for, because there was no difficulty in getting in. And then the wedding cake was brought in – oh, a beautiful cake with candles on it – and I was completely intrigued, so much so that I sort of lost control and I pointed at the cake and said, 'There are candles on the cake!'

And someone said, 'Yes there are. It's the bride's birthday. It's a dual-purpose cake.'

Well, I don't know what age she was, but the heat was *desperate*!

And this woman with the long nose was seated opposite me and I was trying to ignore her without being rude, because it's so easy to be rude, but I was fascinated by her nose, and what she could do with it! Why, I watched her pick up a bun from the floor!

And then it all happened. Someone, inadvertently I suppose, nodded to her. And as she nodded back, she cut the cake! Of course the bride was in tears. So was the cake. So, as we left the hall, you know the tramlines which run in Blackpool – well, *they* don't run in Blackpool, but they allow the *trams* to run in Blackpool – we crossed the tramlines, oh, an interesting ceremony, and this long-nosed woman was at my back. I knew that because of the constant prodding I was getting. At least I was *hoping* it was her.

And then she slipped, and as she slipped, she fell. Fortunately I was leaning forward at the time, otherwise I might have been dissected! And she fell face downwards and straight as a die she made for the tramlines. And her nose lodged in the aperture of the line – the aperture that allows the wheels to run freely to Fleetwood or, well, I've never gone the other way, I don't know where it goes! Anyway, we took a chance and a few of us bent down. We tugged and pulled but we couldn't dislodge her nose and someone beside me, an engineer from Motherwell or somewhere said, 'It's the heat of her nose and the cold of the steel doing this.'

I said, 'Oh *no*!' [At this point, Chic grimaced at the horrendous dilemma confronting them, shaking his head at the vivid memory.] We ended up picking her up by the legs and wheeling her along to the depot, and someone had phoned the mayor because he took the salute at the North Pier – did it very well, I must say.

But she was frightened. I didn't know that until she whispered out the side of her mouth, she asked, 'Could I be electrocuted?' Well, I hadn't thought of that and dropped her leg immediately. 'No, I don't think so,' I replied, 'not unless you throw your other leg over the top wire.'

Patron
HER MAJESTY THE QUEEN

We the undersigned,
tender our sincere congratulations to

Chic Murray & Maidie

on being one of the Representative Artistes
selected to appear at the
Royal Command Variety Performance

held at the

LONDON PALLADIUM

on November 5th, 1956

✦

The Performance being in aid of the
VARIETY ARTISTES' BENEVOLENT FUND and INSTITUTION
for INDIGENT VARIETY and CIRCUS ARTISTES

CHAPTER 7
THE BIG TIME

Chic and Maidie were a hard-working couple and Billy Marsh was an unrelenting taskmaster. They were never off the circuit, criss-crossing the country, and yet found time for television appearances on shows such as Vera Lynn's *Tonight at Nine*, *Young and Foolish* and *Camera One*. But still Billy was reluctant to bring them to London. His policy was deliberate as he wanted to hone and shape their act to the highest standards of professionalism in the 'sticks' before their metropolitan launch. And there is little doubt that the learning curve was working, with regular rave reviews, increasing popularity and instant recognition as a unique brand. One spin-off from their success was Chic's willingness to talk to the press. His earlier reticence was subsumed by a growing awareness of their place in the country's entertainment hierarchy. In an interview with a journalist fan, Philip Diack, Chic talked candidly of his approach to humour.

> *I think that story-telling – the telling of real yarns, fantastically tall stories – is a lost art. I think to do it, you have to be a terrific liar, and there's a terrible shortage of even competent liars. I mean, the man is rare who can tell a tall tale and get away with it. You may know full well that he's a liar, but you enjoy it just the same. The great thing is to make a bond between you and the audience. It isn't what you say, but how you say it.*

He added tellingly, 'What I enjoy most is a real night of good talk with friends. *Real* people, I mean. Ordinary persons are ten a penny, but characters, *real* people are my main hobby.'

With no prospect of a London venue, Chic would persist in

That boy needed a good hiding. So I took him away and hid him where they'll never find him.

*I got on a bus and went
upstairs. The conductor asked
for my fare. 'A single to the
West End, please,' I said.
'We don't go to the West
End,' he said.
I said, 'But you've got
West End on the front of the bus.'
And he said, 'We've got Persil
on the back but we don't take
in washing.'*

*'Excuse me.'
'Certainly. I'll grant you a full
pardon if it will help.'*

raising the London issue. 'You're not ready yet,' was the standard reply which Chic, just to annoy Billy, would repeat out loud to Maidie.

'We're still not ready yet, pet!'

But the day did dawn. 'Okay, Chic, you're ready and it's all set. September. You go straight into the West End at the Prince of Wales!'

They were booked to appear with an all-star cast: Jimmy Wheeler, David Nixon, and, in top billing, Mel Tormé. Chic was a tad apprehensive. London critics were a savage breed apart and how would they take to a Scot in their midst? Nonetheless, he didn't want to compromise his act apart from some minor adjustments such as, 'I was walking down Piccadilly, one foot in front of the other – oh, that's the best way . . .' He also said to Maidie, 'I might fling in the odd Enigma Variation.' She stared blankly back at him but he followed his instincts and pursued a familiar track that had served him well across the country. The night before the big launch, they wandered past the theatre where the previous signs for the *Folies Bergère* show were being removed. They passed the Academy Cinema on Oxford Street. 'My kind of hall,' Chic commented.

'It's not for me,' Maidie replied, 'they only show films with subtitles there.'

'That's right, Maidie. You know how I enjoy a good read!'

As they returned to Piccadilly Circus the Prince of Wales came into view. They picked a window seat in a restaurant across from the Prince of Wales to have a bite to eat. Outside the theatre, workmen were displaying Mel Tormé's name in huge lettering. They delved around for other letters for the remainder of the cast. The next letter went up, immediately below Mel Tormé. It was a C. The H, I and a further C followed. 'Could this be Chic Lamour, the famous French fandango dancer?' he quipped before he uttered, 'Aw! God! Maidie, it's far too big! They'll be expecting too much!' The theatre's frontage was now dominated by the words CHIC MURRAY & MAIDIE. He'd come a long way from Bank Street in Greenock and Maidie, quite overcome by the sight, ditched her knife and fork.

'God! I can't eat another thing,' she moaned.

'Oh well, I suppose I'll have to finish it for you!' Chic magnanimously volunteered.

Rehearsals took place most of the following day, with Chic doing his best to soothe Maidie's anxieties. 'Remember, Maidie,' he said, 'just do what we've always done, keep it clean, keep it simple and keep it moving. It's much harder to hit a moving target, you know!'

A host of good wishes and telegrams greeted them in their dressing room from Duncan Macrae, Harry Secombe and Jack Milroy amongst many others including Granny Murray and one from Jack Anthony which read: 'A big opening, Timothy Tighthole. Love to Maidie. Good Luck!'

Things went swimmingly, and although her tummy was knotted Maidie left the stage to warm applause, only to leave Chic there, alone on the stage to face the unseen press assassins in their serried ranks. Now she was doubly anxious, but she needn't have worried. Off he went.

A case of whisky, please, and two cases of assault and battery.

Good luck telegrams came
from the famous and the unknown

79

I got up this morning. I like to get up in the morning, it gives me the rest of the day to myself.

Laughter broke out in the auditorium.

Oh! I prefer it!

The laughter increased and Maidie began to relax just a little.

So I dressed. I always dress. I like to be different, but I think undressed you're just a bit too different! As I walked out of the door, I turned left. I usually turn right but this time I turned left – it's the spirit of adventure! I walked down Piccadilly, one foot in front of the other – oh, it's the best way. Then I went to cross the street – it was the only way to get to the other side – and a fellow says to me, 'Is that you?' Well, I could hardly deny it, with me standing there!

By this time, Chic had the audience on toast and Maidie knew she could unwind.

You know, it's a funny thing, I can look at anyone and say whether I know them or not. It's a gift I have!
  A wee man started jumping up and down, clapping his hands together like this . .

Chic gave a demonstration with the audience now in pain from laughter,

. . . and I said, 'Excuse me. Would you mind telling me what you're doing?' He told me he was trying to catch Genumphs.

Maidie, who hadn't heard this surreal nonsense before, began laughing herself as she thought maybe this is what Chic meant by Enigma Variations!

I said to him, 'What's Genumphs?' He said, 'I don't know. I haven't caught any yet!'

The audience rolled around in hysterical, helpless laughter. Maidie composed herself at the end of Chic's triumph to come back onstage to sing 'Nobody's Darling But Mine', a musical finale that brought the audience to their feet. They were an absolute knock-out and with the throng hollering for an encore, Billy, ecstatic, joined them backstage, leaping up and down, embracing them both, shouting, 'You did it! You did it!' redolent of the plaudits paid to Professor Higgins in *My Fair Lady*. Without doubt, this evening in the Prince of Wales Theatre in London's West End, when Chic swept the critics off their feet, must rank as one of the greatest moments of his life.

Billy Marsh treated them to dinner, champagne thrown in. 'You've justified every particle of faith I had in you,' he said over

Chic and Madie with Mel Tormé
(seated), David Nixon (right)
and Marty Paich (left)

a glass. 'If people like me have any talent at all, it's in spotting talent – and I like to think that's a talent in itself. You know the definition of a critic, Chic? That's someone who criticises someone who can do something, although he can't do it himself. At least I'm on the positive side, pushing talent I believe in – and folk like you make it all worthwhile.'

After a pause, Chic, rolling his glass around in his hand, interrupted his musing. 'Look,' he said, 'it's time for some straight talking, Billy! You're a wee bugger in my book for keeping us away from the West End – our goal – for over a year. Well, guess what?' Chic paused again, smiled and raised his glass, 'You were dead right, you wee blighter!'

Maidie, the morning after, seized the papers and frantically raced through the pages to the showbiz columns. Chic looked at her quizzically after her scrutiny of the notices. He raised an eyebrow. 'Don't worry, Chic, they're better than good! They're marvellous!'

Donald Zec of the *Daily Mirror* wrote, 'The narrator of the night was Chic Murray, a hefty Scotsman with a humour as dry as champagne.'

The Stage's judgement, written by Andy Gray, said, 'Tall Chic Murray, with a honey of a partner in Maidie, makes an impressive London debut with his inconsequential patter which has a freshness all its own.'

And back in Scotland, the local papers were warbling with enthusiasm including Glasgow's *Evening Times*, 'The Chic Murray manner took a trick last night at the Prince of Wales when Chic and Maidie made their West End debut. Chic, as imperturbable offstage as on, hadn't altered the style of the act for the occasion, and the first-night applause proved he was right.'

But the jewel in the critic's crown went to Harold Hobson of the *Sunday Times*, an intellectual and respected theatre critic who could effectively snuff out the career of a budding actor or the fate of a production which fell below his exacting standards: 'I thought the Scottish comedian, Chic Murray, first-rate. His dissection of the process of getting up in the morning is Proustian in its detail, Beckettish in its innumerable qualifications and wholly his own in irresistible delight.' Chic had missed the review but his friend and fellow thespian, Iain Cuthbertson (*Sutherland's Law*), wrote to him in the following warm terms:

'Can you spare me a fiver, sir?
I only have six months to live.'
'Och, never mind. It'll soon pass.'

Telephone Nos.
Reception Waverley 7277/8
Visitors Waverley 7050

R.S.A.C.
A.A.
R.A.C.

Proprietors: Trust Houses, Ltd.
CARLTON HOTEL
North Bridge
EDINBURGH 1

16th September 56

My dear Chic,
      I want simply to
say how glad I am that
Harold Hobson in 'The Sunday
Times' saw fit to give you such
an excellent notice. He's a clever
man, a big voice in the theatre,
and one whom the public place
great reliance on for his level-
headedness. His appreciation of
you will go far, I feel, in creating
a wider audience for you – an
audience which I have felt for
a long time you have every right
to.

Being up to the neck in the
business myself, it is very far
from easy for a comedian to
make me laugh deeply. You have
always been able to twist me
into kinks, and all I'd want
to see in this matter, is you
getting the audience and
recognition you so amply deserve.
      Give my love to Maidie.
And keep it going! You have
all my sincerest good wishes,
            Yours,

            Iain Cuthbertson.

Within a few weeks, to underline their earlier triumph, Chic and Maidie were invited back to the Prince of Wales, this time to accompany an American comic, Jerry Colonna. And then they were hit by a bombshell! Billy phoned and told them that they were to be invited to appear at the Royal Command Performance at the London Palladium on 5 November, the eve of his birthday. Reminiscing, Chic said,

We were both flabbergasted. Billy swore us to secrecy, but it wasn't necessary. I was too petrified to talk to anyone – about anything! – until it became official. It was just totally unbelievable. Maidie was dying to tell Mum, Nana Dickson and the kids, but we just couldn't. I had the feeling right up until the actual invitation arrived that it was all a mistake, that somehow they'd

got us mixed up with the Oberkirchen Children's Choir or something, but no – there it was. And to think they could have had Mel Tormé instead of us!

Then confirmation arrived. Chic rushed to the telephone. On breaking the news to Annabelle, his daughter, she joyfully returned him the traditional good wishes in show business. 'Break a leg, Dad!'

'Mmm,' thought Chic, 'how's she picked up the lingo so fast? I'll need to watch this one!' Congratulatory telegrams arrived in avalanches and sycophantic hacks buzzed around them. But on that morning of 5 November, as rehearsals got under way, the headlines in the newspapers all spoke of the Suez Canal crisis. With Tommy Trinder acting as MC, Alma Cogan set the ball rolling, followed by Syd Millward and his Nitwits, Sabrina next,

The unofficial invitation

Variety Artistes Benevolent Fund and Institution

THE HOME, BRINSWORTH

Patrons: H.M. THE QUEEN
QUEEN ELIZABETH THE QUEEN MOTHER
President: PRINCE LITTLER
Vice-Presidents:

Organising Secretary: HARRY MARLOW   HM/CR

Hon. Treasurer: DAVE LEE   Trustees: BARCLAYS BANK, Ltd-
Assistant Secretary: Miss L. M. MILES

'Phone: Temple Bar 6310/3985   'Grams: Orchestoe,Lexquare,London.
18, CHARING CROSS ROAD   LONDON, W.C.2.

PRIVATE & CONFIDENTIAL   October
Fourth.
1956...

Chick Murray & Maidie,
c/o Olivelli's,
35, Store Street,
W.C. 1.

Dear Chick Murray and Maidie,

We are now compiling our programme for submission to the Queen for the Royal Performance to be held at the Palladium on Monday evening, November 5th, and I should be glad to know if you would be available to appear if selected.

When replying please send me a couple of photographs for reproduction.

Yours sincerely,

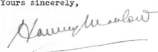

and then Chic and Maidie. Later Laurence Olivier, Vivienne Leigh and John Mills were pencilled in to do a white-tie-and-tails routine but were unable to make it. But the Crazy Gang, led by Bud Flanagan, stepped manfully into the breach and Liberace took the stage to complete the finale of the first half when everyone downed tools for a tea break.

With a cup of tea in his hand, Liberace crossed the stage and introduced himself to Chic and Maidie. 'Call me Lee – everyone else does,' he gushed, 'but I just had to say how wonderful I thought your routine was. You'd be a sensation in the States. Do you have any plans to appear there?'

'We'd like to try,' Chic replied, 'but you already have Burns and Allen – how would you see us fitting in?'

'Look at another parallel: Jeannie Carson,' Lee argued. 'She's a Scots girl new to the big city. There's lots of scope there to develop, folks, but it's a tough market – the toughest, I should know!'

'Aye, but you've cracked it!' Chic said with a sardonic grin.

'Sure I have, Chic, but if I'm an overnight success as people say, why, it must be the longest night on record!'

Rehearsals for the second half of the show were announced which was to reach its finale with Eric Delaney and his band, supported by the stars of the fifties, Dickie Valentine, David Whitfield, Beryl Reid and Gracie Fields. However, as Tommy Trinder prepared to make his introductions (with a sprinkling of topical gags thrown in), Val Parnell, the producer of *Sunday Night at the London Palladium*, strode purposefully to centre stage. 'Ladies and gentlemen,' he addressed the players, 'I am sorry to tell you that I have just received a message from Buckingham Palace that I know will be a dreadful disappointment to all of you who have worked so hard to make this show a success. The Royal Family have decided they cannot attend tonight because of the international situation, leaving me with no option but to cancel the show.'

A pin-drop silence ensued, followed by tears and sobs of distress from Lee who was led away by his brother George. It was difficult for people to take in at first. Chic and Maidie just stared at each other in stunned silence. 'Let's go and get changed,' Chic said. He gave Maidie's hand a wee comforting squeeze and they made their way to their dressing room and to

I made a stupid mistake last week. But, come to think of it, did you ever hear of a clever mistake?

the support and commiserations of Archie McCulloch who joined them backstage.

Then word came through in the spirit of 'never say die' that Winifred Atwell and her spouse, Lew Levisohn, wanted every bewildered living soul in the Palladium to attend a party that night at their Thameside home – what might be referred to in Scotland as a 'greetin' meeting'. But this was no wake – far from it! 'Wi' reaming swats that drank divinely', the tension of the day was loosened.

Lee was dressed to kill in black and a smidgeon of lurex ('isn't it stunning?'), had recovered his pout and swivelling hips from what he termed 'the biggest blow of my life', and circulated with his mantra of comfort to the assemblage: 'Don't worry! You'll be asked back.'

The performance is cancelled
(Gracie Fields to Chic's right and Dickie Valentine to his left)

Chic introduced Alma Cogan's mother to Lee as Joan Crawford. This thrilled Lee but somewhat discomfited both the singer and her elderly mum. Chic, who, on such occasions simply couldn't help himself, then found himself juxtaposed on both sides by his hostess, Winifred, and Lee. 'Is there anyone here in the company who could do a turn on the piano?' he roared above the throng. Winifred gallantly volunteered to tickle the ivories in contrast to Chic's wonderfully unpredictable method of social bonding.

'Is there something special you wanted, Chic?' she asked.

'Well, thanks Winnie, I'll have a cheese sandwich and a glass of champagne!' This was followed by the alternative Chic, swathed in innocence, 'Oh, you're going to play the piano? Och well, in that case, give me a C!' Thereafter, Winifred and Lee took turns on the piano, not as established worldwide entertainers, but as accompanists to Chic and Maidie singing 'country'. You can't keep a good man down!

It was not, apparently, unprecedented for the Royal Command Performance to be cancelled – it had happened before on the death of Queen Mary. But Chic and Maidie were the first Scots to be so honoured since Jack Radcliffe featured at the end of the war a decade earlier. Prior to that, in the thirties Robert Wilson and Renée Houston trod the boards. Chic and Maidie, unlike some who reached their heights, were recognised as being where they were on merit. Unusually, there was no backbiting, an unfortunate Scots trait that manifests itself from time to time. And this was exemplified at the Empire in Glasgow where they returned to heartfelt good wishes for their Christmas show, entitled *We're Joking*. Jack Anthony wrote, 'May this be a *definite* Royal success.'

The 'Dear' Girl

I had a most interesting day today. I took a stroll along Piccadilly. I wasn't forced to go. I wanted to walk that way at the time. I did it in my usual manner, one foot in front of the other, so as not to attract too much attention. I got about halfway along or maybe more than halfway. I wasn't measuring the distance at the time. I never do. I'm careless that way. Then I

THE CHIC MURRAY STORY

stopped. So I said to myself, 'I've stopped.' I said that in case I walked away and left myself standing there. I felt a touch on my shoulder. I said, 'That's a spot of rain.' It could have been, but it didn't really matter what it could have been. So I took shelter under a nearby canopy. I just went nearby to save me scouting the town.

A girl passed me and she said 'Hello' in passing. Well, she didn't say 'Hello' in passing, because she'd passed me and then said 'Hello'. I said to myself, 'That girl has spoken.' I didn't say that to her because she must have known she had said something. I said to myself, 'I wonder who she is,' because she kept walking the way she was facing and you would have needed to know her pretty well to be able to tell who it was from the rear. As I wondered who she was, she returned and retraced her steps. I said to myself, 'She's coming back,' because I knew it was up to me to acknowledge her salutations. In other words to acknowledge her 'Hello.' I couldn't place her name. I knew her face but couldn't place her name, so I said, 'Oh, hello dear.' She had two horns sticking out of her head. Probably the bad weather had driven her down from the hills.

She said to me, 'Charlie's looking for you.'

I said, 'Charlie who?'

She said, 'Not Charlie Who, Charlie Smith.'

I really don't know what made me say Charlie Who because I don't know a Charlie Who either. Probably her horns disconcerted me but she was quite nice about it.

She said, 'Perhaps you thought you knew a Charlie Who.' I replied that maybe I did think I'd known a Charlie Who, although I didn't, of course, but if she thought that I knew a Charlie Who, that was up to her. However I did know a Charlie Smith because Charlie and I used to run about together. Well, we didn't run all the time, only when it was necessary.

I said, 'Where is Charlie?' because I wanted to go.

She said, 'He's round the corner waiting,' and I was very eager to see Charlie.

So when I got there, Charlie told me that I must come up to the house and see his birds. The house, when we got there, was full of canaries and budgies flying all over the place. I hid my disappointment when he asked me what I thought of them. They were getting me down – well, the feathers were anyway. He said

88

he'd a wonderful idea and I was all for it because it was going to cost me nothing. He said. 'I'm building cages with a difference. I'm building cages without bottoms for canaries you can trust.' We tried it out but it fell through. So did the canaries. We were dreadfully upset and when one canary started whistling backwards, Charlie choked it. He thought it best in case anyone enquired where the sound was coming from. They might have thought we were developing a new strain . . .

CHAPTER 8
HOME AND AWAY

Another full diary stretched out in front of them including a visit back to the Hippodrome in Birmingham, that venue that had occasioned their earlier flight in a three-seater refrigerator. Travelling south in their faithful Standard 10, the Furies struck once more when a Morris Minor, on the wrong side of the road, crashed into the driver's side of the car despite Maidie's efforts to swerve to avoid it. They were just a few miles north of their destination. Chic was badly winded with cracked ribs, but it was Maidie who gave most cause for concern, concussed with a nasty gash on her brow. Chic and the Morris driver (also in a state of shock) gently lifted Maidie from the car, now a write-off, and laid her on a blanket. 'Get an ambulance, man! Be quick!' Chic ordered. Mission accomplished, the Morris driver returned from a nearby house carrying a flask of brandy.

In hospital, Chic was corseted to help relieve his discomfort. Maidie, still concussed, had fourteen stitches to close her wound. 'Your wife has concussion, Mr Murray,' the hospital A & E doctor said, stating the obvious, 'and she's weak from loss of blood. There is no question of her performing in Birmingham tonight. Perhaps later this week . . .'

'Just get me to the theatre!' Maidie interrupted, raising herself from her bed.

'But what's the point?' Chic asked, with concern.

'Look,' she said, 'all I've got is a sore head and I'm feeling better already!' Her determination was stunning in its intensity and, with grave misgivings from her frustrated carers, this great trouper set out for the Hippodrome by taxi. At the theatre, together they saw their routine through to the end and without a single hitch.

Understandably, Chic and Maidie had a few days off to fully

That man plans to cross the Atlantic on a plank. Trouble is, he can't find one long enough.

'What do you think of Red China?'
'I quite like it against a white tablecloth.'

91

recover, but not for long. They were rehearsing in London for a television show when Billy shunted them north to cover for Harry Secombe at the Glasgow Empire. Acute laryngitis had laid him low. They were about to return south when Harry's show, *Rocking the Town*, switched to Edinburgh, and with Harry still *hors de combat*, Billy leant on his 'ever-reliables' to cover for him again. Then, at last, they completed their television mission in the big smoke before they joined Petula Clark in Aberdeen at the start of Harold Fielding's *Music for the Millions* UK tour. They became good friends with Petula, exchanging gossip and banter, yet she pined for her then boyfriend, Joe 'Mr Piano' Henderson.

Later the same week, they learnt that in October they were scheduled to make a tour of the army bases in Cyprus. 'I just hope the natives are friendly,' Chic commented.

BERNARD DELFONT AGENCY LTD.

DIRECTORS: BERNARD DELFONT — WILLIAM MARSH — KEITH DEVON

TELEPHONES: WHITEHALL 1525/6/7/8
GRAMS: BERDEL, PICCY, LONDON

WM/JD

MORRIS HOUSE,
1-5 JERMYN STREET,
HAYMARKET,
LONDON, S.W.1.

Chic Murray, Esq.,
Theatre Royal,
PORTSMOUTH.

28th June 1956.

Dear Chic,

I have had a special visit from Mr. George Brightwell and Mr. Watson of the Combined Services Entertainment Committee who would very much like you to go and entertain the troops in Cyprus about mid-September. You have been particularly requested Chic since there an enormous amount of Scottish troops in Cyprus. As you probably know, many of the star artistes do this, and all receive a nominal fee of £50. plus everything found.

Think it over and let me know what you decide.

Yours sincerely,

Billy Marsh.

Off to the sun.
The invitation to Cyprus

92

'Don't be so daft, Chic,' Maidie countered, 'why the hell do you think our troops are over there?'

Chic was as excited as a schoolboy on his first class excursion (he had never been abroad before), as he practised his foreign language vocabulary in front of the mirror. 'Fa-ma-gu-sta. Nic-o-si-a.' Those two words were recited ad nauseam until Chic reckoned he was able to take on the Greeks!

Jimmy Edwards, the moustachioed comic actor, counselled Chic, on hearing of his trip abroad, 'Don't go on the army aeroplane they offer you! *Please* don't! You'll be rattled out of the bleeding sky!'

'What's the alternative? Banana boat, perhaps?' said a cheeky Chic.

'No, you bloody idiot!' Jimmy boomed, 'Don't be such a miserable bugger! Fly in civilian aircraft. Pay your own fares! I'm telling you, it'll be worth it!'

Maidie didn't have to predict whether Chic would accept Jimmy's wise and experienced advice; they boarded an army Blackwood DC6 for their flight to Nicosia. They sat in their cigar tube, miserable and cold on the ground for in excess of an hour. Finally they took off, the plane heaving, groaning and shuddering to reach its flight altitude as, quite literally, sickness bags were circulated to every passenger, reassuring them that, as and when they were sick, there would be no need to make an unhygienic mess on the fuselage. Maidie was mightily relieved to arrive in Cyprus after the rollercoaster journey, during which she had thought of nothing except the freely given advice of Jimmy Edwards!

Chic loved the sun. He couldn't get enough of it. But it was not vanity that made him the sun-seeker he was. It was because (something he never discussed) he suffered from psoriasis, a nervous disorder of the skin, which was relieved, certainly in Chic's case, by exposure to the ultraviolet rays of the sun. This was also a chance for Maidie to relax and enjoy the weather; it was the nearest thing to a holiday she had experienced since her marriage had begun.

Wherever she went, however, picnicking, sightseeing or shopping, she was escorted by a member of the military. Makarios and ETA were formidable enemies. On one occasion, Chic was being driven by a 'squaddie' with an officer beside him

'Sergeant! Get those screaming women into my tent this minute!'
'But there not screaming, sir.'
'They're not in my tent yet, you fool!'

93

in the back of the Land Rover. 'What would you do, McKay, if a grenade was flung from hiding at your vehicle?' the oh-so-smooth Sandhurst captain enquired.

The driver replied: 'Ah'd ram mah fuckin' foot richt doon tae the flair. *Sir!*'

The shows were a huge success, doubly so because the boys were so grateful to be entertained by familiar faces from home. They roared their pleasure wherever they went. But, into the second week, Chic, like a wounded soldier, limped with difficulty into the hotel room where Maidie was relaxing. 'Maidie, my big toe's throbbing with pain. I think I tripped over a shell of some sorts after a wee swim. I'm sure it's broken.' The doctor, summoned by the hotel's management, confirmed Chic's diagnosis and the toe was strapped tightly in bandaging. When he had left them, Chic pleaded for advice on the way forward (literally!), 'Maidie, I've got to be able to walk but I don't want the punters knowing my difficulties.'

Maidie looked at the pathetic sight of Chic's bare foot with what appeared to be a tennis ball stuck on the end of it and fought hard to keep a straight face. 'Well what can you do? You're never going to get a shoe over that!' she said, pointing at his huge white protuberance.

But Chic had a brainwave. 'I've got it!' he said. 'Maidie, get down to the quartermaster's store and get the biggest army-issue boots that they can lay their hands on. Tell them it's for a sketch. Tell them bloody anything! Just get them!' The requisites were duly procured and signed for. Chic had huge feet by any standards, but these almost freakish bulbous toe-capped boots seemed more suited to a circus ring.

'How on earth are you going to explain those away to an audience?' Maidie asked, as they studied the newly acquired items.

'Oh, that's easy. We're on a forces tour, for goodness sake. It's my way of identifying with the boys. We're here at the behest of the British army, let me remind you!' Then he tried them on as he winced and squealed with pain – symptoms which received only a modicum of sympathy from his spouse.

'You said you wanted to identify with the British soldier. So a wee bit of the "stiff upper lip" won't go amiss, will it?'

Their final gig in Cyprus took place in the open air, in an

That woman has a tongue on her that can clip hedges.

94

amphitheatre surrounded by palm trees. Their act was predictably going well – anyone could have seen that – until, inexplicably, the audience got up off their seats and ran like demented lemmings from their view of the stage. This was a new one for Chic. 'I've heard of unprofessionalism among performers. But this must be a first time for an unprofessional audience!' he commented, in a state of shock. An official-looking 'wally' then ran onto the stage to inform Chic and Maidie that there was a bomb scare. Unfazed, Chic ambled off the stage as Maidie unbuckled her accordion. 'Watch it!' Chic turned and shouted in frustration, 'the bomb could be inside that accordion!' And as he took further giant strides in his indescribably ill-fitting clumpity boots, he turned to his partner, 'That's rich, isn't it Maidie? We're the entertainers. It makes sense that we're the last to know. Can't you see the headlines? "Chic Murray and Maidie go out with a bang!"'

As Chic presumed (it was, in this instance, a fortuitous presumption), the incident turned out to be a hoax, a false alarm. His main concern lay elsewhere. Addressing a support comedian who had come out to Cyprus on their death-defying flight, he confided, 'I know that we didn't finish our act, but I can't see, in the circumstances, that the army would be asking for a refund. What do you think?' He received unqualified reassurance that in no way could he or Maidie be held responsible for terrorist hoaxes, designed to undermine the morale of the troops. (But it remains something of a doubt that this solicitous adviser was directly in touch with Whitehall at the time.)

For the five sun-sizzling weeks that Chic and Maidie had spent in Cyprus, wherever they went they met an adoring crowd who simply loved them. Their time on a troubled Mediterranean island was an unqualified success. And, in spite of his concern, even the British army hadn't the brass neck amongst the brass hats to ask for a rebate! How could they? And that must tell us something!

Chic's act was now second nature to him. He never lost the sharpness or immediacy of his routine, but that in itself began to be a problem for him. It was the very 'routine-ness' (to coin a word), the predictability of his stage life, which made him look to new horizons and address fresh challenges. He was thinking, more and more, of the United States and the vision of his name

'This shirt,' the salesman said,
'will laugh at washing!'
He was true to his word. I got
it back from the cleaners with
its sides split.

Pat lost both his ears in an accident. Clean off! When he returned to work, the foreman greeted him, 'Good to see you back, Pat, especially since your eyesight's improved.'
'Why?' Pat asked.
'Well, you've managed to do away with the specs and that's a great start!'

He was the first killer executed by the electric chair. When he heard the verdict, it came as a bit of a shock.

in lights on Broadway was a longed-for dream. Billy Marsh understood that and recommended that he contact Neil Kirk, an agent based in the Big Apple who hailed originally from Dundee. He had started out as a comedian but crossed the pond in the 1930s and set about organising Scottish kitsch shows across North America. 'Heederum-a-hooderum' was a winning formula for any American with a smattering of Scots blood. What was required was to throw in a Bonnie Prince Charlie dirge here and a Highland fling there, add a touch of Grannie's Hielan' Hame and then package the lot in swathes of tartan! This was a heady cocktail, tried and tested, that proved irresistible year after year! It was disparagingly referred to amongst the swinging-kilt show-business *mafiosi* as the 'milk run' (surprisingly *not* the gravy train!). By way of contrast, the tartan thing was never Chic's scene (indeed his only concession to his origins was his trademark tartan bunnet). However, he agreed with Billy that Neil was familiar with his market and that he was at least a starting-off point. Maidie opted out of the trip. She rationalised they both needed a break and, after all, she rightly pointed out, she had hardly spent a complete week, uninterrupted, at home since the 1930s.

Chic was sizzling with excitement as he landed at Idlewild Airport, a sizzle that rapidly disappeared on account of hours of delay at US customs. His visa lasted only four weeks and there were further statements to be made that his visit was 'non-political' and that he had never been a member of the communist party – the last wretched thing on his frustrated mind at the time! (McCarthyism was officially ended by the Senate in 1954, but old habits died hard.) After eventually being cleared by officialdom, he went to collect his luggage. Neil Kirk appeared out of the shadows. 'Hi, Chic,' he said effusively, 'I'm Neil Kirk. Pleased to meet you.'

'How did you know it was me?' Chic quizzed him

'"Look for a tartan bunnet," Billy advised me.' (For a man who had left Scotland those many years before, Neil had never lost his Dundonian accent.)

They grabbed a cab and headed for Manhattan. 'As you probably know, Chic, my main activity is organising the Scottish tours,' Neil explained, 'but that doesn't mean to say that I don't know a number of guys who would be willing to manage you. It's

vital you get the right person, someone you're comfortable with.'

But Chic, half listening, was transfixed by the skyline as lights began to sparkle in the early dusk. 'Is that the . . .'

'Yeah!' Neil cut in, 'That's the Empire State Building. The other one's the Chrysler. They're beauties aren't they? Look. You check in to your hotel. I'll give you an hour to freshen up. We can go and get something to eat and get you back for an early night. Tomorrow I'll show you the sights.'

True to his word, he collected Chic an hour later. Chic was in a melancholy mood. He was touched how Maidie had packed everything he was likely to need. He was missing her already. They ate enough to choke a horse (Chic had a horse's appetite!) and then they talked for hours. 'I can't make out your humour at all,' Neil said earnestly, 'it's so *different*! I truly can't classify it. You're *so* original! That very originality might make it tougher for you, though.'

'That's nothing new for me,' Chic opened up. 'To begin with, when I was going piggy-back on Maidie's shoulders, folk couldn't understand what the hell I was trying to do. It took time and tears but I think they finally got the message.' They were silent for a short time until Chic spoke with a smattering of anxiety, 'Have you heard of anything I've done, Neil?'

'Only a record Maidie sent over,' he replied. 'Apparently it was your first broadcast together. Something about Betty Grable trying to get a night's sleep. It was the sweetest, daftest story I've ever heard. Don't worry, Chic, I'm a committed fan!'

They met again the following morning. 'Where would you like to go first, Chic?' Neil asked, bang on time again. (Chic had been up wandering the streets at 4 a.m. before the penny dropped and his watch was readjusted.)

'The Bowery,' Chic answered.

'Skid Row, Chic? You've got to be kidding!'

'Between you and me, Neil, the Bowery Boys are cousins of mine. Go on, Neil, humour me!'

Down Eighth Avenue they went and shortly, with a wave, Neil announced, 'This is it!'

Chic got out of the car. 'I'll just stretch my legs. Won't be long,' he said as he headed across the road to a small coterie of unshaven, raggity down-and-outs huddled together as an unidentifiable bottle wrapped in brown paper was circulated.

I love driving the hearse and, of course, you've got the added bonus that you're not bothered with back-seat drivers.

'For God's sake, be careful, Chic!' Neil shouted at his back, advice that fell on deaf ears. He walked on.

'Any chance of a wee go at your bottle?' Chic asked the assembly, pointing at the said bottle. The welcome was somewhat muted, and a particularly mean-looking, hirsute spokesman suggested that he 'fuck off', as much in surprise as in indignation. His 'colleagues', in shocked silence, stared open-mouthed at the sheer brazen effrontery of the stranger and it was clear that their spokesman spoke for them all. Yet Chic looked genuinely hurt, 'I was told Scots were made welcome in New York. Obviously what I was told was wrong,' he muttered.

'Bloody hellshit!' shouted Hirsute, 'he's from the Old Country and Scots *are* welcome here! Sit down, Scottie. Give him the bottle, Chuck!' Chic sat with his new acquaintances for a full twenty minutes as Neil rubbed his eyes in disbelief.

'Christ,' he said to himself, 'this guy is a total one-off! I've never seen anything like this in my goddam life!'

Eventually Chic got up. To each of the motley crew, he handed a 'greenback'. 'I had to dispel any myth about Scots' meanness even if it buggers up my budget,' he commented, back at the car. 'You know,' he continued, 'we can all be down on our luck and everyone deserves a break. I got a break when I met Maidie. It wasn't like that for my poor old dad or my uncle Tom. The war saw to that – poor devils!'

Chic went on to be treated to a number of shows on Broadway and experienced American television with fascination for the first time. The two weeks sped to their conclusion but a firm friendship had been established, a dynamic manager was promised for Chic's return visit, and a wealth of memories waited to be related to Maidie.

A month or two on, back in Blighty, Chic bounced in as Maidie was loading the washing machine. 'You're going to love this, Maidie!' he announced airily, 'I've arranged for the whole family to spend a holiday at the seaside. There's a wee bit to do when we're there, but nothing we can't handle!'

Maidie was delighted. 'That's marvellous, Chic,' she said, 'our first *real* holiday as a family! Did you say we had a wee job to do when we're there?'

'Yup,' Chic chortled, 'a real family break with the added bonus that it'll pay for itself!'

*'Good evening, madam.
I'm from the Environmental
Health Department – Pest
Control Division.'
'Aye, ye'd better come in.
He's nae hame frae the pub yet.'*

A rare family outing

98

A hint of anxiety influenced her next question. '*Pay* for itself? Don't speak in riddles, Chic. What do you mean by that?'

'Oh, you'll love it! We've been booked for a full summer season at the Winter Gardens in Rothesay and, what's more, we're the bosses. We hire the rest of the bill *and* we'll get a percentage of the take! Just think of all that free sun, too!'

Maidie sat down clutching a handful of shirts. 'Wait a minute! Is this what I think it is? Two performances a night, plus matinees and only Sunday to ourselves?' She wailed, 'What kind of a holiday is that?'

'Well I was going to mention the Sundays, if you'd given me a chance . . .'

'Oh! Don't tell me. This so-called family holiday includes Sunday work as well!' Maidie cut in.

'Umm, well, I was coming to that,' a sheepish Chic rejoined. 'You know how much you like being out on a boat? Well I've arranged for STV to pick us up, nice and early, every Sunday, and ferry us over to Wemyss Bay and then, *wheech*, off we go – smart limos guaranteed – into Cowcaddens for a new show they're putting on. Wouldn't that be great? Och! Come on, Maidie, you know you'll just love it out there on the boat, twice every Sunday. What more do you want?' He continued to press any button that might appeal to Maidie. 'I went to all this trouble,' he pleaded, 'and all you do is act awkward!' Maidie began to thaw on account of Chic's persistent wheedling. 'Oh! And I've kept the best to last!' he said. 'We'll be staying on a farm just outside Rothesay. Won't that be fun?' If ever there was a case of accentuating the positive and eliminating the negative, this had to be *the* outstanding example!

'Oh, Christ!' Maidie wailed, 'Don't tell me! I suppose I have to feed the bloody chickens, clean the shitty stables and milk the effing cows as well!' Even this doughty dear couldn't hide a smile at Chic's irrepressible cheek.

'No, no,' he said jokingly, 'the only thing you'll be required to do is a wee bit of ploughing.'

Being a non-confrontational, good-natured soul, Maidie relented in the face of Chic's overpowering blandishments! The family were Rothesay-bound!

As fate would have it, the children had the time of their lives. Plootering about on the farm, and with trips to the seaside and

'I can't tell you how pleased I am.'
'Why?'
'Because I'm not a bit
pleased. That's why!'

100

Rothesay itself, their days were never dull. Meantime, inevitably, Chic and Maidie's days were long, finishing almost every night with a visit to Tony's Place for a plate of spaghetti bolognese, then back to the ranch for a large dram for Chic and a cuppa for 'herself'. The Sunday trips to Glasgow meant that the couple had to rise at the unearthly hour of three thirty in the morning; a motorboat was laid on to cross the Firth of Clyde. Some of their memories of the peace and tranquillity of those early trips, as the dawn came up, remained with them throughout their lives. And the journeys to the STV studios were not in vain either. They featured every Wednesday on *Holiday Showtime* and the inevitable spin-off from these recordings (which outperformed the network shows in the ratings) meant that they played to full houses twice nightly. Somehow, too, Chic managed to squeeze in a series of voice-overs for commercials – a nice little earner.

The season over, they returned to Edinburgh. Domestically, Chic was becoming a 'tad' grumpy and Maidie's suspicion that there might be some health reason for his behaviour transpired to be well founded.

On the first night of a new show in Blackpool, fish suppers were delivered to their dressing room after the performance. They then drove back to their private hotel, but all the way there Chic complained of pains. 'It's like birth pains,' he said. (Maidie's imagination wandered as she debated whether Chic had experienced parturition in an earlier incarnation, but chose to remain silent for fear of agitating the Tall Droll's wrath). On arriving at the address, the patrons of the establishment greeted them and informed them that they were going out to meet friends but would be back in good time for breakfast. Chic's discomfort increased, 'The pains are getting worse, Maidie. Honestly!'

It was clear this wasn't play-acting and Maidie suggested that they get a doctor, a proposition roundly rejected by her husband. They tried aspirins to no effect. She then proposed that he have a bath, a course of action, for a change, that met with his enthusiastic approval. After an hour, steeping in a hot tub, she tentatively asked how he felt. 'Did that help ease your pain?' One look at him convinced Maidie that she had no alternative but to drive him to hospital. He was in agony. She helped him to dress swiftly and headed for the door, only to find they had been

Glasgow is lucky in having all these entertainment units. Whenever boredom sets in, they can drive anywhere within the city boundaries and dig a hole.

locked in. 'The fire escape! That's the only other way out.' Maidie cried, as they climbed from their window on to a far-from-safe fire escape. To add to their misery, a steady drizzle ensured they were well soaked.

Eventually they reached the car, but not before Chic, climbing over wooden fencing, managed to impale himself on some of the sharp ends. A squawk of pain signalled his release. 'That's bloody marvellous, that is! Now I only need two operations!' he moaned in a vague attempt at humour.

At Blackpool Infirmary gallstones were identified as the root of the problem. He was given a painkiller and put to bed as Maidie returned to an empty house. The following day, a meek, downcast, shaky Chic sat licking his wounds. 'They're never going to let me out of here, that's for sure. You'd better inform the theatre they'll need to get Frank Sinatra to stand in for me.'

Maidie thought, 'Crikey, he really is seriously ill, if that's the best gag he's able to come up with.'

Then, in something of a contrast in the unfolding melodrama, a young smiley doctor popped in. 'Right, Mr Murray, Chop, chop (hands clapping)! It's time for you to bounce back up! Let's be having you! Out of bed you go! Get dressed and off you go home! Oh, and don't forget to take plenty of liquids! You'll be back climbing Everest in no time!'

There followed some minutes of serious foot-dragging as Chic came to terms with the diagnosis. In the taxi back to their hotel, he hissed, 'Bloody barbarians, what the hell do they know?' Somehow, they both knew, his histrionics had been blown clean out of the water. Chic was not a happy bunny!

Chic was vindicated of any suspicion of hypochondria some months later when he was admitted to the Edinburgh Royal Infirmary for a successful operation which resolved his gallstone problem once and for all. But, sadly, his unremitting 'love of life' was fraying at the edges; one moment he was sweetness and light, the next he showed callous indifference. Rows became commonplace between Chic and Maidie. When looked at from the distance and perspective of the ensuing years, one can sympathise with both parties. Any show-business couple working cheek-by-jowl for so many emotion-sapping years would be subjected daily to a degree of stress that the nine-to-five civil servants could never comprehend . . . and it was taking its toll.

I hear he fell badly from the train. That was hard lines.

On one occasion, to illustrate the ups and downs of their relationship, Chic thoughtfully suggested that Maidie should have a break from the kitchen. 'Just for a change, why don't I pop out and bring back four fish suppers? It's food for the Gods!' This was greeted with joyful enthusiasm by the children who had no inkling of the drama still to come. Chic duly set off in the car while Maidie prepared steaming mugs of tea and piles of buttered white bread, both compulsory ingredients in Chic's fish supper routine.

He reappeared about a quarter of an hour later in a state of agitation. 'Oh God! Maidie,' he said, 'come out and see what's happened.' He had been unable to find a parking place and double parked instead, effectively closing the street to through traffic. Worse, on placing the fish suppers on the roof of the car, he had left the engine running with the key in the ignition and with the lock button down he somehow had managed to close the driver's door; not an inconsiderable feat – locked out, but with the engine running. Quick as a flash, Maidie rushed inside to fetch a wire coat-hanger whilst urging Chic to try and placate the angry motorists queuing up behind the delinquent car. She succeeded in her mission in a matter of minutes but not before one enraged motorist demanded to know Chic's address before he reported him to the authorities. As Chic disappeared inside, clutching his precious fish offering, he shouted back at Mr Angry, 'The Conservative Club, Moscow!'

Once inside, the relief was palpable and Chic was hugely grateful for Maidie's cool-headed initiative. 'I tell you this, folks,' Chic purred, 'in the unlikely event we obtain our own coat of arms, we would have to include two crossed coat-hangers rampant!'

The fish and chips were still piping hot and delicious. As the last of Chic's chips disappeared from view, Douglas asked, 'What would you have done, Dad, if Mum hadn't thought of the coat-hanger?'

'Well,' Chic replied, 'you're good at history, son, so you'll know that every page of it is made up of "what ifs". For example, what if your mum and I hadn't met? Like a pal of mine from my school days, you might have been your auntie's bairn by the lodger!' This amused Douglas no end, so much so, that he left his fish supper unguarded. 'And,' Chic continued, 'I wouldn't

We have stained-glass windows. Those damned pigeons!

*He's as funny as rabies in
a guide dogs' home.*

be nicking half your chips as I am now!'

'You can have some of mine, Dad!' Annabelle sweetly offered. This was just a little cameo that illustrated the shared happiness that every family should expect to enjoy.

But in contrast to the idyllic life sketched above, a couple of days later he tormented Maidie (unfortunately, not for the first time) at a gig in Glasgow. Minutes before curtain-up he announced, 'I'm not going on tonight. You'll have to go on on your own! No. I've had enough!'

'Please, Chic,' Maidie pleaded, 'these threats terrify me. My stomach's in a knot!'

The cue came for their entrance, as Maidie called helplessly to Chic's disappearing back. On she went with her accordion and began to sing, 'Be sure it's true when you say you love me . . .' Chic's voice broke in from the wings: '. . . it's a sin to tell a lie.' Chic made his entrance to generous applause. But for Maidie, these incidents provoked not only tremendous relief but also an inner rage, in equal measure, that intensified each time this unmerited threat was played on her.

Doctor's Surgery

I was in Glasgow last night and I've got an aunt here, well, it's not my aunt, it's someone I've always called auntie. I think we've all got this problem – this is my auntie but it's not my auntie at all. In this case I know it's not my auntie, it's my uncle, he just likes to be called auntie.

So I met him today in Sauchiehall Street. I knew him, otherwise I would have never allowed him near me. He said, 'Look! I would like you to do something for me.'

I said, 'What is it?' because you get some strange errands.

He said, 'When you pass the butcher's shop could you pick me up some pigs' trotters?'

I said, 'I can't pass the shop, I will have to stop and go into the shop and see what I can do.'

So I made my way to the butcher's when I felt a sharp pain and I said, 'O Ho!' – now was it 'O Ho!' or was it 'A Ha!'? – anyway it doesn't matter, this would happen to me on television, and I changed my mind: no butcher's, go to the doctor.

104

So I made my way to the waiting room of the doctor's surgery. I didn't go straight into the surgery – you've got to know the doctor fairly well before you can force yourself into the surgery. I sat down. There was a bench there, otherwise I would have never attempted it. And there were other patients, at least I presume they were patients, as far as I could see. I didn't say, 'Are you a patient?' I am not a curious person, I am a loner. And I sat there and they were looking at me like I am looking at you and you are looking at me.

After some time the door of the waiting room opened and I looked just to give myself something to do, that was all; I've seen a door open before, there was no novelty in it, and someone opposite me tried to gain my attention and they said, 'There is someone coming in.'

So someone did come in and although there was ample room in the waiting room he chose to sit beside me. I realised that as soon as he planked himself down and he was in close proximity, I could Ffff . . . You know. I thought that's a bit close and I thought I felt a nudge but I could just have been . . . you know! Then he started speaking to me, this stranger, about this and that, of which I know very little. He said, 'What do you think about this?'

I said, 'I don't think much about that.' I thought if he comes out with a bag of toffees, I'm off; so just as I am contemplating this, the door of the surgery opened and the doctor made his appearance . . . TARRA!

I didn't know it was the doctor at first but this and that knew who he was, 'It's the doctor,' he said, and nodded, and the doctor nodded back and I thought the next time I'll get in quick and I'll say, 'Oh! It's the doctor!'

The doctor was wearing a kilt – probably a Scottish doctor, although you can never be sure these days – and it was a bit on the short side. You didn't notice the kilt immediately so he came swinging gaily into the waiting room and he looked at us all, which he has every right to do; it's his own waiting room, he can do what he likes, then he took a little run and he stood on his hands and he said, 'How's that for a table lamp!'

So a few applauded, probably panel patients or something – regulars or panel beaters – I don't know what they where. So when he got on his feet, which I thought would have to happen,

he couldn't stay up there for long, there's only a certain amount of time you can spend on your 'Germans'! So he got on his feet and said, 'Who's next?' and the rush for that door, I've never seen anything like it in my life. I don't know how I managed to get in first. He was pleased, oh, I knew he was pleased the way he shut the door. He said, 'You're new.'

I said, 'I am hardly unwrapped.'

He said, 'I like someone that's new. What's wrong with you?'

'Oh,' I said, 'I don't know, I don't know what it is.'

And his expression changed and he said, 'I detest when patients come in and they don't know what's wrong with them, it makes it so difficult for me.' He said, 'It means I've got to go into the little room there and look up the medical dictionary. You could have anything! My eyes are bad, what do you think it is?'

I said, 'I don't know what it is.'

'There must be something.'

'Well,' I said, 'I get a pain six inches above my head at night.'

'Oh! I can cure that, I can give you something to take half an hour before you wake up,' the doctor said. 'How long have you had this?'

'Oh,' I said, 'I've had it before.'

And the doctor said, 'You have had it again so it's recurring.'

I said, 'You could say that.'

He said, 'I've just said it and I've no intention of saying it again.'

'This has been on and off for a few years.'

The doctor said to me, 'Have you got a war record?'

I said, 'Of course I have, I've got Vera Lynn singing "The White Cliffs of Dover".'

The doctor said, 'I like that and I'm going to take a personal interest in you.' He said, 'You had better strip. Take your clothes off.'

I said, 'Don't you think you should take me out a couple of times first?'

He said, 'Take your clothes off.'

I said, 'Where will I put them?'

And he said, 'Put them on top of mine.' He said, 'I want to see you walk, we doctors can tell a lot from a walk, let me see you walk. Mmmm. Ahhh,' he said, 'you turn nicely.' I had to turn, I was up against a wall, I just did it on my own initiative.

He said, 'That's a great walk you have, the best walk we've got in the surgery. I wish my partner were here,' he said, 'he's always out on these occasions. Have you been practising?'

I said, 'No, I haven't.' I do a nice walk as it happens. [Chic then walks.]

'Let me see you do it again.' He was pleased, I knew that the way he patted me. 'Well done,' he said. He missed me the second time, I shortened my step.

He said, 'I hope you don't mind?'

'Oh,' I said, 'Feel free.'

Then the doctor said, 'You had better bend over,' so I bent over and the door of the surgery burst open. I had placed myself rather badly. I never thought of a door knob like that before, you know, I must have been three feet in the air, so I looked between my legs and there was a huge fella there built like a rugby three-quarter, so I straightened up immediately.

I said, 'Doctor,' with a little gesture that surprised him.

He said, 'Now, look, don't call me "doctor", I feel as if we are on first names – call me Lance.' [Chic does a double take.] He says, 'I will write you out a recipe or something.'

So I made my way to the nearest pharmacist and I was approached by an assistant and I said, 'I was just going to take a gander round the shop.'

She said, 'As long as it's house-trained.'

Just at that moment a woman came in with a rush. She placed the rush on the chair. The pharmacist said, 'Madam,' and she looked at me.

I said, 'It's you he means.'

She asked for some invisible hairnets. She said, 'Are you sure they are invisible?'

The chemist said, 'Of course they are. I've been selling them for three weeks and I've been out of stock for six months.'

The pharmacist said to me, 'You are due some pills. Shall I put them in a box?'

I said, 'Well, it will save me rolling them all the way home.'

CHAPTER 9
CHANGING TIMES

In that summer of 1959, Chic and Maidie took on a new challenge. They were invited to participate in a spectacular show, produced by Larry Parnes, at the seaside resort of Great Yarmouth. What concerned Chic was the age of the stars under Larry Parnes' management – they were all kids to him. At forty, Chic had filled out his not-inconsiderable frame, was being threatened by a receding hairline (which shouldn't have bothered him under his instantly recognised tartan bunnet), and was making the odd visitation to his neighbourhood optician. However, Larry Parnes, cleverly, had brought Chic and Maidie into the scheme of things to widen the appeal of the show. Top of the bill was Billy Fury, appearing alongside Joe Brown, Marty Wilde, Karl Denver, the Tornadoes and the Vernon Girls. 'Well, there's one thing for sure,' Chic said, 'I'll be damned if we're going to introduce rock 'n' roll into our act just for the occasion.' They did tweak their act, as it happened, with Chic, for example, introducing a comedy version of a recent chart-topper, 'When Mexico Gave Up The Rumba'.

Any misgivings he had were soon extinguished, thanks to the lovable cockney Joe Brown. He was an avid fan of Chic's and though his attempts to mimic Chic were hardly accurate with his East End twang and Oor Wullie hairstyle, nonetheless they were highly amusing to the company. He was described by Joe – even then – as a cult figure. Chic feigned indignation at such a notion, but secretly loved it! And so, with Douglas and Annabelle accompanying them, the whole family enjoyed a very successful and lucrative season. By this time, variety was regularly being featured on television, marking the decline of live variety shows in theatres and music halls. The combination of contemporary music and variety undeniably arrested this trend in Great

'Doctor, I've got butterflies in my stomach.'
'Oh. What have you been eating?'
'Butterflies.'

Chic 'addressing' the ball

*'You didn't have the Rolling
Stones in your day, Granddad.'
'No, but we had rickets and
diphtheria so it sort of evens
itself out.'*

*'I'm going to have to do
something to keep the bills down.'
'Have you ever thought of a heavy
paperweight?'*

Yarmouth, but it was something that, in times to come, could not be sustained.

The family left Montague Street the same year as their sojourn to Great Yarmouth, moving to a smart address in Bruntsfield overlooking parkland and not far removed from the famous sixteenth-century alehouse, the Golf Tavern, on the other side of the Links. They were barely settled in when an adjoining terraced house came onto the market. Thinking on his feet, Chic saw a commercial opportunity in developing both properties into a hotel, but still leaving ample living space for the family. 'It would provide future employment for Douglas and Annabelle,' he added, 'and, of course, I would drink exclusively in the hotel!' This comment was met with a somewhat lukewarm response from Maidie as Chic was becoming increasingly fond of the dram! 'We can call it the Chic Murray Hotel; how's that for a bit of originality, eh?' (Actually, it was a shrewd suggestion, because such was the widespread public consciousness of his name, it gave the business an established air, even before it began to trade.)

The idea appealed to Maidie: if property was a good investment, two of the same was twice as good, she figured. And, from Maidie's point of view, what could be more ideal? She and Chic were about to embark on an eight-week tour of Australia so all the conversion work could be left in the capable hands of Anne Dickson. Unlike the proverbial mother-in-law, Chic had a deep respect for her and for her organisational skills. Maidie, thus, would be free from the day-to-day hassles and snags that a clerk of works might encounter. And the bonus was, mercifully, that Chic would be well out of the road!

The sale proceeded towards completion and plans for change of use and alterations were duly approved, coinciding with details of their itinerary under the Southern Cross. First, they were to fly to New York to meet Neil Kirk again, who had arranged a television appearance for them on the *Jack Parr Show*; then they were to plane-hop to Chicago; and then there were brief stop-overs in San Francisco, Los Angeles, Las Vegas and Fiji before landing in Melbourne. In all, they were to be away for ten weeks, with two shows in Scotland on their return before heading for the Hippodrome, Birmingham, for the *Lonnie Donegan Christmas Show*, to share joint billing with Miki and Griff.

Chic took a delight, as an old hand, in showing the sights of New York to Maidie (but no mention of the Bowery Boys!). They visited Chinatown, Little Italy and Staten Island on the ferry, and climbed to the top of the Statue of Liberty to admire the view in amongst her spikes. But the weekend soon came and went. Neil Kirk treated them to dinner to round off the Sunday night at Jack Dempsey's. The ex-World Champion boxer introduced himself, 'Neil tells me you're as hot as hell in the old sod! Just remember, when you make it big over here, I saw you *foist*, Chic! Okay?' He insisted on a photograph of them all together, to adorn his walls, already crammed with the images of celebrities and stars in his company, and, before they left, they had to observe the 'signing of the menu' ritual, only granted to those whose names had previously appeared in lights!

The following day, Neil phoned to say the Jack Parr television appearance was off. A major show-business scandal had cropped up and guests were put on hold so that the show's

At home in Edinburgh

producers could extract an hour's questionable entertainment exclusively at the expense of some high-profile victim. They set out on their journey with a promise from Neil to introduce them to someone who would be ideal to handle their affairs in the States but that would have to wait for their return from Australia. From then on, their trip was too brief for more than snatched postcard-like remembrances including the City by the Bay and a giant redwood forest after a ferry ride to Sausalito.

Down under, they worked for the Chevron hotel chain and they went down a treat. There was a surfeit of goodwill for entertainers from the Old Country, particularly with Australia's young, raw history that so often featured the pioneering Scot, but Chic and Maidie excelled themselves anyway. 'Whingeing pommies' was, in general, reserved for those from south of the border! Chevron pleaded with them to stay. 'You could run for a year here in Melbourne alone,' they cajoled, but Chic and Maidie had commitments back in New York, back in Glasgow, and back in Birmingham. If that wasn't enough, Maidie's heart was bursting for want of her children and home. They moved on with mixed feelings, to be a smash hit on Australia's Channel 7 TV before the tour ended in triumph in cabaret in Sydney.

After a stretch-the-legs break in Las Vegas, Neil was delighted to welcome them back to New York. 'I'm a hundred per cent sure, folks, I've got the very man for you! His name is Nathaniel Silverstein. Sadly, he's stuck in Chicago which is not much use, but his plane gets into Idlewild two hours before you guys head home tomorrow. At least you'll have time to get acquainted; you'll have time to talk.'

Next day, Maidie packed their things, withdrawn. At length, Chic broke the silence: 'What's bugging you, Maidie? Let's talk about it. I can't stand atmospheres at the best of times. Just tell me. What's on your mind?' It was as if Maidie was steeling herself for this moment because her directness stunned Chic.

'I'm quitting the act. That's just as soon as we've fulfilled our commitments back home.'

Chic visibly paled. 'Quitting Maidie? *Quitting*? How the hell can you come out with that when we're seeing Silver-whatshisname in a couple of hours?'

'Look, Chic, I've been taking a back seat more and more. The public come to see you. I'm just an added extra. Get this into

There's a new slimming treatment that's all the rage. They surgically remove all your bones. Not only do you lose a helluva lot of weight, you look so much more relaxed after the operation.

your head – *you're* the star! Besides, I badly need a break. Don't forget I've been doing the same routine – admittedly it's changed over the years – since I was four. Come on! Don't play the helpless ticket! You can get a jeely piece wherever you go! You don't need me, Chic, that's the honest truth and, in all honesty, the constant travelling has become a dreadful chore for me. Don't worry, I'll still back you and I'll only be a phone call away! Now, let's get cracking and meet Mr Silverstein.'

The gentleman in question appeared cool, self-assured and rather distinguished-looking. 'Neil's told me lots about you. What I've heard sounds intriguing. And I'll tell you something more at the outset. I won't take you on if I thought you couldn't make it big in the States. What's the alternative, after all? Failure? Or a small-time two-bit turn in Hicksville? Nuh! I don't do that for my people! So, let's you, me and Maidie have a right good talk in the time we've got.' Chic hesitated. He was breaking new ground. 'Mr Silverstein . . .'

'Call me Nate, please!' he interjected.

'Nate, the act is *me*. Me alone. Solo.'

Chic's comment met with a smile from Nate. 'Maidie wants to take no part. That's okay. That doesn't stop us talking.'

That reassurance brought relief to Chic. The talking bit came easy to him. He was, after all, a master of chat: amusing, provocative, stimulating, original, humorous. After an hour of sheer, brilliant 'Chic-anery' with Chic firing on all cylinders, Maidie thought to herself, 'Dear God, if it was me, I'd have signed him up half an hour ago!' Throughout this *tour de force* Nate remained his cool, collected self although Chic was sure he detected the early beginnings of a smile on a number of occasions which ran counter to Nate's professional imperturbability.

An hour went by, and, as if he'd heard enough, Nate addressed Neil Kirk, 'I have to say Chic makes a big impression on me and I believe we can do something together. I'm already thinking along certain lines but I need a day or two to get a fix on just what that line of thought comes to.' Then Nate turned to Maidie, complimenting her on her selflessness and assuring her that there was a real possibility that her husband could be on the threshold of great things. Lastly he turned to Chic, 'Give me a day or two, Chic, and I'll be in touch with Neil.' He said his farewells and left.

A statesman's just a politician who you can sometimes agree with.

'That sounded very hopeful,' Neil said. 'What did you think, Chic?'

'Hard to say,' Chic replied, 'but I suppose I'm in with a shout. I don't know the guy, after all, but I will say, whether he was impressed with me or not, I was well impressed with him!' Shortly thereafter, there were warm goodbyes as they boarded their plane home. They settled down for the flight where Maidie's thoughts increasingly turned to her young family and home whilst her partner – understandably, after the trial of the last few hours – thought only of Broadway.

Neil Kirk phoned the Murrays a week later. 'You might have thought Nate a bit stand-offish, Chic, but that's his manner. He's not typical of the species and he never gets carried away. Nevertheless he was very enthusiastic about you and gave the green light for you to work with him. This is what he plans. Initially you'll be working in cabaret in Greenwich Village where the up-market chattering classes hang out and, hopefully, the word will circulate that there's a new comic on the block! With the helping hand of regular television appearances, Nate wants to steer you into your own one-man show, just off Broadway, before the year's up. He's going to fly over to see you, amongst others, obviously, to discuss availability and, most important, to see what kind of a timetable is available for the launch. Is that good news, or what?' Chic's first reaction was mild disbelieving shock. After a while, when the news had been fully absorbed, the family were informed and whoops of delight were heard on the Links as congratulatory hugs and kisses were exchanged.

In the short term, Chic had other fish to fry, and one in particular, Lonnie Donegan, as he and Maidie headed south for rehearsals for his *Christmas Show*. For some reason, Chic couldn't abide Lonnie Donegan. This was hard to fathom – they had never even met! 'I just hope he has no illusions about acting the big star with *me*!' he boomed in sonorous tones.

'Och! Behave, Chic,' Maidie said sensibly, 'give him a chance. What's wrong with you? You've never blinking met the poor devil!'

'Ah! That might well be,' replied a grumbling Chic, 'but I'll just keep my powder dry and if he starts to come the bag with me, I'll just blast him off the face of the earth! No bother!' Maidie could scarcely forbear to smile because Chic's views on

Then there was this enormous bang! There was sand everywhere. Hurriedly, I filled the egg-timer . . .

the singer, for no apparent reason, were so over the top.

'I'll bet,' she said, 'Lonnie's a wee sweetie-pie!'

Chic rejoined, 'Oh! A *pie* merchant! Have no two doubts about that! He's a pie, all right! He's even signed with the Pye label. And there I am, a recording artist with Parlophone. Okay! Okay! I know it was only for one day! But you can't compare them. Parlophone's like royalty compared to a sweaty-socks *pie*! Imagine! A fusty old pie! I shouldn't even be talking to him, never mind appearing on the same bill!'

And daft as it sounds, all this was no more than huff and puff, blustering bravura, because, almost from day one, Chic and Lonnie became good friends. His *Lonnie Donegan Christmas Show* at the Hippodrome was some reward and recognition for his string of smash hits nationwide, ever since leaving the Chris Barber Skiffle Group to strike out on his own. Maidie drew comfort from the knowledge that if Chic wasn't with her, he wasn't too far away, with his new-found friend, Lonnie, either reminiscing on their earlier experiences on the stage or, more likely, slagging each other off, toe to toe, with no holds barred! It was a sort of ongoing verbal tennis match where only taking the huff, followed immediately by a storming off, could clearly identify the loser. One of the favourite items of discussion took a form not dissimilar to the following . . . 'Of course, you *do* know that I invented skiffle in this country.'

Chic would state in a statesmanlike manner. 'Aw! Give us a break, you old codger!'

Lonnie would hit back, 'How did your addled, warped mind work that one out? And where did I fit in then, in the scheme of things?'

Then Chic would move up a gear, 'Look here, laddie, you weren't even a plucked string on your daddie's guitar when this all happened! Nobody doubts that! You've no right even to question the facts in your pram. Listen! I laid the groundwork for you! It was I who opened the doors to a new musical genre and it was froth like you that saw and heard what I was on about and used it to turn a shilling for yourself!'

It was almost as if this gifted story-teller believed his own script – perhaps with treasured memories of those halcyon days of Chic and the Chicks with Gooey on the washboard those many years before in Greenock – but how much provocation,

even if the banter was essentially good-natured, could any man reasonably absorb without an alternative plan of action? And Lonnie often was unceremoniously pushed beyond the absorption limit when Plan B, the counter-offensive, had to be wheeled in. 'I hear your recording career began and ended with one measly Parlophone record. Is that the case, Chic?'

Viper-like, came the reply 'What? Just *one* of my Parlophone records, and fine you know it, is worth a million of your 'Pyes'. You're nothing but an out and out *pie* merchant! Imagine getting a gold disc for flogging a few dozen pies?'

'And what about 'My Old Man's a Dustman?' (One of Lonnie's most popular hits.)

'I have to give you credit for one thing, you've got a wee bit of honesty. That was the one and only autobiographical hit ever pressed in music history. And everyone knows the job was rubbish but how did your dad get into that racket? Did he just pick it up as he went along?'

Lonnie Donegan, like Chic, had many redeeming features (in amongst a number of foibles), so that, even when they wanted to go in for the kill, there was a degree of gentleness in their ribbing. And these exchanges were literally a daily occurrence, so much so that Maidie, in exasperation, suggested they form a double act. 'Don't give him ideas above his station!' Chic remarked, 'building up his hopes like that will all just end in tears!'

To which Lonnie replied, 'Maidie, tell me, for God's sake, what do I want with another roadie?'

On Christmas Eve, Chic was taking it easy in their hotel suite before setting out for the theatre whilst Maidie was busy packing a change of clothes for a party at Lonnie's. The phone rang. Maidie lifted the receiver to hear Neil Kirk's voice asking for Chic. She left him to it in the lounge. After several minutes, ash-white, Chic entered the bedroom, his face strangely contorted. 'What's up, Chic?' Maidie asked, concerned.

'It's Nate Silverstein,' he said slowly, barely audible, 'he's been involved in a multiple pile-up on the New Jersey Turnpike. He's dead, Maidie.'

That evening was an immense challenge for Chic but his professionalism saw him through one of the lowest points of his life. The news had hit him like a thunderbolt because all his future dreams of Broadway lay smashed alongside Nate on the fateful

He'd make someone a wonderful stranger.

New Jersey Turnpike. They explained their non-attendance at the party to a hugely sympathetic Lonnie and quietly repaired to the hotel. Chic had prepared a special gag book exclusively for his American adventure which he showed Maidie for the first and last time. He threw it into the fire and as the flames consumed it, the scene was a metaphor for his own feelings. 'Yup,' he said, still staring at the fire, 'it's all going up in smoke, just like my American conquest.' He fell silent again, shaking his head in disbelief. Maidie looked on, powerless to comfort his very private grief. Then he interrupted his meditation to throw some light on his thoughts, 'Y'know, Maidie, every single bloke who has climbed up on a stage to try and entertain his fellow man, needs someone like Nate who believes in him. He believed in me,

Behind the bar at
the hotel in Bruntsfield

honest! And I mean it when I tell you that if he'd asked me to jump into the Hudson, I'd have done it.'

Back in Edinburgh, the Chic Murray Hotel was granted its liquor licence and with the alterations complete, trade began in 1963 with Douglas, now seventeen, working under the supervision of the newly appointed manager. They were both assisted by Black Bottle Bill, so called because he never deviated from his two favoured tipples, Johnnie Walker Black Label and Guinness. Despite his proclivity to imbibe copiously, he was a handy handyman and factotum. True to his word, Chic did most of his drinking in the hotel bars and was a terrific draw for the Edinburgh public, but it didn't take long for Maidie to suss there was a downside to his presence. He was every stocktaker's nightmare. For example, a pint glass, on occasions, was near half-filled with dark rum before cheekily enquiring of Maidie whether the said glass and its contents were 'roughly a measure'. Unsurprisingly, this had a very limited effect in furthering the interests of domestic bliss and harmony.

That summer, they had another loosely termed 'holiday' à la Chic, a booking for the season at Gwrych Castle, a holiday complex of sorts, near Abergele in Wales. It boasted a miniature railway, a mini-zoo and a chamber of horrors, amongst other horrors, presumably designed for couples and their young offspring. Chic and Maidie both entertained the public in a huge marquee but, in spite of performing a matinee in the afternoon, with two shows in the evening, it was hardly taxing to either of them and, in truth, with Douglas, Annabelle and Nana Dickson in tow, it was something of a holiday after all. They lived in a large luxury caravan with all mod cons. And the weeks were carefree with the exception of the occasional telephone call to the hotel. Black Bottle appeared to be the harbinger of nothing but ill tidings. (Maybe he was missing them!) Either the roof was packing in or the toilets were yet again flooded. Luckily there was no mention of a fire.

But in fairness to Black Bottle, on their return, they were confronted by a number of tribulations and mishaps. For example, Black Bottle had fallen off the roof whilst attempting his handyman bit, erecting an aerial. It was probably safe to conclude that this episode was the result of a good number of alcoholic tinctures. His fall to earth – he was miraculously

unhurt – had been cushioned in part by Maidie's rose bed; the Bottle remained unbroken but the roses had had a fearful seeing-to.

As they unravelled the various snags and must-dos, their attention was diverted by an invitation to tour South Africa with Kenneth McKellar and Moira Anderson. 'Oh, goody goody!' Chic said, rubbing his hands and grinning like a demented hyena. 'All that lovely sunshine! Oh! I'd love to go to Durban in a turban! Here we go, here we go, here we go!'

'Here *you* go, Chic!' Maidie cut in, 'I told you in the States that once we'd finished the gigs we had already agreed to do, as far as I was concerned, that was that! I don't care if you are touring the Caribbean, or any other exotic destination for that matter, that would have no bearing on my decision.'

Chic pleaded with her but she was adamant. She was going to stay at home and act as assistant manageress. Full stop, no ifs, no buts – eventually Chic threw the towel in and accepted the inevitable. 'No more Chic and Maidie,' he muttered, crestfallen, the euphoria of minutes before just a passing chimera. 'I can see the headlines: 'Small Doll Leaves Tall Droll!' or, maybe, 'Tall Droll Throws Himself into Large Hole!'

Maidie couldn't resist a smile. 'Why should there be any need for headlines? Just be discreet about it! We've got one more show at the Gaiety in Ayr, then we can simply split up with no announcement, no kerfuffle and no fuss. That's the proper way, the dignified way, to tackle this and you know it makes sense, Chic. It's just that, sometimes, you don't think things through.'

Grudgingly, Chic accepted the inevitable but the day marked a watershed in his life. A period of readjustment had to begin for him which, to some extent, never reached completion . . .

'I've just run over your cockerel. I'd like to replace him,' the motorist informed the farmer's wife. 'Fair enough,' she said, 'the hens are round the back.'

CHAPTER 10
ON HIS OWN

Without Maidie, it was as if a part of Chic's very essence had simply seeped away. He missed her hugely, something which he freely discussed with his show-business colleagues, Moira Anderson and Kenneth McKellar, as they toured South Africa. And they, in turn, did their level best to give him support and a sympathetic ear. No matter his heartache, it never hindered his remarkable turn of phrase, his psychotic 'hyper-humour', or his wonderful and original take on life. The public, wherever he strutted his stuff, took him to their hearts. Simply put, Chic continued to make people laugh out loud and unashamedly. He was good at it whatever the circumstances.

They were in Durban when, out of the blue, Chic received a phone call which he was unable to authenticate. Was it a wind-up? Or was it for real? He wandered down after the conversation to the hotel lounge where Kenneth and Moira were having coffee. 'Have you been at it?' Chic asked Moira (she was a known practical joker).

'Of course,' she replied, 'I'm always at it! No, Chic, seriously, I haven't a clue what the "it" is that I'm supposed to be at! Go on, spill the beans! What's happened?'

Chic frowned. He was still far from convinced. 'Well, it seems that the producer of *What's New, Pussycat?* is making a James Bond film with Orson Welles as the villain, the main man representing SMERSH, the baddies, with me as some kind of a sidekick, a sort of heavy, I suppose. There were all sorts of questions. When was I back in the UK, what was my availability and so on. Are you *sure* it wasn't you, Moira?'

In response, Moira burst into innocent laughter. Secretly she would have loved to have worked the big fellow up, but not on this occasion!

Colour television! Whatever next? Me, I won't believe it until I see it in black and white.

Chic in *Casino Royale*. (© 1967 Famous Artists Productions, Inc. and Danjaq LLC. Courtesy of MGM Clip & Still Licensing)

I don't recognise this court, your honour. Was it painted blue recently?

On his return, back in the UK, all became clearer to Chic. It transpired that a certain Charles Feldman, producer, had had an unexpectedly successful response to *What's New, Pussycat?* He was the flavour of the month and despite the film receiving a good pasting from the critics, he was so pleased by the box-office response to the movie, he even gifted Peter Sellers a brand new Rolls Royce. For whatever reason, the rights to Ian Fleming's *Casino Royale*, somehow, had been missed by the usual Bond producer, Cubby Broccoli, and landed on Feldman's lap. The film was to be a send-up of the James Bond genre, starring David Niven, Ursula Andress, Woody Allen and a peppering of other stars in cameo roles, including the ultimate heavyweight, Orson Welles. But one major uncertainty remained over Peter Sellers. Would he agree to sign up, or would he not? Without him, Feldman reckoned the project was a non-starter. So did Columbia Pictures. Meantime, understandably, Chic lived in hope that Sellers would resolve his dithering because, subject to Sellers' signature in the affirmative, he, himself, had been offered a cracking deal: a fee of £4,000, all his expenses and plenty more if they overran the scheduling of sixteen weeks. And during Sellers' make-your-mind-up time, this delay had no material effect on Chic's career as he busied himself with both television and radio. Eventually the bugle sounded the advance. At long last Sellers had signed.

Chic made a number of excursions to London to get measured up by the costumiers, not to mention a number of bookings across England. When things began in earnest, he was duly introduced to the director, Joe McGrath, a fellow Scot. Columbia were not happy with the appointment but acquiesced on Peter Sellers' insistence. The studio, in fairness, were concerned with his limited experience in film and they were worried that he had no experience whatsoever of a large-budget movie.

Nevertheless, the cameras began to roll at Shepperton Studios with Peter Sellers warmly welcoming Chic to the set. The latter was pleased that he was familiar with much of his material, including, even, a working knowledge of Genumphs! But the whole time that shooting took place thereafter, not a word passed between either of them. He was a strange bird, Sellers, and insecure to the point of absurdity at times. For

Chic signs up in a James bond film. The original contract for *Casino Royale*

122

FOSTERS AGENCY LTD.

Piccadilly House, Piccadilly Circus,
London, S.W.1.

TELEGRAMS :
CONFIRMATION,
LONDON.

I hereby acknowle...

Confirmation of Contract for :-

Famous Artists Pro...

One week comme...
Feb.11th 1966.

To open on

Also

Also

Also

Also

at a salary of   £4...

Signature ....

Date sent   17.2.66.

Returned   ....

WEEKLY SALARY ENGAGEMENT

An Agreement made the EIGHTH day of

FEBRUARY   One thousand nine hundred and sixty   six   BETWEEN
FAMOUS ARTISTS PRODUCTIONS LTD.   of   Shepperton Studios, SHEPPERTON, Middx.
(hereinafter called "the Company") of the one part and

CHIC MURRAY

of   "Hawaain Bar" Murray's Hotel, 5, Bruntsfield Crescent, EDINBURGH.
(hereinafter called "the Artist") of the other part

whereby it is agreed as follows:—

SECTIONS

The B.F.P.A. Equity Agreement.
1. This Agreement shall incorporate terms identical with the terms of the Agreement made between the British Film Producers Association and the British Actors' Equity Association and dated the Fifth day of December, 1947, as amended and extended by all supplemental agreements made between the same parties which shall be operative at the date hereof (hereinafter called "the B.F.P.A. Equity Agreement") so far as the same are applicable hereto provided always that during such periods as the engagement of the Artist shall not be on a daily salary basis the said terms of the B.F.P.A. Equity Agreement shall for the purposes of this Agreement be deemed amended in accordance with the provisions set out in the Schedule hereto.

Engagement.
2. The Company hereby engages the Artist and the Artist hereby accepts the engagement to perform the part of   "ILYA"   in a film entitled   "Casino Royale"   and the engagement shall continue until the Company has completed the Artist's part in the production of the film.

Guaranteed Period.
3. The Company shall be entitled to the Artist's exclusive services for a period of   ONE   weeks (hereinafter called "the guaranteed period") commencing on the first day on which the Artist shall, following a call by the Company, attend to render services in the photographing or recording of the Artist's part, or travel to a location such day being on or about the   Eleventh   day of   February   1966 i.e. not earlier than seven days before such date or, failing such call, on the seventh day after such date.

Extending Engagement
4. The Company may retain the exclusive services of the Artist after the guaranteed period for such further period as the Company may require to complete photography of the part.

Weekly Salary.
5. Save as otherwise provided in this Agreement the Company shall pay to the Artist (a) the sum of   FOUR HUNDRED POUNDS   (£ 400.0.0.) per week for each week of the guaranteed period and, (b) the sum of   FOUR HUNDRED POUNDS   (£ 400.0.0) per week for each week of any period of extended engagement.

Daily Salary and Half Daily Salary.
6. Save as otherwise provided in this Agreement and save when the weekly salary is payable, the Company shall pay to the Artist the sum of   ONE HUNDRED POUNDS   (£ 100.0.0.) per day (hereinafter called "the daily salary") for each day (or subject to the provisions of Clause 15 of the B.F.P.A. Equity Agreement, for each night) on which the Artist attends, following a call by the Company, to render services in the photographing or recording of the Artist's part in the film provided that :—

(a) the Company shall pay to the Artist a sum equal to one half of the daily salary in the circumstances provided for in Clauses 9 and 10 of the B.F.P.A. Equity Agreement, and

(b) the Artist shall not be entitled to more than the weekly salary for any period of a week or less than a week.

Artist's Warranties.
Delete words which do not apply and initial
7. The Artist warrants that until fulfilment of this Agreement :—

(a) The Artist is and will remain a British Subject (or if not a British subject) The Artist is and will remain ordinarily resident in a Commonwealth country or the Republic of Ireland.

(b) The Artist is/is not a minor.

(c) The Artist is, to the best of the Artist's knowledge and belief, in such a state of health that the Company will be able to effect insurance under normal conditions upon the Artist against loss, howsoever caused, arising from the Artist's inability to perform the services required hereunder and upon the conditions as to medical examination which are provided in Clause 20 of the B.F.P.A. Equity Agreement.

(d) The Artist will not incur any liabilities on behalf of the Company nor pledge the Company's credit.

(e) The Artist shall comply with all the regulations of the Studios or location (especially the "no smoking" regulation) and shall provide at the Artist's own expense such sun-glasses or other protection for the Artist's eyes as the Artist feels necessary while working in the Studios or on location.

continued over

FAMOUS ARTISTS PRODUCTIONS LTD.   (The Company)

CHIC MURRAY.   (The Artist)

CALL SHEET No.30

PRODUCTION "CASINO ROYALE"

DATE Tuesday, 22nd. Feb. 1966

UNIT CALL 8.30 A.M.

WHERE WORKING INT. CASINO - Stage 'C'

ARTISTE	CHARACTER	DRESSING ROOM	MAKE-UP	READY ON SET
		Old Hse 23	To be notified	
	TREMBLE	26	" "	"
PETER SELLERS	VESPER	C/D 94	11.00	11.30
URSULA ANDRESS	MATHIS	76	8.30	9.00
DUNCAN MACRAE	WAITER	58	"	"
JOHN BLUTHAL	CHEF DE PARTIE	90	"	"
DAVID BERGLAS	PEDRO	"	"	"
JONATHAN ROUTH	ILYA	76	"	"
CHICK MURRAY	PETERS	A/B 42	8.00	"
BOB GODFREY	CASHIER	C/D 72	"	"
MONTI DE LYLE	GREEK	91	8.30	"
HENRY GILBERT	MR. LEE	"	8.00	"
ROBERT LEE	JONES	"	"	"
IAN QUARRIER	BUSINESS MAN	81	7.30	"
JOSEPH DUBIN-BEHRMANN	MRS. GOSS	99	7.00	"
HELEN GOSS	ALEX	"	"	"
DIANE LLOYD	MISS RUSSELL	89	"	"
CHRISTINE SPOONER	GIOVANNA	85	"	"
JACKY BISSETT	GLORY	"	"	"
JEAN STEWART	SPLIT	"	"	"
JAN RENNISON	CHOCOLATE	"	"	"
GINA WARWICK	MELBA	99	"	"
DANI SHERIDAN	CHARLIE	"	"	"
HEATHER LOWE	JAKE	"	"	"
JUNE ABBEY	ROBIN	"	"	"
ROBIN TOLHURST	REGGIE	70	"	"
ROSEMARY READE	JACKEY	"	"	"
VERONICA GARDENER	LILY	"	"	"
KARINA STERRY	BLOSSOM	"	"	"
MAGGIE WRIGHT	VIOLET	"	"	"
BARBARA FRENCH	ROSE	99	"	"
SUE BARDOLPH	TULIP	70	"	"
CATHERINE LANCASTER	DAFFY	99	"	"
DIANA BURFORD	HEATHER	89	"	"
VIRGINIA TYLER	PENNY	85	"	"
FIONA LEWIS	FARTHING	99	"	"
CHRISTINE ROGERS	ANGEL	"	"	"
SUSAN BAKER	"	81	7.30	"
JENNIFER BAKER	MISS BRINDLEY	70	7.00	"
MADGE BRINDLEY	PANSY			
ALEXIS DRURY				

SCENE NUMBERS

		C/D 93	8.30	9.00
Special Talent: 1 Man	Croupier			
		A/B 22	8.00	8.30
Stand ins:	For Miss Andress	Crowd Cut 2	"	"
BETTY ROGERS	Mr. Sellers			
LYNDSEY HOOPER				

P.T.O.

example, he became obsessed that Orson Welles would 'steal' every scene where they filmed together. And, because of this mini-attack of paranoia, he flatly refused even to appear on set when the great man made his entry, despite the requirement for them to be filmed playing cards together. The sequence had to be filmed with only one of them on set at any one time and the resultant shots then had to be cobbled together.

Even Chic thought this behaviour was passing weird but, to compensate, he got on famously with Orson Welles himself who liked Chic and his humour. When asked by a journalist if he was enjoying the moment, Chic replied, 'Great! But it's been work, work, and then more work! I've been in two scenes and uttered five lines so far, but no, no, I can take the strain! Oh, and I nearly forgot! I'm setting up an Advice to the Lovelorn bureau to cater for the lassies, Ursula Andress, Joanna Pettit and Daliah Lavi. I'm doing my very best to help the poor lambs, but it's not easy, you know!'

Matters were not running smoothly on the film set itself. McGrath was given the heave-ho and the studio tried to square the circle by issuing a statement that it was always their intention to use the services of more than one director. (The real reason was the very strange complexity of Peter Sellers' nature himself – the warmth between the men, by this time, had gone decidedly frosty.) Chic had more or less done his stint, but he was quite agreeable to staying on (for extra loot, of course!) to be included in a pipe-band sequence. Could he help in advising where a pipe band could be provided? 'Nae bother!' Chic phoned Maidie. As quick as 'next, please', the Edinburgh Police Pipe Band were flown down for a short filmic excursion which included Peter O'Toole and the indomitable Chic banging on the big drum. (Somehow anything less than a large drum would have been inappropriate for Chic!)

Feldman kept reassuring Columbia that they had a smash hit on their hands but the studio could only see a budget exploding through the roof. That, and a procession of directors, including John Huston, Ken Hughes, Val Guest and Robert Parrish coming and going in the night hardly assuaged their misgivings. Chic wasn't bothered by the internal frictions, 'It was all just funny money to me,' he said afterwards. 'I wasn't exactly carrying the film, though I wouldn't have minded carrying some

Chic wasn't the only star to appear in this film, as the call sheet shows!

125

of the cast, if I'd been asked nicely, of course. I could have started with Ursula Andress, for example!'

The film was heading for the buffers and matters were aggravated further by Sellers refusing to take part in the closing scenes which might have made some sense of his role. There was to be no Rolls Royce presentation this time round. Chic attended the premiere in April 1967 in aid of a charity and then zoomed north to hear the critics simply shred, decimate and annihilate the production off the face of the planet. The only saving grace from Chic's point of view was that he never merited a mention – a bonus in the circumstances.

Charles Feldman never recovered from the public's judgement. The box offices remained steadfastly empty, as did his credibility, and he died the following year, a broken man. 'Oh well,' Maidie observed, 'at least you came out of it unscathed, Chic, and in years to come you can always say you were in a Bond movie!'

Chic agreed. 'Yet the whole damned thing seems to me to have been such a waste!' he said. 'All that parading of egos while the money and the film itself went down the plughole. But for goodness sake, I've made a few thousand smackers out of it and I'm several million wiser!'

A week later, he was back down in the big smoke, fulfilling a BBC engagement. As he wandered past Leicester Square where *Casino Royale* was showing, he literally cringed as he thought to himself, 'I just hope to hell nobody recognises me here in this unfamiliar territory!' Yet Chic was entirely blameless for the press attacks. He had done what was asked of him in the film with panache. The discomfort he felt was an indication of how much the botched production affected his morale, which, sadly, was exacerbated by weightier considerations.

As is so often the case, fate lent a hand – he bumped into an old friend, Archie McCulloch, who was first to hire him (almost by accident) in those far-off days in Carnoustie! Archie was accompanied by his bonnie wife, Kathy Kay, who sang as one of the leading members in the company of the *Billy Cotton Band Show*. 'Have you seen the film?', Chic asked anxiously. 'He cheered up a bit when we told him we hadn't. We were staying in a hotel in Bayswater and asked Chic to join us for dinner.' (Kathy had been recording that same day for the BBC.)

'Do you still have your gun?'
'Yeah.'
'Well, keep him covered.
I'll fetch a blanket.'

126

Archie continued, 'I had never seen Chic quite so down-in-the-mouth before. I think he was badly in need of company but, as usual, he raised himself to the occasion, so much so, that our three boys simply loved him!' Chic found the breadsticks which accompanied their Italian menu something of a novelty. 'He took one or two of them to our room after the food, to conduct an imaginary orchestra,' Archie went on, 'which had the young ones rolling in the aisles in helpless laughter.' As the evening lengthened, Kathy could see the 'black dog' begin to affect Chic again. And they realised it wasn't the film's ratings that troubled Chic, it was much closer to home.

He was having to come to terms with reality. Maidie and he had lived too many years living out of suitcases. He could see with great reluctance that their double act was now a thing of the past. He found it tough to accept, yet understood, that Maidie now embraced a new challenge in life in the management of the hotel. He began to appreciate that the wear and tear of their tension-filled lives together had inevitably taken its toll and that the chance to repair and renew their relationship had come and gone some time before. In short, the penny had dropped – Chic knew that from now on, he was on his own and the prospect filled him with foreboding.

The cold war between Soviet Russia and the West was at its height and so it was for Chic in his personal and professional life. There was the prospect of divorce on the horizon and relations with Billy Marsh were cooling too. *Casino Royale* undoubtedly was an influential factor, but Chic had single-handedly negotiated a deal in Perth to perform over their summer season, along the lines he and Maidie had enjoyed in Rothesay, including a profit-share arrangement and the right to hire and fire the supporting cast. Thus his ties to the Delfont agency began to seem something of an irrelevance to Chic and, in due course, they simply fell away. As it happened, a dispute arose in Perth over an alleged breach of contract which the parties settled out of court but, as so often happens, with neither side entirely happy with the outcome.

He immersed himself in work, partly as a distraction from events around him, and took up temporary residence in Hillhead, Glasgow, conveniently close to Queen Margaret Drive, the home of BBC Television (Scotland) at the time. He piled into

'I've been a foreman now for fourteen years.'
'Gosh! That's a helluva long time doing nothing.'

CHIC MURRAY
"As Ever Was"

Telephone messages received at
041-221 7236 (Week-days only
between 9 a.m. and 5 p.m.)

the work schedule, appearing in a show with David Frost, another with Leslie Crowther, *Does the Team Think?*, and *Joker's Wild*. William Davis, editor of *Punch* at the time, asked him to write an article on Scotland. He was trying to avoid the trap of gathering together a bunch of Sassenach hacks to denigrate their northern neighbours and intended that most of the input would be by the Jocks themselves. Chic's piece was entitled, 'How mean are the Scots?' As soon as he received his fee, what Chic considered to be a measly, miserable sum of sixty guineas, he suggested he should do a follow-up article entitled, 'How mean are the English?' and then, one for the Welsh, 'How mean was my valet?', based on the lord of the manor and his tight-fisted retainer.

> *What is a Scot? This is the question people keep asking me. I can only say that a Scot is somebody who keeps the Sabbath and everything else he can lay his hands on. Joking apart, is the Scot really mean? Are all these stories about Aberdeen true? Well, you can judge for yourself. My father was an Aberdonian and a more generous man you couldn't wish to meet. I have a gold watch that belonged to my father. He sold it to me on his deathbed, so I wrote him a cheque.*
>
> *Is the Scotsman's thriftiness hereditary? Maybe my uncle can help to answer that question. An American lady in hospital needed three blood transfusions to save her life and my uncle, being the unselfish man that he is, volunteered to be a blood donor. For the first pint, the lady gave him $50. For the second pint, she gave him $25. And, for the third pint . . . nothing! So you see – it's in the blood.*
>
> *When I was a kid, my mother hired a woman to push my pram and I've been pushed for money ever since. But, please don't think we are all just money grabbers in Scotland. We realise that money isn't every-thing – women are the other 5 per cent! After all, what is money? The Mint makes it first and we've got to make it last. The Scot is not as tight-fisted as some people make out. I read in a newspaper only last week where a Scotsman had actually offered £50,000 to the first man*

to swim the Atlantic in gumboots. And in business, the Scot has few equals. My father once told me that my grandfather was one of the most successful men in Britain, so much so, that that one businessman in London wrote to him asking the secret of his success. My grandfather wrote back and told him it was all a matter of 'brain food' and that he would give him a correspondence course at 2 guineas per lesson. Each week my grandfather sent him a pair of kippers which cost him 2 shillings and for which he received 2 guineas by return. But about six months and 48 guineas later, He received a letter which read:

> Dear Mr Murray, I have had a feeling for some months now that two guineas is rather a high price to pay for a pair of kippers. I am now almost convinced that the charge is much too high.
>
> Yours faithfully
> Cedric Smithers

My grandfather was equal to these aspersions. He wired back: 'Imperative you continue course. Undoubtedly, it's beginning to show results.'

Of course, thriftiness is not the only characteristic that the Scot has to take a bit of stick for. Take the kilt, for instance. He is very proud to wear the kilt and display his clan tartan, but he's all too often the butt of the alien's tongue. I wore my kilt only last week down south in enemy-held territory when I was approached by the usual inquisitive young lady who wanted to know the age-old secret. I thought, 'Here we go again!' She said, 'Pardon me, Mr Murray, but my friends and I would like to know what is worn under the kilt?' I said, 'Madam, nothing is worn. Everything is in fine working order!' I think it's about time we did something about this question. Could see-through sporrans, perhaps, be the answer? . . . Just a thought.

One cannot mention the Scot without mentioning whisky, the national drink. There are only two rules for

drinking whisky: first, never take whisky without water and, second, never take water without whisky. The Scot is very proud of being able to hold his drink. I remember being out with a friend of mine one night, and we had a real ball. The next morning I met him, I said, 'You had a real skinful last night. Did you manage to get home all right?' He said, 'I was getting home fine when a big policeman tramped over my fingers.' Then there was the Scot in London on holiday who had been out on the bevy. He was making his way home when he was set upon by a gang of thugs. The Scot, a born fighter, and with ample whisky courage, put up a very stubborn resistance. But after a long and bloody struggle, he was finally overpowered. The gang leader, after such a battle, was expecting rich booty but, after turning his pockets inside out, he found only one measly sixpenny piece. 'Sixpence! Only sixpence after a stramash like that!' But his mate sagely commented, 'Maybe we're lucky. Can you imagine what it would have been like if he'd had a shilling!'

Still, Scotland has much to recommend it. For example, we gave golf to the world. St Andrews is the home of golf but I'm sure St Andrew never played it or he'd never have become a saint. I don't like to boast, but I'm a very accurate golfer myself – straight down the middle, that's me. It will give you an idea of how accurate I am when I tell you that last week, I lost my first ball in ten years . . . the string broke. I was taught golf by an old Scottish professional, a real purist with everything done according to the book. I'll never forget my first lesson. I went onto the tee and he gave me a seven iron. I was so nervous, I could hardly hold the club. He placed the ball on the tee. Then, taking my courage in both hands, I swung through the ball and, to my amazement, it flew through the air, right onto the green and rolled into the cup. As I waited for congratulations, the pro said, 'Naw, naw, laddie. That'll nae do at a' – ye're using the wrang grip!'

What else do we have to blow about in Scotland? – the bagpipes, what else? Many a hungry garrison has

been relieved to hear the skirl of the pipes in the distance. How is it, then, that so many people can't stand them? And how does a piper learn to play? I took up the bagpipes once. I was blowing away merrily, marching round the room, when my wife came upstairs. 'You'll have to do something about that noise,' she said. What could I do? So I took my shoes off and marched around on my stockinged feet. Oh, you have to come and go in life.

Well, I hope I have enlightened some of you foreigners who have been reading this. Remember that Scotland has produced many things that make this world a better place. She gave the world chloroform invented by Simpson, penicillin invented by Fleming, television invented by Baird and 'Funnyosities' invented by Chic Murray. What more could you want? (In answer to the last question, please send on a Rolls Royce Silver Phantom and, in return, I will write on a plain postcard a minimum of twenty words telling you exactly why I like it.)

P.S. In case of fire, cut along the dotted line.

Chic ran into two notables through serendipity. Willie Woodburn, his old chum, invited him to an Old Firm game to watch Celtic and Rangers lock horns in their seasonal battle for supremacy. He brought Sean Connery with him. Introductions were duly made and mutual compliments were exchanged before they both started nattering about James Bond movies. The game kicked off and ebbed and flowed. Willie and Chic were utterly thrilled by the outcome, a comprehensive win for Rangers. Sean, at that time a Celtic supporter, was less than thrilled.

Towards the end of 1970, he and another 'worthy', a certain Spike Milligan, were booked to appear on the same television show in Glasgow. They were, like Sean and Chic, fans of each other, and, as they shook welcoming hands, Spike said, 'I believe you and a certain friend of mine, Monsieur Sellers, have worked together, *n'est-ce pas?'*

To which Chic swiftly replied in martyr mode, 'Am I ever to be tormented thus?' They got on famously and after filming finished for the day they repaired to the canteen for a long chat.

Ah! You must be the woman with the drip-dry wedding dress.

Are you growing a beard or just acting the goat?

Spike Milligan, one of Chic's
close comedian friends

'I've read your *Puckoon*, Spike. Total crap, I regret to say.'

Spike graciously accepted this in-depth critique by announcing that he would dedicate the next edition to Chic. 'I can visualise it all now!' he said with an assumed Scot's burr, 'To a little-known wee Scots comedian I happened to come across one day in the meadow!'

Again, the swift reply, 'How dare you bring my lady wife into it!'

In reflection, Spike said this of Chic: 'He made me mindful of W.C. Fields, with a healthy disdain for the human race and he'd found his own ways to keep it at arm's length. "Did someone make you up?" he asked me. "Yes," I replied, "someone did. But nobody made *you* up! You made yourself up!" To me he was one of the top comics in the world.' Which was hardly to damn him with faint praise from a very gifted fellow entertainer.

Chic's divorce in 1972 coincided with his son's news that his young wife was expecting a baby. In the settlement Maidie compensated Chic for his half share in the hotel, whereupon he promptly went out and purchased a spanking new Reliant

In the Olympic village a man in trainers, carrying a long stick, was asked by a stranger: 'Are you a pole vaulter?' 'Nein. I am German. But how did you know my name was Walter?'

Scimitar, much to the disapproval of his son Douglas who had become something of a motoring expert. Chic countered, 'If it's good enough for Princess Anne, it's good enough for me!' A strange remark for Chic to make as he had never before been noted as a keen monarchist!

He was due to be interviewed by Pete Murray on the fateful day itself. He made one final appeal by telephone to Maidie to no avail and, after a brief sojourn to a café, made his way to the BBC. Pete Murray, a live wire, did his best to keep the subsequent broadcast light and fluffy, but it was a daunting task which challenged his undoubted professionalism as Chic, his voice flat, his remarks little more than a grunt, made the interview a near impossibility to conduct. Thankfully the conversation was brought to its pained end and it wasn't hard for Pete Murray to discern that something was seriously troubling Chic. Chic was frank in explaining his melancholy and he received nothing but profound sympathy from his colleague.

But life moved on and, in the weeks to come, Chic spent much of his time in the BBC's Scottish headquarters. Ian Christie, a producer at the BBC (who later in this book pays tribute to Chic) introduced him to Jenny Wales from the music department. He regularly looked in on her and she looked forward to his visits. One day, he was in her department, sorting out records for a request programme. He was enjoying himself tickling the ivories of the studio piano when Jenny poked her head round the door. 'Chic, I'm off. Are you staying on for a while?'

'I'll lock up, Jenny. Have a good evening,' he said as he continued to play some of his old favourites. He became nostalgic as memories flooded his senses. Dipping into the plastic bag he'd brought with him, he rummaged amongst some recent scripts and pulled out a photograph of his father as a young man, now somewhat threadbare through the passage of time. 'Hello, Dad,' he said. He stared at the image for some time, deep in thought.

Slowly, he closed the piano lid and took his leave in the Scimitar to a nearby shop for a double helping of his favourite fish and chips. Fifty yards on, he was home; he devoured his supper and drank a steaming hot mug of tea, then fell fast asleep in his chair. He woke up close to midnight. He knew from experience that sleep wouldn't be an option for some time to

Unfortunately, at the AGM of the Unspeakably Shy Society (Rutherglen Branch), nobody was able to attend.

come, so grabbing another cowboy yarn by Zane Grey, he settled down to read accompanied by a large measure of rum. The hours ticked by as the rum bottle played a significant part in the evening and early morning. On an impulse, he decided to retrieve his scripts from the car, but as he picked up the bag, his father's photograph tumbled out. He sat in the car for some time, gazing at his dad's image under the light of a street lamp.

His next recollection was a voice asking him to get out of the car – a voice which carried some authority. Chic shoved the photograph back in the scruffy plastic bag, opened the car door and fell prostrate at the feet of two officers of the law. When asked if he owned the car, he replied that he didn't know. 'Who does the car belong to, then, sir?' the younger constable persisted.

'I'm sorry. That's far too soon to ask me. I only stole the thing yesterday,' chirped a cheeky Chic. He was less chirpy at the police station, however, when he apologised for being 'terribly obstreperous, having assaulted so many'.

It was probably a first when the officer in charge felt constrained to deny this self-inflicted indictment, 'Nah, nah, sir. You werenae. Just a wee bittie tired, maybe.' (Chic later commented that he thought it something of an achievement to have uttered a lengthy word like 'obstreperous' at the time, given his state of health.) Nevertheless, justice prevailed because Joe Beltrami, the well-known defence lawyer, kicked the allegations of 'drunk in charge of a vehicle' firmly into touch and Chic walked from court into sunlit uplands.

The Door

I was staying in a hotel in London and I must say at the outset, I'm not a complainer, but I went downstairs and I could see the manager looking at me. He said, 'What is it?'

I said, 'I would like a door in my room.'

He said, 'You're funny, aren't you?'

I said, 'I *prefer* a door in my room. I'm *used* to a door in my room.'

'Oh well,' he said, 'in that case we must get a door for you somewhere.'

So after some time a door arrived – not on its own, of course, two fellows brought it up – and one of them said, 'I'm the carpenter. Would you like a handle on the door?'

I said, 'Well, it sounds like a good idea,' just to give him confidence, as it were. So once the door was fixed I made my way out, because I wanted to get out, you see, and turned the handle. There was one on the other side, I noticed that on the way out, really useful, otherwise you'd need to put your arm round the door. [At this point Chic attempts to bend his arm in two, with the wrist cocked in demonstration mode!]

So I went down and the manager said, 'Have you got the door?'

I said, 'Yes, the door's in the room.'

He said, 'You've no sooner got the door in than you start to go out. When you made your way in here, I thought, "Oy! Oy! Here's trouble!"'

'Well, I don't think I'm causing a great deal of trouble. I just wanted a door in my room.'

'Well, you should be grateful because now you've got one!' he said.

So I said, 'Yes, yes, I have.'

'But you're going out for a while,' he commented in a hurt voice.

I said, 'Yes.'

'Why?' he asked.

'Because I don't want to stay in, that's why!' Oh, I told him!

Eventually I made my way downstairs. The stairs led down to the street – they led all the way up too, of course – which saved them having two stairways really . . .

135

Chic's outline for The Battersea Dog

As I was perambulating along the sidewalk, this fellow approached me. I knew him otherwise I'd never have allowed him near me. And he stopped. So *I* stopped – just to let him see I could do it. And he was surprised. He didn't say he was surprised, but I knew he was surprised, I could see it in his eyes. He'd found someone as good as him! 'Oh!' he said, 'it's you!'

I said, 'Yes.' I couldn't deny it, standing there.

He said, 'I thought it was you.'

'Oh,' I said, 'it's me all right.' I could, after all remember coming out. I said, 'You've got a nice dog with you.' He had a dog with him otherwise I'd never have mentioned it. He had it on a lead. He didn't seem to be too sure of it.

He said, 'Yes, it is a nice dog.'

It wasn't. It was a *dreadful* creature. It wasn't trained properly – you just had to stand there and hope for the best. I always think, if you can teach them to beg, you could surely teach them to look up and read your lips, just an extra kick would probably suffice. Then he said, 'Do you know the Battersea Dogs Home?'

I replied, 'I never knew it had been away.'

Then he said, 'This dog, just watch this! This will amaze! This dog can talk! *Speak*!' he ordered the dog, '*Speak*!' he repeated. 'This would happen!' said the dog owner. Actually nothing had happened. 'I'll just have to give it a touch of the hobnails, that'll liven things up.' So he had a quick look round. Again he said '*Speak*! *Speak*!'

The dog looked up. 'What'll I say?' it asked.

'Och,' he said, 'anyway it doesn't make any difference, I'm getting it destroyed.'

I said, 'Why, is it mad?'

'Well,' he said, 'it's not *pleased*!'

Chic with canine friend – no hobnails in sight!

CHAPTER 11
NEW FRIENDS

It was around this time that I first met Chic. I received a telephone call from a friend to join his party for an MMT at an early hour – a very early hour, because we were to meet in Edinburgh and I had still to drive down from Inverness (being self-employed, I was fortunate enough to be able to drop things at a whim). 'What's an MMT?' I asked with some trepidation.

'A Magical, Mystery Tour!' came the reply, which did little to reassure. However, I visualised a trip to the Lakes, Blackpool, Newcastle, whatever. Yet these destinations were very far from where a wing and a prayer can end up and it never crossed my mind to carry a passport.

I arrived at a hotel on the north side of Edinburgh around breakfast time. The hotel had been purpose-built for the first Commonwealth Games to be held in the capital. I trod with a less-than-lofty step into the main foyer to be met by a number of disparate individuals, all gathered under the instructions of the host. There was no Agatha Christie about, but the mystery part rang true because none of the assembled seemed to know where we were heading (or if they did, they weren't letting on!). I recall a taxi driver was there, an entertainment agent from Shotts (best known for its state-of-the-art penitentiary) and a chunky, overweight, wheezing bookmaker's son who popped air tickets to London Heathrow into our top pockets. I was informed that the flight to London was only a 'starter for ten' – there was more to come!

We duly landed at Heathrow to be greeted by the host and a large, tartan-bunneted man. His strong features and character-istic straight face rang big bells but Chic was a far more easily recognised person in Central Scotland than in the Highlands where television was provided by Grampian, not STV. And,

I passed my vicar the other day. 'Hello, Father,' I said, 'still on a one-day week?'

At the airport, travelling abroad on holiday. 'Och! I don't half miss the piano.'
'Why?'
'The flight tickets and passport are on it.'

The Hotel Phoenicia, Malta, where Chic was a regular visitor (reproduced by permisssion of Hotel Phoenicia Malta, The Mall, Valletta, Malta www.phoeniciamalta.com)

'Thank you for pulling in, sir. This is a routine spot check.'
'Nae bother, officer. If I remember correctly, I've currently got two pimples and a boil on my bum.'

It's always nice to help those people that money can buy.

because there were far fewer chimney-pots up north, advertising revenue and coverage were that bit smaller. (The station was known locally, and with some affection, as 'Grampian the Wonder-Horse' and the local news was always good for a laugh!) I remember in sharp focus queueing at the flight desk to embark for Malta, vexed by the absence of any travel documentation which was dismissed as an irrelevance by the organiser. Chic did one of his stage stumbles, tripping himself, followed immediately by a scowl at any who had the temerity to react to the incident! But to the unknowing public it never failed to provoke a giggle which, knowing Chic, was the whole point of the exercise in the first place!

Three hours later, we arrived in Malta and were driven to the Phoenicia Hotel on the outskirts of Valletta. (The hotel was the pride of the Trust House Forte group, and back in the late forties was the favourite venue every Saturday night of Princess Elizabeth who would dance with her consort Philip Mountbatten, a young officer with the Royal Navy.) As the hotel register was being signed, a telegram was handed over at reception which read:

Arriving later this evening.
The Wine Taster

I was to learn later that this claim to be a bon viveur, gourmet and wine buff was given the stamp of authenticity by his furrowed brow of affected study of any establishment's cellar, followed by an order for the most expensive wine on the *carte des vins* for which, going Dutch, we all had to pay!

Having unpacked and smartened up a bit, we descended the stairs for dinner and we were greeted by the Wine Taster. Drinks in hand, we entered the dining room. Many of the diners wore evening dress – there was a hint of the Raj, I thought – and tables were assembled round a generous dancing area. A gently elevated stage featured three ladies, a pianist, cellist and violinist, playing the old standards, perhaps a dash of Gilbert and Sullivan and, even more *risqué*, the occasional selection of favourites from musicals such as *South Pacific*. This was the Palm Court Orchestra in miniature!

Against this tableau, the Wine Taster reached for his wallet

and produced a five-pound note to be matched by all others who were non-combatants. The wager was that Chic and Stewart, an overweight member of our party, would dance together, waltz tempo, and complete a full circle of the dance floor before returning to their dessert courses. Unhesitatingly, Chic rose to his full height, made a deep bow to his partner, then, proffering his hand, escorted his partner to the floor. It seemed an agony of ages passed before Chic set forth on just the right beat of the music, and as he masterfully guided his partner his expression of studied concentration never altered. The miracle was that the ladies continued to play, because without the music there was nothing but slack-jawed, outraged silence from the black-tie brigade – all the shock and horror of an H.E. Bateman cartoon. After what seemed an eternity, they returned to base camp, whereupon Stewart, Mr Heavy, twirled deliciously beneath the outstretched arm of the male lead who then chivalrously pulled out a seat to accommodate his 'other half'!

In the next intermission, the frenzied buzz of hissing disapproval could be heard behind every whispering hand, with all eyes staring with disbelief and animus at our corner table. And then the maître d'hôtel came to the table in a starched white waistcoat and claw-hammer jacket. He cleared his throat. 'Patrons are respectfully advised to dance only with the opposite sex. We have a policy of disallowing same-sex dancing at the Phoenicia Hotel. Thank you.' He bowed as the nudges and winks were reactivated by the visitation. But to any fair-minded person, this was one of the most hilarious acts of spontaneity ever witnessed and the efforts made to suppress outright laughter were Herculean.

As with most Magical, Mystery Tours, nothing had been planned, so most time was taken up exploring round and about. Chic stayed at the hotel most of the daytime, sunning himself and writing scripts. At the time, the common belief was that 'writing scripts' was an excuse for Chic to enjoy some peace and quiet, sunning himself on his balcony, but now that I've read some, thanks to his family, he should never have been doubted. His output was prodigious. He did make one trip with the others, travelling to the north of the island and then by ferry to Gozo, Malta's verdant sister island, where we lunched in a wonderful Italian restaurant allegedly owned by the Sicilian

The hotel was so posh, the waiters tipped me.

Mafia. (As the crow flies, Sicily is almost a neighbour.) And on another occasion, we dined at Wheeler's – an offshoot of the celebrated London restaurant specialising in fish, where Chic bumped into his old friend Frankie Howerd who had an apartment on the island. It was, after all, Frankie who had alerted the Delfont agency about Chic those many years earlier.

There is yet another story worthy of retelling from this week in Malta. Chic had earlier commented on the nuisance factor caused to guests when there was a telephone call for any hotel resident. Clearly the management of this establishment considered the installation of a Tannoy system to summon guests frightfully vulgar and *infra dignitatem*. Instead, they employed some young lads as bellhops à la Waldorf Astoria, who would trail through the hotel's public areas shouting out the person they sought in a high-pitched treble voice and carrying a sign with the name chalked onto a blackboard on both sides. We were back in the main dining room one evening, when the music was hastily interrupted by this young lad in uniform summoning a guest to the phone. 'Paging Mr Pile, please. Paging Mr Pile,' he cried as he circled the floor. To our surprise, Chic suddenly rose from the table and, with his elbows firmly tucked into his sides, he walked in tiny paces with the cheeks of his backside clenched so tight they could have cracked walnuts in the direction of the dining room entrance.

'I'm your man!' he shouted to the bellhop. 'I'll be right with you!' Those around us didn't know whether to feel sorry for his extreme discomfort or laugh at the coincidence of his unfortunate surname. It really wouldn't have mattered because everyone at our table was in tears of laughter! What was so professional about the episode was that Chic never once explained how he had obtained an outside call in Malta to the Phoenicia Hotel, nor why, for the evening, he had changed his name to 'Pile'! No one could better maintain a straight face. It was part of the glory of his humour.

Our return to Scotland was not without its problems because I was exiting a sovereign country without a passport. Eventually the British High Commissioner gave me a temporary pass but not before I was delivered a stern flea in the ear. That same day I drove Chic to a gig at Fochabers Cricket Club, a place more recognised for its soups and preserves than for its cricket. There

Charlie Chester

"The Glen",
Chestfield,
Nr. Whitstable,
Kent.

14th October, 1967

Chic Murray, Esq.,
c/o Snow's Hotel,
Cromwell Road,
LONDON, W.

My dear Chic,

        Such a pleasant evening the other evening at
the Eccentric Club and it was a joy to spend such a
while with you.

        This is to let you know that it was not empty wo
words when I talked to you and I haven't forgotten
the yodelling song but I am just off to Hastings
and from there I go to Birmingham for a week and from
there to Belfast and I have made a note to set up
something on my return.

        In the meantime, my kindest regards to
you and my love to Madie.

                As ever,

                Charlie

Charlie Chester was another
fan of Chic's yodelling.

were two things I admired him for that day. First, he asked an official where the changing room in the hall was located. He was told such a thing didn't exist. He never deigned to comment further on the subject and, uncomplaining, changed in the open air. Second, I had never before heard Chic yodelling onstage. I can't say I've listened to plenty yodellers in my life but I was hugely impressed by this unexpected talent.

Variety, with its origins in music hall, was in decline some years previous but it became more marked in the seventies. The obvious alternative was television. Bruce Forsyth, for example, was a natural front man for game shows and the like, as indeed was Bob Monkhouse, both of whom had previously appeared on the same billing as Chic. He was perhaps less aware of the

I wouldn't say she was a big girl. But I remember once using her knickers for hang-gliding.

*I'm very proud to be standing
before you. I never dreamt I would
sober up in time.*

*Are men smarter than horses?
I don't think so. You don't get
horses betting on men.*

Chic as the fiddlemaker in
The World of Chic Murray

trend. He did appear from time to time on 'telly' and unquestionably he was comfortable with the media. But his main
activity became voice-overs, radio work and secondary roles in a
series of fairly down-market films: *Secrets of a Door-to-Door
Salesman, What's Up Superdoc!* and *Ups and Downs of a
Handyman.*

Later in 1975 a script landed on his lap – a specially commis-
sioned work by Joe McGrath, the first director of *Casino Royale*,
for a one-hour special for the BBC. Chic had uniquely always
written his own material so this was a potential sea-change. It
was entitled *World of Chic Murray* and was a zany collage of
off-the-wall sketches. Chic read it for most of that night and he
loved it. He contacted Bob Hird, the producer-in-waiting, and he
saw this as a new and exciting window of opportunity, so much
so that he was pleased he'd rationed his appearances on
television largely to guest appearances. This was the big one!

However, the time scheduled for rehearsal and production,
for whatever reason, was derisory compared to that given to
others such as Stanley Baxter. And then, of all things, the transmission date was fixed at 8pm on New Year's Day, 1976 –
blasphemous to most hungover, liverish Scots. Chic had grave
misgivings about the timing of the programme and he was right
to have them. It was slagged off for being too convoluted,
disjointed and unfunny – hardly criticisms that should have been
levelled at the performer alone. To be fair, it was pioneering in
what it set out to say and do; one critic wrote, 'It was ahead of
its time . . . the Beeb should show it again in ten years' time and
it would get a rapturous reception.' The BBC, unfairly, many
commented, never aired the show again.

Engagements round and about occurred in a haphazard
manner until, in the summer months of 1976, he was booked to
share top billing for a three-month season at the new Eden Court
Theatre in Inverness.

Chic was booked into a popular howff, the Beaufort Hotel
(owned by Barbecue Bill, so named because of his main
occupation as an undertaker). My mother's house was next door
so I saw plenty of Chic during this time – plenty socialising,
plenty laughter too, and in the theatre where he would name-
drop any guest I had with me into his routines. (No single Chic
routine was ever an exact repeat of previous versions which

somehow lent credibility to the stream of total nonsense that flowed so effortlessly!)

After a few weeks, my mother, who couldn't really understand Chic (the poor soul!), began to tire from his daily demands for a mug of tea, a 'jeelie' piece and the appropriation of her newspapers to the garden lawn for his perusal in the summer sunshine. She phoned me. 'Look, dear, I don't wish to cause any offence but what am I going to do about your friend Chic?' She explained she couldn't even get 'a read' of her beloved papers until well after lunch. If it wasn't so funny, this would possibly have been sad!

I said, 'What do you do with your front door? You keep it locked, don't you?'

'Yes,' she agreed.

'Well, the answer's simple, do likewise with your back door.'

'Ooh! I never thought of that!' (Lateral thinking, you see!) The following day, she was telephoning one of her friends when she heard a half-strangulated voice from the scullery door.

'Kay! Kay! There's been some mistake here,' the voice bleated.

'Just a minute, Mary,' she said, 'there's someone at the back door.' She put the receiver down to confront the unforgettable vision of Chic, trying his best to look her in the eye but better placed to receive the axe on Tower Hill: lying prostrate, all six feet three inches of him, with his head through the cat flap and his bunnet still in place! She dissolved into helpless laughter (she'd finally cracked the code!) and, better still, the matter was resolved within a few seconds of extricating Chic's head from the aperture. Jeelie pieces and mugs of tea were reinstated forthwith and from then on, the papers were circulated equally between both parties. God was in his heaven and all was well with the world!

Chic had a wide circle of friends which he tended to compartmentalise. They rarely, if ever, got to meet each other. All his life Chic remained a private person and paradoxically that remained the case even onstage. As Barry Humphries famously stated, when confronted by cameras and an audience of thousands onstage, 'Thank heavens I'm alone!'

One such friend was the well-known Glasgow criminal lawyer, Joe Beltrami. They had met originally on a lawyer/client

'If I buy a thousand currant buns from you for cash, would you give me a discount?'
'That all depends, sir. Are they for taking home or would you be eating them on the premises?'

Joe Beltrami (left), a friend
of Chic's who was anxious not
to miss a moment of *Ups and
Downs of a Handyman*!

147

There are three other things besides
sex. Nothing you'd want, of course.

basis over a motoring offence and in due course became good friends. Chic badgered Joe into viewing *Ups and Downs of a Handyman* which in 1976 was on general release. Joe was not a regular cinema-goer. He and his wife arrived early and had to endure a supporting short film, the trailers and the advertising slots prior to the main feature, but they were well positioned in the dress circle. However, an unsuspecting ice cream sales girl was partially obscuring their view as the lights went down. Joe, with his courtroom stentorian voice, said, 'Look! Could you please get out of the way! I've come specially to see this picture and I don't want to miss a single minute. Is that clear?' As the unfortunate waif scurried from the scene, even before the titles of the film were screened, a naked couple in bed were busily employed in explicit scenes of lovemaking. As the balcony audience gasped at the couple's feverish athleticism, Joe could hear the whispers, feel the nudges – 'Nae wonder Joe Beltrami wanted no tae miss anything!'

Later Chic asked Joe whether he had enjoyed the movie. 'Terrific!' Joe replied, whereupon he burst out laughing and related the embarrassment of events on and off screen to general amusement and mirth.

Joe Beltrami remained at the top of his profession as a defence lawyer, enjoying a reputation of considerable standing, particularly amongst the villains of the west of Scotland. He was on a par, perhaps, with his predecessor, Lawrence Dowdall who had written an autobiography entitled, *Get Me Dowdall!* (He, incidentally, had met my mother on a cruise ship and rechristened her Tiger Eyes!) Joe's practice was known as Beltrami and Dunn, the latter name belonging to his partner, Willie Dunn, a man of diminutive stature. On one occasion Chic accompanied Willie to HM Prison Peterhead to carry out a precognition with a prisoner in the north-east. The interviewee remarked with a sneer on being introduced to Willie Dunn, 'I asked for Beltrami, not Mickey Rooney!' (Chic loved recounting this anecdote.)

However, despite Chic's cordial relations with Joe, he received a frosty reception from him when he informed Chic that he, too, was writing his own biography and did he have any suggestions for its title? Quick as a flash, and mindful of Lawrence Dowdall's book title, he replied, *Get Me Dunn!* Glassy-eyed, Joe stared at Chic – for once, stumped for the bon

mot. Relations were only normalised a few months later when Joe's Christmas good wishes dropped through Chic's letter-box.

Another pal was Israel Kaye (Issy to his friends) who was a furrier in Mitchell Street in Glasgow but who he first came across in Aberdeen. Chic would drop in on him from time to time and Issy made a point of never acting deferentially to the big man. (He liked a bit of deference, it would be fair to say!) Anyway, sometime after Chic's divorce, he resurfaced in scruffy order – baggy breeks and frayed collar. Issy insisted on a smarten-up programme and marched him to his tailor for a number of suits. He took ages to square the bill and the tailor being an elderly friend of Issy's, provoked Issy into a bout of finger-waving, 'You're such a miserable bugger, Chic, you're hoping the tailor will pop off and the bill with him!' Chic was careful with items of private expenditure; for example, at the local hostelry his view was that others could provide the sustenance because he had offered his wit, charm and a rich supply of stories! Dammit – what more did they want?

Issy knew also, despite Chic's denials, that he still pined for Maidie and there was a pervading sadness in Chic's demeanour (as with so many gifted clowns) that cast a shadow over their friendship. On one occasion he was asked back to Issy's apartment for dinner. His wife had prepared roast chicken and on Chic's plate Issy had thrown in a roasted head of chicken as an optional extra. 'What the hell is that?' Chic grumbled, recoiling at the sight of the gruesome object. Whether it was Issy's intention, future offers of hospitality were politely declined. 'Oh, you don't go back to his place for a meal. He serves up hens' heids!' rued Chic.

They regularly popped next door from Issy's showroom for a drink in the Gordon, a popular howff of the press. There was always a pretence that Chic didn't like being fussed over. But he was only human and inwardly it gave him deep satisfaction. It was in answer to a question from one hack that Chic replied, 'What am I currently doing? I'm off to Saigon to make a movie for Thames Television.'

'That's where you had to be so careful with Chic,' mused Issy. 'Everyone thought he was "at it" again. He was telling the truth!'

Three other notables deserve mention. Many years earlier, Jack Milroy (with Rikki Fulton, of Francie and Josie fame) and

I don't care if he was the head of the light brigade. There will be no charging here!

I wouldn't say she was ugly,
but when she sucks a lemon,
the lemon pulls a face.

his dear wife Mary Lee went backstage after Chic had performed at the Victoria Theatre in Paisley. Later, in a hotel in Blackpool, they bumped into Chic in the breakfast buffet queue. He was hard to miss, dressed as he was in a Teddy boy suit and a ginger wig. 'I'm waiting for them to pick me up, Jack,' he said, 'They're planning to film me as they throw me off the North Pier into the sea. Is that a sensible way for a grown man to earn a living? I don't think so.'

They always seemed to meet by accident. The next time Jack and Mary caught sight of Chic, he was limping badly, but bunneted, in an airport in Ibiza. He had injured himself against a jagged piece of steel on board a boat, requiring several stitches. They saw to it that Chic was looked after on their return flight: he stretched out over three seats and was waited on hand and painful foot by doting cabin staff. Jack and Mary saw him home and provided him with their lawyer's coordinates to sue those responsible. When next they met, Jack asked how the claim had panned out. 'We got the name of the captain,' replied Chic, 'but we cannae find the bloody boat!' He then began chortling as only Chic could.

Tom Walsh was a buddy from STV who, with his wife, had put Chic up once or twice. They arrived at a charity 'do' together and heard a familiar voice as they entered. A certain Father Joe Mills, a priest from Dumbarton, was doing what many Scots at play still do: performing a Chic Murray impersonation! 'How can I compete with that?' Chic complained to his pal, attempting to look distraught.

'Come on over,' said Tom, 'and I'll introduce you.'

They shook hands, 'pleased to meet you' noises were exchanged, then promptly Chic turned his back on both of them. Their discomfort was for seconds only as he spun back into full view, this time with a beaming grin. 'That's not a bad wee act, you've got there.' Father Joe visibly relaxed. They were to meet again.

Months on, Father Joe was on holiday in Majorca with two other priests, Larry and John. They were pooling their resources to see if they could afford to rent a vehicle when Joe spotted Chic heading for the beach with a rolled towel under his arm. Chic was on the island, the location for a film in which he featured. They greeted each other with enthusiasm and arranged to meet

Jack Milroy, who always seemed
to run into Chic by chance

150

up in the evening. They shared a delight in mounds of spaghetti bolognese accompanied by a copious libation of Valpolicella. Father Joe said to Chic: 'We have Italian evenings every Wednesday back in Dumbarton. Loads of spag bol, and plenty good wine for a good natter! You'd be very welcome, Chic.' The Fathers didn't have to wait long to receive an affirmative from Chic.

Meantime he entertained the holy brigade with his Philip Marlowe transatlantic asides, 'Suddenly it got to be four-thirty. After a big lunch and a hard afternoon sunning myself, I was ready for something long, cool and sparkling . . . "Where's the Alka-Seltzer?" I asked myself.'

If something's neither here nor there, where the hell is it?

They treasured his company, keeping them in a state of helpless laughter day after day, so that when they returned home Father Joe was quick to remind Chic by phone of their Wednesday Italian bacchanalia. 'Well,' said Chic, 'it's not so easy to get to Dumbarton . . .' The crafty devil ensured that from then on, their evenings of excess commenced with fetching Chic by car from Glasgow which they were more than happy to do since. In exchange, he supplied generous gargles of Valpolicella as his part of the deal! Whenever Chic was in the west of the country, he never missed his visitations to the Fathers. They loved him for who and what he was, and were with him to the end at his funeral on the other side of Scotland.

It would be wrong to assume that Chic was indifferent to the emergence of new Scottish talent such as Billy Connolly but he had no appreciation of his own contribution and influence in its genesis. Here Billy states his case: 'I'd always wanted to get laughs and had admired the quips that the smart buggers in the yards came out with to the bosses, but the desire was unco-ordinated until I saw Chic on the telly one fateful night. That was it. I realised that was what I wanted and, from then on, Chic was the master funny man as far as I was concerned.'

One day in an art gallery in Glasgow, Billy spotted the unmistakable outline of Chic as the latter studied a painting by Magritte. Billy was already established by this time, yet he hesitated before finally approaching Chic and introducing himself. Suspicions were soon allayed and Billy was relieved and reassured that Chic admired his work; he was a fan, as Billy, in turn, immensely valued Chic and his surreal, inventive genius.

Lord, forgive them that trespass against us. Me? I'm different. I just shoot the bastards!

This man came home to find his wife in bed with three men. 'Hello! Hello! Hello!' he said. 'What!' said his wife.'Are ye nae speaking tae me?'

Chic was Billy's hero, it was as simple as that. They talked for perhaps ten minutes before they both recognised the need for less of the niceties of chat and the need, instead, to scratch beneath the surface. 'Let's have dinner and a proper talk,' Chic suggested.

'Great.' came the reply, 'Where?'

'Your place!' And so it was to be.

They dined well and twenty-four hours later, they were still talking. It was a revelation to Billy just how smart his guest was. They discussed politics, sport, music, theatre, films – Chic, remember, was a film fanatic since his formative days in Greenock – and, most importantly, Chic talked with authority on the three men who he maintained had influenced and shaped him the most: W.C. Fields, Damon Runyon and, most of all, Mark Twain. Even art was touched on. He was drawn to Magritte because he sensed a kindred spirit: the surrealism of the perfectly ridiculous, the lurking humour, the absurdity.

They were to meet often from this starting point. On one occasion, sharing a drink in the BBC canteen, a vertically challenged lassie behind the bar struggled to replace an empty half gallon of whisky with another brimming with John Barleycorn on the optic. After sustained endeavour on tiptoe, the barmaid believed that a clicking noise confirmed the whisky was secure on the gantry. But it was not. The wee soul managed to duck as the half gallon loosened its stays and plummeted towards inevitable destruction, the awful vision of its flooding contents enough to break the heart of any maltster as they spewed out across the BBC's floor. 'Stop that!' shouted Chic in high-ranking decibels. (It's easy to visualise the scene in detail – he loved the drama of the unexpected.) Then he turned back for further discussion with Billy, utterly cool, relaxed and unperturbed. And what remains a touching memory of this tragic incident (as far as the whisky was concerned, at any rate!) was that Chic took it upon himself to give the manager something of an uncomfortable time. 'Look,' he said, 'if you choose to employ wee lassies, don't expect them to be lifting half-gallon bottles to fix them to a ropey dispenser a foot and a half above their eye-line. Why not make her responsible for stacking the miniatures?' This had the effect of saving the young girl's employment at the Beeb!

The stories of their meetings were legion, unpredictable and

often hilarious. On one occasion Billy gave Chic his very private telephone number and as with most people who have made the big time, he was paranoid that the number might fall into the wrong hands. Subsequently he received a phone call that heightened his anxiety. 'Is that Billy Connolly? Please hold on, I have Chic Murray on the line for you.'

They talked for a while before Billy voiced his concern, 'I hope you haven't been handing out my number willy nilly!'

'Oh God!' Chic responded, 'hang on just a minute, Billy . . .' So Billy hung on for fully five minutes, maybe more. He was past the unamused phase when Chic returned. 'The thing is, Billy, I gave your number to a Chinaman last night and the little bugger won't give it back!' There was more than a hint that Chic was, to put it politely, 'coming the bag', and this very real possibility was dawning on poor Billy.

'You dirty dog!' Billy exclaimed, then burst out laughing which was met by something similar at the other end. It was hard to better Chic!

Annabelle, Chic's daughter, particularly loves the following anecdote which reflects the innocence of childhood and it was told to Chic by his new-found friend, Billy. It made a profound impression on Chic and that in itself shines interesting, unexpected light on his persona. It involved Franz Kafka, the Czech author. Billy told him of a chance meeting Kafka had in Prague before the Great War. The writer had gone for a walk and, on turning a corner, he came upon a mother comforting her five-year-old daughter. The little girl was inconsolable, sobbing her heart out. He bent down, so as not to alarm the little one, and asked why she was so distressed. 'She has lost her beloved doll,' her mother replied – established news that brought fresh grief to the child.

'Can you describe the doll for me?' he asked.

'She's very pretty, sir,' the mother replied, 'with shiny blonde hair and blue eyes. She's called Helene.'

'My goodness!' Kafka said, 'I just passed Helene on the street not that long ago!' The little girl instantly stopped crying, transfixed, and he added, 'She's safe and well and has gone on holiday. She has gone to the seaside and she said that she was very, very sad to be leaving her young mistress, even for a short time, but that she would write soon.'

To be fair, when I said it was rough whisky, you never had a hangover from it the next day. No . . . You got it the same night!

153

'Can you fix my car, please?
I think there's water in the
carburettor.'
'Sure I can. Where's the car?'
'In the river.'

I'm not often right, but it
doesn't matter too much
because I'm wrong again.

Billy Connolly, who became a close
friend of Chic's and who took Chic's
place at Annabelle's wedding

The small child, wide-eyed, whispered to the great but troubled man, 'Did you really speak to my dolly?'

'Most assuredly, young lady,' he replied, 'I'm sure you'll be hearing from her soon. Give me your name and address so that if I bump into Helene again before you do, I can let you know.' Both mother and daughter left with spirits uplifted, and this surprisingly caring person – a man full of torment and inner conflict – now had the personal contact details of two fellow travellers in life. As things panned out, Kafka *was* heading to a seaside resort only days later. He wrote a postcard to the forlorn child: 'I am safe and well but missing you very much. Love, Helene.' Franz Kafka never met the little girl or her mother ever again but from wherever and whenever, loving postcards from Helene were sent to her mistress until his short tragic life ended in 1924, aged forty-one. Helene's mistress, by then, was a teenager.

One day Billy was indirectly hugely flattered by Chic. He announced he was heading to Edinburgh to meet up with Annabelle, his daughter. It was her birthday and she was a very special person to her father. And Billy emphasised that, for him, Chic had no peer, then and even now, he was simply *the* master of comedy, a pioneer, a genius. 'Billy,' Chic said, 'give me a "wee Connolly" to take to Annabelle.'

Reflecting, Billy said, 'I was touched enough at the time, but thinking about it again later, I could have wept. He'd asked *me* for a "wee Connolly" – this guy I'd admired so much – I felt like I'd been paid the ultimate compliment. Thank God for him, and the fact we had so much in common.'

As a footnote, Chic, in a sense, reciprocated. He told a friend, 'Connolly's okay, me and him speak the same language.'

Billy recalled a joke which was a favourite of another ardent fan, the actor Michael Caine (Sir Michael told this gag on Michael Parkinson's farewell programme in 2007 with Billy in attendance); it illustrates that Chic's approach to life was not so much distorted as oblique: Looking for accommodation, Chic enquires of a landlady whether she has a room to let. 'Do you have a good memory for faces?' she asks.

'Oh yes,' Chic replies.

'That's good. I do have one room available but there's no mirror in the bathroom.'

CHAPTER 12
ILL-HEALTH

It was now 1978. His friendship with Billy Connolly had a two-pronged effect. Billy was on the ascendant, continually breaking new ground, enlarging his fan base, whereas Chic's career was hardly in decline but it was becoming static. Yet, in contrast, their burgeoning friendship was a great fillip to Chic's morale. The nosedive of *The World of Chic Murray* still hurt him, particularly because the responsibility for its failure lay largely elsewhere. He was still occupied with engagements but it was just that the momentum was unquestionably slowing. And as is so often the case in life, his health, it transpired, was the root cause.

It would be fair to say Chic's personal life was somewhat shambolic, unplanned and lacking roots and routine. The combination of meals at haphazard times, sometimes the substitution of alcohol for solid food, the constant travelling, the unlaundered suitcased shirts, and a general lack of energy, all of these things, combined with the ageing process (he was nearing sixty), were taking their toll. 'Time to visit the quack,' Chic thought to himself. 'He'll give me some kind of a tonic and I'll be firing on all cylinders again!' But it didn't work out like that. His doctor, Reggie McKay, was an old friend who was shaken at Chic's appearance. He was given a very thorough medical check-up before the doctor gave his diagnosis. 'This doesn't bode well,' thought Chic, when Reggie, very deliberately, asked him to take a seat.

'It's far from good news, Chic, I'm afraid,' the doctor began. 'I would venture to say you are not an alcoholic but you undoubtedly have liver damage caused by excessive drinking. You're also anaemic which leads to the lack of vitality you mentioned to me, and you're also very short of iron. The

I was making tea in my pyjamas. I must remember to buy a teapot.

Me? Fit? Are you mad? I can get winded playing draughts!

Back on form. Chic thanks the nurses at Stobhill Hospital

situation is all the more serious because you are suffering from duodenal ulcers. I suspect, Chic, you've not been taking good care of yourself, my lad, and you've not been eating properly either. I'm going to give you an immediate blood transfusion as a matter of urgency.'

'I see,' said Chic, injecting a modicum of black humour, 'but apart from that, I'm in tip-top condition, would you say?'

Reggie chose to ignore Chic's rhetorical question and instead had him admitted to Stobhill Hospital within the hour. They spoilt him rotten for the next three weeks and a selection of lucky nursing lovelies, under the supervision of Reggie McKay, tended to his every need.

Three weeks were to go by, interrupted towards the end of his stay by an exceptional trip to London to appear on *This Is Your Life* to pay tribute to Jimmy Shand, accompanied by not one, but three nurses! (There was, of course, much pleading and arm-twisting before permission was granted.) Reggie said of Chic's stay, 'Apart from his various illnesses, he needed a damn good rest. His nonchalant act was just that – an act. He was an inward worrier and never gave himself a break. His hospitalisation did him a lot of good, with Stobhill's glamorous nurses vying for the big man's attention. Oh, and an army of visitors we had to hold back.'

Amongst this army, none was more welcome than Douglas, Annabelle and Maidie. Chic was very touched that Maidie had elected to visit and said so. 'Did you think I would do any less?' she asked as she held his hand.

'Do you know I am very popular with the nurses in here? They seem to really like me,' Chic said conspiratorially.

'Of course they do,' Maidie observed, 'when you're on your best behaviour, there's no one nicer. One of them was telling me you've been a model patient.'

'Maybe I've mellowed, then,' he said which prompted a smile from her. Then, concerned, she asked Chic how he had ended up in need of hospital treatment. Chic stared into the middle distance and after a delay, he replied, 'Everything just seemed to get on top of me. I've been busy enough and yet not busy – you know, hunger or bust. And generally overdoing the drinking, I dare say. On top of that some of the charge has gone out of it. When you're not getting very positive feedback it

makes for a hard grind, Maidie.' He went on to ask her how life was for her which led to the banter of happier days. Leaning over, he fetched an aspirin from his bedside table, 'Here, take this for your headache.'

'But I haven't got one, Chic!'

'Great!' he replied with a huge grin, 'in that case just jump into bed!'

Maidie couldn't resist a smile. 'It strikes me, you're on the mend, my laddie, my boy!'

'Well, you've cheered me up, Maidie,' he said, 'Do you know what they say about extra-marital sex?'

Maidie continued to humour him. 'Go on,' she said.

'It's okay so long as it doesn't hold up the wedding! Mind you, I'm like the guy who was asked if he got any extra-marital sex. "Extra? I'm not getting *any*, never mind the *extra*!" Then Chic stretched his powers of self-control to the limit by trying to remain serious for two minutes. In hushed tones, he asked gently, 'Is this you making the first move? Are you a wee boomerang on the way back, Maidie?'

'What! Back to the frying pan?' Maidie answered, smiling. 'That *will* be right! Just assure me of one thing – that you'll take better care of yourself when they give you your release papers. Don't forget, you're next door to sixty now.'

Chic's eyebrows shot up as he quickly scanned the horizon for those who might have been within earshot (he was ever so secretive on anything which touched on his private life). 'Don't be daft, Maidie,' he whispered, 'according to the papers, I'm only fift—'

'Aye and the rest,' Maidie interrupted. Putting one over on your ex-spouse was one step too far even for Chic's capabilities. 'But if you're more careful with your work schedule, your diet and your drinking, your best years are still ahead of you.' Chic was unable to take that last remark on board. His mind wandered back to the fifties when, as a double act, they had headed the billboards. 'You have no idea, Chic,' Maidie could see his lack of belief in her remarks, 'you are, whether you like it or not, becoming a legend in your own lifetime. There's never a week goes by on the telly or the radio when you're not mentioned, or someone does a Chic Murray story or impersonation. You could be bigger than ever, Chic, but no one can get a

hold of you. You seem to spend most of your life in limbo – endlessly travelling back and forth on trains and buses and planes. Push yourself, Chic. Get a master plan worked out and stop ricocheting about from one daft project to another.' Maidie could see Chic was visibly tiring, it was time to leave the big fellow.

'I'll try,' Chic said feebly, 'but maybe we could reform the double act.' Maidie prepared to leave.

'One Pinky and Perky's quite enough in the business,' she countered with a smile. She gave him a loving kiss and left the bedside.

Another pal called in on Chic at Stobhill. 'I'm going to have to ca' canny on the booze,' Chic said, 'because if I don't, I could be "potted heid". How's about a wee holiday in Tenerife when I get out? Think of it, two ageing teetotallers toasting in the sun . . .'

His friend recalled their stay in Tenerife. 'We had a great time, lying in the sun, eating plenty, gambling a bit, and it was good to see the big fellow get his strength back. He thought a great deal on what Maidie had said and he was chuffed to have Billy Connolly as a good buddy. He seemed to be renewed by Billy. Mind you, if Chic was careful with the pennies before the holiday, they were watched over slavishly on our vacation island. I worked out that I had spent three times Chic's outlay. That was until Chic informed me he had been talking pesetas, not pounds sterling!'

But in spite of the reconstructive holiday and Maidie's words of advice which had made a deep impression, Chic was back in Stobhill Hospital three months later to be treated for 'complete nervous exhaustion'. After his earlier release, understandably, there were only a handful of engagements to fulfil. 'Out of sight, out of mind' gave him too much time on his hands and old habits died hard. He appeared on *Looks Familiar* for Thames Television, some overdubs for McEwan's Lager and an advertisement for Butlins holiday camps – hardly the level of activity he had become accustomed to. He regretted the years that remained untended by Billy Marsh but had to admit he was largely responsible for being cast loose. Billy gave him direction, whereas now, he felt he was simply drifting. As usual, the nursing staff fussed and pampered Chic until the spark in him

'Are you disturbed by improper thoughts during the night?'
'Crikey, no, doctor, I love them!'

I call that Jimmie Smith 'Thrombosis'. He's nothing but a bloody clot.

reignited and his old self slowly re-emerged. The staff maintained, jokingly, that they could measure his route back to health, not so much by charts measuring temperature, pulse and blood pressure, more by the frequency and piquancy of his cheek which they had to sustain!

Dr Reggie McKay, in conversation with Chic, found out by sheer accident that they had a mutual acquaintance in Anna Young. Chic recalled how she, her husband and two sons had been very welcome when they visited him backstage at the King's Theatre in Glasgow, years before. It was a case of 'I've started, so I'll finish' for Reggie because he felt that Chic had enough on his plate without increasing his anxiety, but the doctor went on to tell how Anna and her husband returned home to find their

'Ah! But what have I got up my sleeve?'
'A broken arm, if you're not careful.'

Chic branches out into advertisements, local and national. The Texaco commercial was never made

"SEE ME I'M...

house on fire with one of the children caught in the inferno. The husband dashed in, in a vain attempt to rescue him. Both were consumed by the fire in front of Anna's eyes. Anna had sunk into a profound deep depression. It was too much for her to bear and Chic thought back in stark contrast to their shared pleasure in the King's, her sparkle then and the radiance of her smile. Reluctantly, Reggie promised he would trace Anna for Chic because the news had touched him deeply.

'I've heard your terrible news,' Chic said when she telephoned him, 'and I want to express my most sincere and heartfelt condolences. When can we meet?'

'Oh, Chic, I don't know,' Anna said on the verge of tears, 'I'm not well, Chic, and I've heard you're not exactly full of beans either . . .'

'Never mind me,' Chic cut in, 'I'm as right as rain now, whatever that means. I'll phone you as soon as I know I'm getting out of here. You and I can have a good long talk.' Two days later, and against medical advice, Chic signed himself out and immediately got back in touch with Anna. The Romans summed up the following passage beautifully – *res ipsa loquitur* (let the facts speak for themselves).

Anna looked back on her meetings with Chic as a miracle:

Chic, purely and simply, pulled me through. I helped him in return, but he did more for me than I ever did for him. He literally nursed me through the terrible depression I was having. And he would do it without my ever being aware of it. He'd start one of his daft stories and I'd be off, out of myself, away into his fantasy world. There was never anything between us other than the deepest friendship. I was his 'big pal'. He would often phone me up and he could tell by the tone of my voice if I was slipping away again. Immediately he'd say he was coming round and I'd watch as he walked up the hill underneath my window. He wasn't well himself and walked like an old man, but up that street he hobbled. People often describe Chic as mean. They didn't know him. Oh, he never rushed in with presents or anything. I think he bought me a bottle of wine once or twice, then there were these crazy postcards – usually free ones from

the hotels he was staying in, but he was generous of
himself – *he gave* himself *unsparingly and unceasingly.*
He made me want to live again.

Nuff said.

After all the setbacks, the bouts of ill-health and the lack of
a compass to steer Chic's boat for a while, it was a pleasure to
see him begin to edge towards more favourable and more
sheltered waters. And there was relief – secret joy, even – when
Billy Marsh succeeded in regaining contact with his wayward,
recalcitrant client. After all, he was one of Chic's biggest
admirers, the man who wept tears of joy those years before when
Chic conquered London's West End at the Prince of Wales. In the
meantime Chic had picked up a number of engagements of
which the most significant was a smallish part in a soap opera
for STV. It was significant because it was a straight part, bereft
of comedy and distanced from Chic's own input – not a
'Chicism' in sight. And surprisingly, Chic thoroughly enjoyed
this new discipline. Talking, like the old days, with their close ties
reconfirmed, he told Billy. 'You know, Billy, there could be
something in this. Believe it or not, it was a great change. And
the joke is, recently they've been saying that this has been very
much *me*, going *legit*! Does that mean that all my life I've been
acting *illegit*? C'mon! Tell me!'

Billy chuckled happily at this welcome renewed interest in
Chic. 'We just lost touch – one of those inexplicable things. After
Casino Royale things kind of fell apart. But now we're close to
the eighties and we've managed to get back together again.' And,
from Chic's point of view, at last, the penny had dropped! It
dawned on him that the public image he had created onstage
was now unique. At long last he realised that it was time, as
Maidie in her understated wisdom had advised him, to begin to
exploit his stage persona, from which much less talented, uncre-
ative mortals were taking greedy bites.

Completely by chance, around this time, Chic travelled by
train to London. Seated opposite him was an up-and-coming
film director, Bill Forsyth. Like most members of the public, he
recognised Chic, and it was no time at all before they began to
talk. The conversation warmed and became more animated and
at some stage it struck Bill Forsyth that Chic was the ideal man

This footman tapped me on the
shoulder with his foot . . .

for a small but significant role as the headmaster in his new venture, a film entitled *Gregory's Girl*. Chic okayed his invitation to play the role subject to fulfilling previous commitments. Had he seen Chic in any earlier films? Bill had to admit he had not. Had he heard Chic onstage? He had of course heard of Chic, but through his legion of imitators! However, he did admit to seeing him once onstage many years previously with 'Maisie'. Chic was quick to correct him with the authority of a headmaster and Bill congratulated himself on an inspired piece of casting.

They continued to chat as the train headed south. 'Did you, Chic, by any chance, see my first feature film, *That Sinking Feeling*?' Bill asked.

Chic replied, 'No, I didn't, but I passed a cinema where it was showing – does that count?'

The budget for the movie, to use Chic's expression, was 'broke to the breek-arse', which in common parlance meant it was financed on a shoestring. With that in mind, Chic's fee was nominal but he was only required to attend two days' shooting. The filming was under way days later; as Chic's role was the final part of the casting jigsaw. It was shot predominantly around Cumbernauld's town centre and principal school. Bill Forsyth insisted that the script be strictly adhered to; there was no room for improvisation. Chic went along with that but with what he called his 'sinister edge' which, of course, had nothing to do with the script; Chic couldn't help himself! There always had to be something original for Chic!

To relax, Chic found an upright piano tucked away and, still in his academic gown, he began to play a little ditty he had first tried out in an office at the BBC. Bill was intrigued. He could visualise a wonderful cameo scene utilising this unforeseen talent of Chic's. 'Would you mind if we worked that in tomorrow?' he asked.

'Not at all, Bill,' Chic replied, 'but, remember, that's my own composition. It's only fair I receive a fee for it.' He scuttled off to parley with the producers and returned offering a stingy sum. Chic, the old fox, ducked the 'yea' or 'nay'.

'Oh, you know me' he said (actually he didn't, but he was getting to know him!), 'I'll have to talk to my agent and I'll get back to you tomorrow.' He left Bill, somewhat crestfallen,

Did you notice the colour of her teeth when she decides to put them in?

Chic as the headmaster
in *Gregory's Girl*

muttering at Chic's disappearing back something about 'tight budgets'.

Bob Phillips was a neighbour of Chic's and a regular of the hotel when it was buzzing. He used to hand out advice to Chic, particularly on matters monetary. Nobody seemed to know why, but he enjoyed his self-appointed role. He and Chic met that night for a drink. 'Bob', Chic began, 'I'm involved in a new film. There's next to no money in the kitty and we're all working for peanuts. Anyway, we'd finished filming for the day and I was unwinding, playing a wee tune on the joanna. "Ooh! I like that," says the young buck director, "I'd like to feature you playing that in the film." "Wait a wee minute," I said, "that's my own composition and I should be paid for it." So he consults the purse-bearers who carry next to nothing in the satchel and offers me a piddling £50. Don't you think that's a bit cheeky? What do you think I should do?'

Bob, wearing his intergalactic financial hat, thought for a minute. 'Did you say you had written the tune, Chic?' He nodded. 'Then you're entitled to royalties, never mind the acting fee. My speciality, as you know, is messing around with property but I think you should chance your arm. Tell them you'll settle for 5 per cent of the world gross takings – that seems fair – and an upfront fee of £500. That'll put the wind up them.'

'Christ! It puts the wind up me!' Chic retorted, 'That's too much, surely?'

The taxi driver packed the job in.
He got fed up with people
constantly talking behind his back.

'Suck it and see,' he replied, 'you've nothing to lose.'

Next day Chic phoned his financial guru, 'That's a drink I owe you, Bob.' (Bob had a secret smile at that!) He went on, 'The tight-fisted buggers went "ape-shit" when I mentioned a percentage deal. But instead, they offered me a thousand smackers which is a damned sight better than £50. Even I can work that one out!'

The final shoot came and the director was desperate to get it in the can before shutting up shop for the night and, possibly, before Chic could extract even more money from his impoverished backers. And, as per usual, Chic couldn't resist a small helping of anarchy.

A scene with Alex Norton (now the star of *Taggart*), a teacher accompanying the headmaster, was due to finish with Chic's words to Alex, 'Fine, I'm depending on you then!' As they hung around for yet another take, Chic took Alex aside. 'Alex,' he said, 'when you're standing with your back to the classroom door and I say, "Fine, I'm depending on you then!" I want you to say to me, "By the way headmaster, did you know Miss Muirhead's been quite ill recently?"'

Alex, ashen-faced, looked as if he'd seen a ghost. 'What for, Chic? Bill will go fucking fitba' crazy. You know that!'

'Just *do* it! Honestly it'll be all right,' Chic gave him a reassuring wink.

Shooting restarted and in time Alex was due to respond to Chic's trigger: 'Fine, I'm depending on you then!'

For a nano-second Alex froze before he spouted the immortal words, 'By the way, headmaster, did you know Miss Muirhead's been quite ill recently?'

'Has she?' Chic asked solicitously as he produced a large green apple from somewhere in his robes, 'Give her this then; it'll make her feel better.' Alex stared blankly at said apple in disbelief before collapsing along with the rest of the film unit in helpless laughter – everyone, that is, except poor Bill Forsyth. As the laughter died down, and with words that were barely audible, he said, 'Very good, Chic. Now, could we do it the other way?'

As a postscript to the shooting of the film, a month or two later, he had lunch with John Gibson, the ageless show-business scribe from the east of Scotland. The waiter suggested they crack open a bottle of Pouilly Fuisse. 'No, I'll settle for a Beaune, thank

'Did you see my picnickers?'
'You shouldn't have
taken them off.'

you,' Chic responded, 'I'm not partial myself to birds or cats.'
(Ever since he'd attended a short course on wine during the
shooting of *Casino Royale*, Chic had developed a modicum of
oenological knowledge.) He waxed lyrical about *Gregory's Girl*.
The talk in the confines of the film industry was already
predicting the movie would be a major home-grown success. But
Chic deliberately understated the reality. He informed John, 'It'll
establish young Bill Forsyth as a major film-maker and me, of
course, as an international superstar.'

I've never asked John Gibson whether he accepted Chic's
opinion in its entirety but he did describe his lunch guest as a
'charming heid-banger'. He was, most certainly, all of that and
more!

There was a heartening buzz of expectancy now in antici-
pation of the general release of *Gregory's Girl*, which, for once,
was entirely justified. Chic was buzzing too. There was a weekly
series on BBC Radio Scotland, cutely called *Chic's Chat* on the
drawing board in which the big fellow would write his own
scripts and select his own records – hardly a major challenge to
Chic on either count! His good friend Ian Christie envisaged a
television special to be shot in the Mediterranean and, all the
while, exciting noises were being leaked from Billy Marsh's desk
of possible movie roles for the self-proclaimed 'international
superstar'.

When *Chic's Chat* hit the airwaves, it was a breath of fresh
air. That was the mega-bonus of the big man. Even if his
programme had turned out ready to be flushed down the pan,
there was one utter certainty – it would never meet that fate
through a lack of originality. And as it proved to be a great
success (with some guidance in the musical department from his
daughter Annabelle), he had, not unexpectedly, created a
programme which hit the high spots in the ratings. Ian Christie
was waiting in the wings.

Chic Ahoy was enormous fun to watch and interesting too,
as Chic good-humouredly cavorted round the Mediterranean in
his best blues and tennis shoes. But it was a tad more stressful
for the BBC producer. Ian Christie had several mountains to
climb – some of them precipitous!

The general idea was to cruise in a chartered boat belonging
to the Chandris Line from Genoa to Cannes, Barcelona, Palma,

*When he knocks on the door,
it usually rings a bell.
'I'm glad I got you in, on
this occasion,' he said to me.
'Well, that's a change,' I told him,
'because I'm forever being
caught out.'*

*'You remind me of the sea.'
'Does that mean you see
me as rough, sometimes
tempestuous, perhaps?'
'No, no. The sea just
makes me sick.'*

Tunis, Palermo and to end up in Naples with Chic doing his cheery commentary under a floppy hat and sun cream along the way. Then they hit on the first major snag. Being a charter, there was a tight schedule that the eight-strong film crew had to adhere to. If the boat, say, was docked for four hours, that was it – up anchor and off she goes, bang on the dot! Any laggards then had to play catch-up and meet the tub at the next port. The timing was critical therefore, so Ian decided the team would have to do the trip twice to clock the precise length of stay in each port and to sniff out suitable locations. (This, of course, suited the bold Chic just fine!)

On the practice run in Tunis, they were boarded by armed, bearded heavies from the Tunisian police force, demanding an immediate inspection of all passports before anyone was allowed on shore. Anxious to minimise the delay, Ian took it upon himself to rush round and grab everyone's documents. Starting

Chic Ahoy!

with Chic, a voice from behind the closed door promised to provide his passport 'in a minute'.

'Okay, Chic, I'll get the others now. Have it ready when I get back,' he said in haste. Five minutes went by before Ian, clutching a pile of passports, attempted re-entry with his free hand on the handle of the star's cabin – but to no avail. Locked! He rattled the handle in frustration.

'I'll be right with you,' Chic shouted, 'I'm just finishing dressing!'

'Well, pull the bloody finger out, Chic, time's marching on, you know.' The minutes ticked by and Ian's patience was wearing thin as he caught sight of tourists, in numbers, trundling down the gangplank. Another five minutes passed. 'I need your passport now! Do you hear me, Chic?' he yelled, now infuriated.

'Won't be long now,' came the disembodied voice. Ian had a fair idea what this immobility was all about. Chic was in denial about his age. There had been recent press speculation about the matter and the consensus was that Chic was aged somewhere between 50 and 55.

Chic's passport, in the wrong hands, would spoil all that, so Ian, bawling at the cabin door, went back into fighting mode: 'Look! I don't care if you're a hundred and bloody sixty-five! Hand over your passport now or I'll get these hirsute gorillas, hanging out here, to bloody well shred you with their shooters!'

The cabin door opened sufficient to permit the passport's transmission to Ian's eager hand. A raised mutter followed, 'Oh, there's no need for that kind of talk!' (Anyone who knew him would confirm these words are vintage and authentic Chic!)

It was all downhill for the poor devil. Now with all documentation present and correct, Ian had to tolerate the sight of Tunisian officialdom taking the BBC's equipment to bits as they meticulously noted down the serial numbers. Eventually, close to breaking point, the emotionally drained producer made it onto terra firma. He hired an interpreter and arranged transport to await them when they returned. 'Is there anything you want, Chic?' he asked.

'A camel,' was Chic's curt reply. The interpreter seemed happy to oblige.

Clearing the air, Ian turned to Chic, 'I take it you got your passport back okay?'

THE CHIC MURRAY STORY

*'What's the difference
between Rice Krispies and sex?'
'Dunno.'
'Pop round for breakfast
tomorrow.'*

'I did,' Chic replied giving Ian a bit of a look, 'but, remember, a passport is a very personal thing. I don't go around telling strangers my inside-leg measurement, you know!'

Ian was too bushed to lock horns again or to mention that his age and inside-leg measurements were a matter of sublime indifference to him. Instead he smoked the pipe of peace, 'Your idea of hiring a camel sounds intriguing, Chic. What do you have in mind?'

'It just came to me,' he said, 'a new angle while you were yapping to the interpreter wallah. I'll give it a bit of thought but I'll work that out in plenty time before we're back here.'

Apart from Barcelona where the footage was constantly interrupted, despite numerous takes, by baying hounds and yapping dogs, everything else had panned out beautifully and Chic had been in top form. Ian planned to use some earlier footage of Barcelona that they had previously shot without Chic, replacing the ear-splitting barkathon with a voice-over and shots of the main man on board the ship. Arriving back in Tunis, they were advised they had five hours on shore, not a second more. The interpreter was waiting for them with two jeeps. The crew and equipment were piled in, whereupon Ian asked, 'Have you found a camel for us?'

'I take you,' came the esoteric reply.

'How long?'

'Soon.' Chic and Ian sat in the front and stared at endless sand for an hour. Effectively, that was two hours – they had to get back after all. Each minute increased the anxiety level which accelerated when they were forced to stop by a lorry straddling the road. Then there was a queue for a ferry and with Ian's nerves at snapping point and the interpreter's neck nearing a throttling scenario, the convoy at last began to creep forward. They were the last vehicles to get on.

A quarter of an hour further into the other side of the backside of beyond, they caught sight of greenery, a small village, a palm-encircled hotel and a camel tethered alongside. It transpired the ship of the desert was there for the benefit of tourists to be photographed on its back, possibly to be passed round at the Puddleduck or Beacon's Bottom Bowling Club's Annual Dinner. Chic turned to address Ian, who felt the relief and euphoria drain from him as he realised there was a major

170

Captain P.O line goes ashore Port Said little boy runs alongside & says filthy Postcard Pretty Girl - anything I can find for you Young man I want the Harbour Master little difficult but I will Try.

Chic often worked out his gags on scraps of paper. This one was written (like many others) on the back of an envelope. It reads: Captain PO line goes ashore Port Said little boy runs alongside & says filthy Postcard Pretty Girl – anything I can find for you Young man I want the Harbour Master little difficult but I will try.

hurdle yet to be circumvented. In a slow, deliberate and deadly serious voice, Chic said 'This is not a *correct* camel, this is a *tourist* camel. It's an *incorrect* camel. That, I'm afraid is the situation – and I refuse to play in these circumstances!'

'Och, c'mon, Chic, a camel's a camel. What the hell's the difference?' Ian argued.

'No, it won't do, Ian,' Chic stuck to his guns, 'I had envisaged an oasis-type scene in the middle of the desert.'

'Well, don't worry about that, we'll just keep the hotel out of the picture.' he said.

'It's no use, Ian. I can't do this on the back of an *incorrect* camel,' he said emphatically. (Perhaps Chic was envisaging David Lean's *Lawrence of Arabia* while Ian pictured John Cleese's dead parrot scene! An *incorrect* camel? Whatever next?)

Meantime, the film crew, who had no idea of the absurd dialogue between the two men, were becoming irritated by the inexplicable delay, compounded by the discomfort of an unforgiving sun. The producer did his level best to explain to the film crew that Chic viewed the wretched beast as 'incorrect' as it rested alongside, chomping on some indescribable bundle of dried vegetation. Redolent of Mark Anthony's address to the citizenry after Caesar's death, so Ian addressed his confused film team: 'He looks an okay camel to me, I have to say, and he probably looks an okay camel to you, but Chic says,' he pointed

*'I suppose I'm something
of a sado-masochist. I'm addicted
to agony columns.'*

at the foul-smelling, farting ship of the desert, 'that he is an *incorrect* camel! Now, go and shoot some background stuff and get back to the wagons double quick!'

Back on the boat, Ian was in a forgiving mood. After all, he rationalised, Chic's the professional here. He should have the final say, and if he feels that he's not happy with something or other, his views should predominate. All the same, it had been a tough assignment that had brought little to the table. When they met for dinner, he gave Chic a fraternal slap on the shoulder and, in view of his earlier intransigence, Chic was pleasantly surprised by the offer of a drink. Better still, there was a tacit under-

Chic and friends on the gangplank

standing that the small matter of 'incorrect' camels was to be consigned to the lost-and-found columns.

Fast-forward to Glasgow, as Ian busied himself editing the Mediterranean footage. He thought twice about cutting out the barking dogs of Barcelona. And after some judicious cutting, Chic's attempts to overcome the noise from the Catalonian canines, when spliced together, produced a side-splitting result. He phoned Chic to get his permission to use the threatened outtakes but Chic, initially, was horrified at the very suggestion. Grudgingly, he agreed to come over and have a 'look-see', but, he was muttering negative thoughts. 'It's unprofessional,' he complained. After seeing the montage through, Ian detected the suggestion of a smile on Chic. 'Run it through again, Ian,' he requested. After the second viewing, Chic said, 'I'll bet this will turn out to be the funniest part of the show!'

'You mean you actually like it?' Ian asked, surprised.

Chic, now beaming, said, 'I'll sue you if you even begin to think of cutting it out!' Chic's words were dulcet music to Ian's ears and, all of a sudden, those painful memories of 'incorrect' camels faded and then vanished out of his sight – a nightmarish mirage beyond the desert haze.

After a sticky start, *Gregory's Girl*, which was first shown in the smallest of three cinemas in the Glasgow Odeon ran for a few weeks only. Chic and his daughter Annabelle were present at an unannounced preview. Afterwards Chic made a number of optimistic noises to the press which were well placed. True, its reception in Glasgow was lukewarm, but when it was rolled out in London, the English critics simply loved it and the film began to take record receipts that films with mega-budgets couldn't equal. Speedily, the film was brought back to Glasgow where it ran for months. In Edinburgh, the family-owned Dominion cinema ran *Gregory's Girl* for two whole years without a break!

And things got even better. David Puttnam, an independent film-maker, had had a massive hit on his hands with the Oscar-winning film *Chariots of Fire*, which broke all sorts of records in America. Like *Gregory's Girl*, it enjoyed a lengthy run in the West End. However, when both reached saturation point and the law of diminishing returns began to bite, he had the creative instinct to re-issue both pictures in a double bill. The synergy worked a treat and both films had a new lease of life. (It was

'You're the sommelier. Why don't you recommend me a wine?' 'Well, perhaps, sir, you would like to try the Macon?' 'What? Are you going to pour it over me?'

*'My boyfriend slings a rope round
my neck and drags me along. Do
you think he's serious?'*
'No. He's just stringing you along.'

ironic, indeed, that long before, Bill Forsyth had offered *Gregory's Girl* to David Puttnam when it was still on the launch pad and the latter had declined the offer.) The spin-off for Chic was considerable and his cameo role in the film received universal praise; his scenes in the film were some of the high spots and, unsurprisingly, the funniest!

As he had previously announced, the cast of *Saigon – Year of the Cat* eagerly welcomed him in Bangkok, including Judi Dench and Frederic Forrest, the two principal stars. The film was a large-budget movie, directed by Stephen Frears but made for television. Chic entranced everyone on the film set. Firing on all cylinders, his humour was such that his colleagues laughed with him until it hurt. (Judi Dench's memories of those hilarious moments are contained in the tribute section of this book.) And, of course, Chic was in his element. Every spare minute he would sun himself to relieve his psoriasis, so he was reluctant to leave the film set once his scenes were in the can. (Such was his fixation with sunbathing, Judi Dench affectionately renamed him 'the old leather bag'.) The crew wanted Chic to stay on in case he was required for any re-shooting of scenes, and he could well have stood for another fortnight's sun, but nobly he kept his word to perform for another director back in Scotland. There is a splendid archive interview with Tony Bilbow where Chic discusses his stay in Bangkok. 'There was one Scottish connection in Bangkok when I was there,' he remembered, 'apart from myself, that is. *Gregory's Girl* was being shown locally and the whole unit trooped down to see it. The cinema was not air-conditioned, which lent a distinctly Eastern atmosphere to the entire proceedings.'

When he was asked how the film went down with the locals, he replied, 'I think they made a curry with it. It certainly seemed to go down very well!'

The Garage

Good evening. Tonight marks the end of a very eventful week for me. Yesterday was my birthday. Twenty-eight. I know . . . I hear you laughing. You thought I was 19! So I had a celebration drink in a pub and a man said I had bumped into his vulture. I couldn't

see any vulture, so I asked him, 'Where's the vulture, then? What vulture?"

'Voucher.' he replied in a low voice, 'my luncheon voucher.'

Anyway, the next day, the phone rang and I picked it up. Well, you have to! You never know who's on the other end. It was the man from the garage to tell me my new car was ready. So I dashed down the stairs – we use stairs in our house now – we used to jump out the second floor window until I realised what the stairs were for . . . I thought they were just for going up. So I got to the garage and I asked the salesman which was my car. 'Oh,' he said, 'it's that one there,' pointing to the one without any doors. I took the steering wheel – (that was a mistake for a start. I should have left it where it was!) – and got out of the garage, and after about 50 yards' driving, I had to stop. I said to the salesman, 'If you can't push any harder, I'll be forced to get the engine with the next instalment.'

Eventually I abandoned the car and took a quick run on the bus – there's not much room on that centre passage, but it was good exercise, just the same – then I realised the bus was going faster and faster down a hill. It was then that I spotted there was no driver – I'm very observant that way. I turned to this fellow passenger, a total stranger. I don't often speak to strangers: a chance remark and you never know where it can lead. I said, 'Excuse me, I can't see the driver.' He said, 'No wonder. He jumped out five minutes ago.'

Well, on the approach to Glasgow Cross, we crashed and I ended up on a ledge between two pigeons. And since I was the only one who couldn't fly, I was the one in an awkward position. I turned to my two companions and said, 'This will not do!' So I made use of my previous dropping experience and landed in the arms of a waiting policeman. He said, 'Are you drunk?' and I said, 'Do you think I'd have gone up there if I'd been sober!' The policeman was very good natured and he was laughing a lot as he drove me to the police station. The next day I was up before the judge. In my defence, I said, 'I'm sorry, Your Honour, I was in a tantrum at the time; but he interrupted me, saying, 'The make of your vehicle has no bearing whatsoever on this case . . ."

CHAPTER 13
YOU'LL NEVER WALK ALONE

So it was a radical change of direction to return to Scotland to be swathed in tartan excess and to act the outrageous part of Sir Rhosis of Glenliver opposite a promising young up-and-coming actor, Robbie Coltrane. The film was a production for Channel 4 entitled *Scotch Myths*, based on a highly provocative but hugely successful exhibition of the same name which had received lavish praise at the Edinburgh International Festival. The director and scriptwriter was Murray Grigor, my brother, and the producer, Barbara Grigor, my sister-in-law. My two outstanding memories of the film include the actor Bill Paterson uttering the memorable phrase, 'hoisted by my own pet bard' (a reference to Robbie Burns, not to the 'petard' of the Stratford Bard) and the image of a concert pianist playing Mendelssohn's 'Fingal's Cave' as his grand piano and candelabra are gradually submerged beneath the waves at the mouth of the very cave that inspired the composer.

Murray secretly loved Chic's anarchic tendencies but had the perspicacity not to let on to Chic. To have encouraged him further would have been to create utter mayhem, confusion and all-round chaos! That was the wonderful element of surprise with Chic. You simply didn't know what to expect, where to expect it and what was it that had come unexpectedly in the first place.

Such incidents were always accompanied by his body language which telegraphed, through the utter blankness of his facial expression, that look of kindly indulgence and childlike innocence – it melted the iciest heart. And it also had the effect of throwing off suspicion, complicating matters further! Mickey Spillane, Sherlock Holmes or F.E. Smith QC, even – none of them would have had a cat's chance in hell of being able to catch

Do you mind if I laugh into a paper bag?

As Sir Rhosis of Glenliver in Murray Grigor's *Scotch Myths*, with Johnny Bett

177

'Can I borrow your lawn-mower?'
'Sure, as long as you don't take it
out of my garden.'

him out! That Chic held this trump card meant that it was virtually impossible to distinguish between the Chic who was in earnest or the alternative persona who, feet up, just relaxed in the 'kidology' department. One unfortunate thespian accidentally stood on Chic's hand, right in the middle of filming on the *Scotch Myths* set. 'You've stepped on my fingers!' he bawled, his hand tucked under one arm. 'In America, you'd get sued for much less than that! Yes! I know it sounds funny – permanent loss of pressure in the pinky – but, today it's a palpitating pinky, tomorrow it could be a malfunctioning pinky!' No writ for damages, however, was issued on this occasion and the pinky soon recovered its 'pre-stood on' mobility!

Late afternoon and late in the year, Chic phoned Murray's wife, Barbara. 'Hello, Barbara, I was just wondering if I could pop over to see you and Murray, since it's New Year's Eve?' Chic, by this time, was well known to the couple. In addition to playing his part in *Scotch Myths*, he had done a superlative job for Murray, as director, acting out various comic parts in a commercial for peppermints: one minute, dressed as a vicar angelically smiling and sipping tea at a garden party (the fully recovered pinky extended), the next driving a vintage car in a deerstalker and Biggles jerkin.

Barbara hesitated, 'We don't actually do the Hogmanay thing, Chic. As often as not, we're in bed before the bells. But you're very welcome, just the same.' They saw the New Year in together, exchanging cordialities, and the following day they were assembled round the table when there was a firm knock on the door of their sixteenth-century townhouse. It was a soldier on leave, helplessly drunk, with rubberised legs which Billy Connolly so brilliantly mimics onstage.

'Ah've jest admired yer hoose for a lang time. An' ah jist wanted tae ca' by tae first foot ye and wish ye a' a guid New Year!' the squaddie stranger slavered. He made his way, just, to the table where Chic was seated, but as luck would have it, there on the table was a lengthy article about Chic with numerous photographs of the comedian in the *Scottish Field*. The rubber man, now fortified by a dram, caught sight of the magazine. 'See that man!' he said, pointing in the approximate direction of the photo spread, 'he's absolutely the greatest comedian o' them a'!'

'Oh, I most certainly don't agree with that!' Chic interposed.

YOU'LL NEVER WALK ALONE

One of the shots from
the *Scottish Field* article

A further half an hour of argument ensued with Chic constantly rebutting the rubber man's assertions regarding Chic, the man he so admired without the slightest clue that the badinage was between him and the very man he sought to praise. How weird is that? Only Chic could have maintained this pretence for so long, so that when the squaddie did eventually leave, he still had been incapable of matching the many photographic images of his hero to the man who had sat opposite him. Chic, of course, never broke cover – what a pro he was!

That night, over an evening meal, Murray explained that Valda MacDiarmid, widow of the poet Hugh, had asked him to auction a number of items belonging to her late husband to provide funds to commission a memorial sculpture. One of the most treasured items, amongst the bits and pieces, was a smoker's pipe, given to the bard by Sir Harry Lauder. Chic's eyes lit up! 'I'll do the auction for you,' Chic offered enthusiastically, 'and we'll have a bit of a laugh but I'll get you Ascot prices! Wait and see!'

At the sale, true to his word, Chic took an interminable time flogging off the items with great hilarity and profit until he came to the Harry Lauder pipe . . . he had spotted Jimmy Logan, the comedian and his long-term friend, in the audience and he knew

*He was so bone idle,
he married a pregnant woman.*

he was a collector of Lauder memorabilia. Chic waffled on about this charred, carbonised, smelly object being a slice of Scottish history and it was pure Chic as he created images of a kilted Harry Lauder belching smoke from the briar, waddling down Sauchiehall Street or blowing his double-twist 'baccy smoke over Sir Winston Churchill, the Prince of Wales, Andrew Carnegie and Henry Ford. (There was probably not a shred of truth in any of Chic's blethers, but who would gainsay Chic in full flow?) 'Sir Harry's last request,' he plugged on, 'was to have his beloved pipe laid upon the pillow of his death bed so that he could lovingly stroke it before his final breath was drawn.'

Jimmy Logan met up with Chic after the sale. 'You're some auctioneer, Chic,' Jimmy said.

'Well, if I'm that good, why did you leave empty-handed without the pipe?'

'It was impossible to know just when the bidding would begin,' Jimmy lamented, 'there's more than me thought you were going to arrange discounted bed-and-breakfast rates for the punters!'

On another occasion, Murray introduced Chic to Sam Fuller, the Hollywood film director and maestro of the B-movie. (They had become good friends ever since Murray, as director of the Edinburgh International Film Festival some years before, had held a retrospective in Sam's honour.) Sam, for old times' sake, had agreed to appear in Murray's film, *Scotch Myths*. He had a strong hunch that Chic and Sam would hit it off, and they did. Chic was ear-marked to appear in a film entitled *Quint's Game*. It was only timing that frustrated events – the finance for the movie hadn't yet been fully raised. Sam said, 'Chic is perfect for the part. The film has been postponed for the moment, but when it does roll, I want Chic Murray in Paris for the shoot.'

Since *Gregory's Girl*, there was real momentum gathering for Chic's career. Having befriended Frederic Forrest on the set of *Saigon – Year of the Cat*, he had enthusiastically recommended Chic to Francis Ford Coppola (the director of *Apocalypse Now*), who pencilled in Chic's name as Owney Madden, a character part as a popular nightclub owner in *The Cotton Club*. It was a role, because of conflicting demands, that ultimately went to Bob Hoskins. There was talk, too, of a 'porridge western' (as opposed to spaghetti!) with Chic as the

There's a lovely blonde who has just moved in next door who took my eye. Well, not really! I need it, you see, as it's one of a set.

baddie, a priest who carried a six-shooter in his Bible, set against Billy Connolly, the goodie mayor of the one-horse town. Again, time, to develop the film and arrange finance, was a commodity in short supply.

In amongst all this excitement, Chic was in Glasgow when he heard from the well-loved Alexander Brothers that Maidie was returning to the stage in a charity event in the Usher Hall in Edinburgh. She had stepped in to cover for a last-minute cancellation. He couldn't believe it. Tom and Jack Alexander agreed to drive him through to Edinburgh. Wide-eyed and unannounced, he kept well out of sight and watched Dainty Maidie perform. Not unexpectedly, Maidie received a rapturous reception both for her performance and as a 'welcome back'. Despite the boys prevailing on him to visit her backstage, Chic would have none of it. They drove back in silence with Chic complaining of an oncoming cold. The boys knew different as tears of sadness, maybe regret and certainly nostalgia for days gone by, were shed in the back of the car.

There was soon to be another interruption to his schedule through ill-health. Back in hospital, Chic was to receive yet another 'hector-lecture' from Dr McKay. 'You ignore my advice, Chic, at your own risk,' he said. 'Nature has a habit of giving you warning signs and one of those is weight loss. Do you realise your weight has dropped from fourteen to twelve stones?'

But Chic looked at himself in the mirror and perversely approved of his gaunt appearance, thinking it corroborated a recent press article which surmised he was in his mid-fifties. 'I've got to remain light on my feet,' he said to himself and he comforted himself with the fact that Billy Marsh was back in tow. 'There'll be no more days on my own without a crust coming in. Things are looking decidedly rosier.'

He was right to an extent. In early 1984, Billy Marsh got in touch with his old comrade. 'Chic,' Billy said, 'I've been approached by the Everyman Theatre in Liverpool but money-wise it's no great shakes.'

'Forget the money, what's it all about, Alfie?'

Billy smiled to himself. 'The company want you to take the lead part in a musical play, *You'll Never Walk Alone*, the subject being Liverpool Football Club's late and much-lamented manager, Bill Shankly.'

She wasn't all there. But I thought there was enough there to make it interesting.

'Dad's just gone out again.'
'Stop fussing! Just throw some more paraffin over him then.'

Back in the limelight

'Oh, I'll go for that, all right,' Chic gushed, 'in any case, some have called me a legend, so that will be one playing another, is that right, Billy? Besides, I love a challenge!' It was a gifted piece of casting. Chic had been well known and well loved on Merseyside as far back as those triumphant days with Maidie when they packed them in, night after sell-out night, at the Liverpool Empire.

Chic, rightly, reckoned his first task was to master Bill Shankly's distinctive burr and staccato mode of speaking. He buzzed off for some peace and quiet and some welcome sun to practise in Majorca for a couple of weeks. And one of the tools of his trade was a small recorder which went with him wherever

he was. It contained lengthy passages of speech from earlier radio recordings of 'Shanks' himself. Even when the show was playing, as it did to full houses every night, Chic would produce this recorder and hold it to his ear, whether in a pub or café or his hotel room, to refresh the accuracy of the man he mimed to perfection. He was never to miss a beat, a nuance, an emphasis, a change in tone, or any characteristic of 'Shanks's' voice. His voice was Shankly's as theatregoers and those that met Chic on a visit to Liverpool FC's Annfield changing rooms can bear solemn witness. Jimmy Logan said of Chic, 'He had an uncanny ear for mimicry.' It wasn't altogether surprising, as South Ayrshire (which produced two other football colossi, Jock Stein and Sir Matt Busby) was next door to Lanarkshire where Chic was raised.

But it was a supreme challenge for Chic regardless, because Bill Shankly was a figure of totemic proportions and a monumental working-class hero to the Scouser, whether they werc supporters of Liverpool or followers of their traditional rivals, Everton. The latter used to receive a bit of good-natured ribbing from 'Shanks' – well, quite a lot actually! He once said of his rival neighbours, 'If they were playing at the foot of ma gairden, son, sorry, but I'd have to close the curtains.' And then, on another occasion, 'A lot of football is in the mind. You must believe that you are the best and then make sure you are. In my time at Liverpool, we always had the best two teams on Merseyside, Liverpool and Liverpool Reserves.' Joyfully both those little passages featured in the show and the likelihood was that there were as many Evertonians as Liverpool supporters at the hundred-plus performances of the show. That surely speaks volumes about how successfully Chic had risen to the occasion, despite small signs that the dusk was beginning to darken his days in the sun.

In view of his general health, the show had not been easy for him. It was physically challenging and his dedication to the star role was exemplary. Back in Majorca, Calamity Chic had again gashed his leg horrendously. Yes – yet again! So over a period of four months as the play ran every night to packed houses, Chic had to have his leg treated and dressed. It must have been extremely painful, yet he was uncomplaining (and, for sure, he could be a Moaning Minnie if he chose to!). The adrenalin rush

My wife's a red head.
Oh you should see her! No hair.
Just a red head!

183

of his nightly performances (which received rave reviews) was some compensation for his private anguish. There was speculation that the show would go on tour to Glasgow and London's West End but, since Chic had made Shankly's part his own, who could understudy him if his health were to give out? Chic *was* Shankly, even to the extent that he told Ken Bruce on a live radio broadcast that he had had to crouch his large frame to align his body mass nearer to Shanks's. (That illustrated Chic not wanting to sell the man short, in spite of Shankly's below-average height!) He was, in truth, somebody that he sincerely and hugely admired, and Chic's family treasure the presentation to him of Bill Shankly's training jersey from his widow Nessie, who came to adore Chic and who died many years after her husband, in 2002. There can be no greater stamp of approval for an actor representing another than to receive the unqualified endorsement of the other's spouse.

For the avoidance of doubt, perhaps it's best if Chic explains his performance in his own words:

> *The accent wasn't too difficult, with Ayrshire bordering on Lanarkshire. He came from a wee fitba'-daft community where he played for the Glenbuck Cherrypickers – a marvellous name that, and absolutely true. The trick is to get the Shankly delivery. With him everything was definite. He spat everything out and didn't waste a word. 'Him up there may have blown the final whistle,' he'd say, 'but I'm playing extra time!'*
>
> *I loved Shankly's style and I loved the stories about him – like the apocryphal story of when he first arrived at Annfield and tested the team by placing eleven barrels on the pitch and having them play against them. 'By half-time,' Shankly said, 'the barrels were winning 3–1!' Another time he was told that a Jewish signing, because of his religion, might not be able to play on a Saturday and commented, 'There are ten others doing the same!' Like me, Shankly was a loner who went his own way and didn't listen too much to other people. He went to one coaching course and said afterwards, 'I do the opposite of what they do and do well. They know nothing about football.' Bill's secret was that he had the*

*common touch. He's a national institution because he
was a character.*

*By the time the play's off, I'll know all there is to
know about fitba' – and since I've got the Shanklyisms
off pat, I'll be the man to motivate the players. When the
run finishes, it'll just be the start of the season in
Scotland. Who knows? – maybe my next engagement
will be in the Premier League.*

Chic returned to Scotland, after an extended run of *You'll Never
Walk Alone*, in triumph and high spirits, even though he was still
not enjoying the rude health of a year or two before. He called
in on his daughter Annabelle before heading round to stay at
Maidie's for the night. (Chic was in the process of moving back
to Edinburgh where he'd bought a cottage but had still to do the
flitting.) He and Annabelle settled down to watch the telly, the
first evening in months that Chic could relax. By coincidence,
Billy Connolly was being interviewed and since he was Chic's
buddy, they listened intently. He was asked to specify his
favourite comedian. He replied unhesitatingly,

*Chic Murray. In my opinion, he is the best in the
world. I think he's the funniest man on earth and I
aspire to be what he is. As he gets older, he gets more
outrageous, which is a lovely thing, and more absurd.
Sometimes I meet Chic and he tells me a joke – and I
don't know it's a joke until he's three-quarters of the
way through. The man's a genius. I hope as time goes
on, I can hone my material as fine as Chic. He goes
into his tales like a story and becomes all the
characters. That's what I, ideally, aspire to as a
comedian – to be as good as him. I'd like to get more
off-the-wall as I get older, the way he has done.*

Chic was stunned at the sheer generosity of the man, particularly
as Billy was at the peak of his professional career. 'No wonder
they call him the Big Yin,' he quipped humbly to his daughter, 'it
takes a big man to come out with that.' Later, having recovered
from the sheer and wholly unexpected thrill of Billy's interview,
father and daughter headed round to Maidie's.

Chic as Bill Shankly

'Did you manage to see the show?' she asked on their arrival, vicariously proud and excited on Chic's behalf.

'Aye, I did and it was nice of Billy,' he replied, 'but I think he's maybe mixed me up with Ruby Murray!' As a grand master of communication, it can be deduced that Chic often thought, 'Why waste a paragraph when a grunt will suffice?'

Chic, over the weeks to come, was somehow driven by a nesting instinct which included stay-overs with Annabelle and Maidie and a general and understandable wish to spend more time with his family. To this end, he realised he needed to resettle back in Edinburgh to be close to them all. So as part of that strategy, he harnessed the affable Harry Meredith as his driver as and when needed. Harry was a Welsh businessman who had settled many years earlier in Edinburgh and, most importantly, was engaged to be married to Annabelle. With regard to Chic's driving skills, it had taken God-knows-how-long for the penny to drop that, for him, he was more likely to win the pools than to be a successful candidate for the Advanced Driver's Certificate. It was suggested that Chic maybe thought that driving was an offshoot of a comedy routine he was developing! In any case, Harry took Chic through to Glasgow on more than one occasion, where he helped pack a pile of Chic's belongings and brought them back to his Edinburgh cottage. Carrying a packing case down the stairs, Harry noticed Chic acting in a very

odd manner. When he arrived at the foot of the stairs, he dumped his load and asked his future father-in-law, 'What are you up to, Chic?'

'Oh, it's just a show-business tradition, Harry. Just tradition, that's all.' Later he was to learn that there was truth in Chic's reply. Where artistes had a legitimate grudge against the landlord or landlady of their lodgings – in this instance the landlady was a notorious busybody – they traditionally lifted the carpet at selected spots, and, with a flat knife, liberally applied a gungy, odorous concoction of kipper, mackerel and cream to the underside! The mind boggles!

During this period, heading towards Christmas, Chic was simply sensational when appearing on *Tarbie and Friends*, a smash-hit television show. Jimmy Tarbuck was a huge fan of Chic's and he was simply in stitches as Chic gave wonderful renditions of 'The Door' and 'The Battersea Dog' routines, both of which are recorded in this book. Having reduced the audience and their host to helpless laughter, Tarbie tried to compose himself to interview Chic, tears still running down his face. In stark contrast, with the hint of a beneficent smile, Chic remained deadpan, giving just a nod or a tilt of the head to Tarbie's questions which simply caused more laughter, even from the cameramen. Tarbie tried a new tack. He tried to do a Chic Murray gag and had the temerity, in front of 'the master' to do so with his impression of Chic's voice: 'A woman opened the door in her dressing gown. I thought – funny place to keep a door!'

As the audience collapsed into more howls of laughter, Chic broke his silence, 'That *used* to go down well, Jimmy!' One of the great tragedies of these wonderful moments with Chic is that not enough have been kept for posterity. Thank providence then, that in this book, some of these delicious ageless moments of unbridled mirth will now be preserved.

Chic's sixty-fifth birthday in early November was not just a joyful occasion, it was, above all, a family occasion attended by his mother-in-law, Nana Dickson, Maidie, Douglas and Annabelle, his grandchildren Douglas and Deanna, and Harry, Annabelle's fiancé. It was a truly happy day of unity but it was to be the last time they would all be together.

On New Year's Eve, 1984, the BBC celebrated the old year's

*I said to the landlady,
'Would you call me early?'
The next morning she stood at the
bottom of the stairs and shouted
up, 'Oh, Early!'*

passing and heralded in the new with their customary Scottish shindig, a Hogmanay show – but with a difference! Inexplicably this year, only one measly day before the live broadcast, some bright spark decided that the show should be transferred from the well-equipped studios of BBC Scotland in Glasgow to the Gleneagles Hotel in Perthshire. Apart from the logistical challenge this effected – equipment, cabling, lighting, etc. – there was the small matter of rehearsal in unfamiliar surroundings and, needlessly, with the clock as the enemy. Timothy Spall, the award-winning actor and devoted fan of Chic's, said of the show (*Neither Here Nor There*, BBC Radio 2, August 2007), 'I remember this Hogmanay show which was just dreadful, all cobbled together and so badly organised. A band would stop and Chic was just sitting there . . .'

Actually, it was even worse than that because Chic's microphone was live. Clearly audible, he complained (with justification) of a total lack of professionalism with snatches such as 'bunch of amateurs', 'this is chaos' and, 'aye, you might well smile, you great buffoon'. The utter lack of direction, his daughter added, was such that when the cameras went hunting for her father, he waved half-heartedly and said (aptly, in the rural surroundings of Perthshire) 'I'm over here, in the long grass!'

The singer Moira Anderson best summed up the late evening's entertainment with one word – 'shambles'! So this was not a day of triumph for the Beeb but the shambles Chic encountered may have been the work of fate; as some commented on that night, no one did more than Chic, albeit in a hugely entertaining career, to create anarchy and chaos onstage. There is a poignancy in that observation because this was to be Chic's last television appearance.

Chic phoned Maidie towards the end of January, 'I'm in London, Maidie, but I'm planning to come north and stay over for a break. I need a few days off – maybe more, because I badly need a rest.'

'Are you all right?' Maidie asked.

Chic sounded rough. 'I'll be fine when I'm there with you.'

'Oh. It sounds to me you want to drop anchor for some time.'

Chic paused on the telephone, 'I've done dafter things in my life.'

I was sitting in a Chinese restaurant, having a business lunch, when a cat bolted from the kitchen and out the entrance door. Nothing was said but I noticed 17 and 26 had been stroked off the menu.

He popped in the following day to find Maidie out. 'Tell her I'll be back later,' Chic said to his granddaughter, Deanna. It was late when he got back, close to midnight, and seeing the lights were out, he chose not to wake the household but to stay next door with his friend Bob Hamilton and his wife, Jean. They were pleased to see him and duly poured him a good dram.

'You're looking tired Chic,' Bob said, 'so I'm not going to keep you up. But you can't fly on one wing. Have another nip and then it's off to bed you go. You can sleep as long as you want in my mother's old room. You know, the one where the wall backs on to Maidie's bedroom.'

Chic drained his glass and put it on his bedside table. He climbed into bed and took his spectacles out to read from a crumpled piece of paper which he smoothed out with his hand. It was entitled, 'That Feeling'.

> *That feeling keeps returning,*
> *It makes me yearn the whole day through,*
> *To hold you close and find*
> *That feeling is shared by you.*
>
> *That feeling lures me to you*
> *Dream-borne it seems I travel on*
> *People seem pale and distant*
> *Only the feeling is strong.*
>
> *The road's been long but nears its end,*
> *Soon, very soon, we'll meet once more,*
> *Moments from now I'll reach for you*
> *With all the joy I knew before.*
>
> *That feeling has rejoined us*
> *Now I will know as I hold you*
> *Whether you share that feeling*
> *I've felt so long for you.*

He replaced his spectacles in their case and set the crumpled paper beside them. Lights out.

It was 6am when Maidie awoke and she stared dreamily at her bed covered in photographs from the good old days as part

of her double act with Chic. She had had an awful job getting to sleep as she had tried to remain alert, fighting sleep, waiting for Chic. It was in the early hours of the morning when she had fetched these memories which prompted so many reasons to smile. Rubbing the sleep from her eyes, she headed off in her dressing gown to make a wake-up cuppa. The phone rang. It was Bob next door who broke the news that Chic had died during the night.

In shock, Maidie inexplicably asked where Chic had slept. 'In my mum's room,' he replied, 'the one next to you.' She realised that Chic had passed away with only the thickness of the wall dividing them, and in all probability while she had been reminiscing with their photographs. She dressed and went next door where she was relieved to see how peaceful her life partner looked despite evidence of blood from a perforated duodenal ulcer. Then, tenderly, she picked up the paper that Chic had read the night before and left.

Chic was no atheist but neither was he a regular churchgoer and, above all, he despised those who pontificated over the arrangements for the departed, often as not people they hardly knew. Accordingly, Annabelle took charge of the funeral proceedings; they were conducted by a lifelong friend in show business, Johnny Beattie, and a more recent but equally true friend, Billy Connolly. Harry and Annabelle collected Billy at the airport and both men gave warm tributes to their lost friend. Then, led by Billy, the congregation sang 'You'll Never Walk Alone', a timely reminder and mark of respect for his recent triumph at the Everyman Theatre in Liverpool. There may well be a perfectly straightforward explanation for Chic's tartan bunnet visibly moving as the coffin began to disappear from view. The BBC, who filmed the service, can bear witness to its wriggling. Was this Chic's way of showing his approval or a final farewell from a great trouper?

With the coffin finally no longer in view, the assembly spontaneously burst into heartfelt applause. Harry Meredith was approached by a curious gardener on the manicured lawns surrounding the crematorium, who had heard the unrestrained laughter coming from the chapel, 'Was that Chic Murray's funeral?' he asked, then added in wonderment, 'What a way to go!'

After the wake, Billy came back to Harry and Annabelle's

house where they sat and chatted for hours. In the course of conversation, regret was expressed that Chic, who was looking forward to his daughter's wedding, to leading her up the aisle and to giving her hand in marriage, was no longer able to fulfil his wish. Billy generously offered to take the place of 'the master' and one year on, he did precisely that. Following the sad death of one of the greatest comedians of the twentieth century, they all deserved their day in the sun.

Months later, Douglas was leafing through his father's papers when he came across a page of previously folded and well-thumbed A4 paper containing some handwritten jottings. One musing in particular stood apart. It read, 'Everyone wants to go to heaven. Nobody wants to die.'

Chic raises a smile even at his own funeral

193

WHAT OTHERS SAY

Chic Murray was a truly unique comedian. I was much influenced by his wry way with words, and I also used his voice, or rather my version of it, for many years in *The Navy Lark* on radio, as Lieutenant Queeg, the engineer. I loved his work.

Ronnie Barker

Chic was that rare bird: a great Scots surrealist; a great comic innovator. *Stanley Baxter*

The first time I saw Chic Murray strutting his stuff was at the Glasgow *Empress* way back in the 1950s. From the minute he came on I was hooked. Other people in that audience were not so sure. This was a whole new comedy experience for them. Over the years critics attempting to describe Chic's style of comedy have used words like Surrealist, Proustian and Beckettish. Chic would probably have said, 'That's just daft!'

For me it was the fact that his persona and material dovetailed so perfectly that made him unique. Some years ago I had the pleasure of saying a few words at the unveiling of a plaque outside Chic's birthplace in Greenock. I could just imagine Chic's take on that: 'Outside what was my house in Greenock there's a plaque halfway up the wall and it says – Chic Murray was born here – and it was very uncomfortable being born half way up a wall!'

Happy memories of our Chic, a one off, a true comedy genius!

Johnny Beattie

I had known Chic for years before his tragic and untimely death early in 1985. Indeed, I read about it when my wife Delia and I were in Las Palmas on holiday. The local *Express* had a photo-

Chic with John Laurie

graph taken at his graveside with all the mourners led by Billy Connolly, laughing, giggling and joking. Just the way he would have wished.

I remember going to the biggest theatre in Edinburgh to see Chic perform as the main act. For fully 45 minutes he entertained the packed house on the piano, no less. Yes, he could 'handle' the piano and, of course, numerous other instruments. He carried the show without breaking sweat. Chic's skill was also evident in front of the camera. On the day of the shooting of his part in the film *Gregory's Girl* – done in a school in sunny Cumbernauld – we met in the 'Muscular Arms' round the corner from my office in West Nile Street 'No re-takes,' he said. 'Not even a rehearsal. Who needs a scriptwriter?' His cameo part halfway through the excellent film included a jaunt on the piano. The film was a great box-office success.

Chic, in my opinion, was a one-off, utterly impossible to imitate, and so very relaxed whether on stage, radio, TV or film. Will we ever see his like again? I doubt it – he had uch originality and natural genius.

Offstage he often looked worried and upset – perhaps the reason was the very prospect of buying a round of drinks. He was careful about his pennies and was slow to buy his round. There would come a time when someone would have to say to him, 'Look, we've been waiting for you to buy a round for the last hour.' Even that lambasting did not embarrass him in the slightest. (Incidentally, many show-biz celebs suffer from the same condition – short arms and long pockets). But this is only a minor fault, and I never once heard him criticise his fellow artists – quite the opposite, in fact.

Although dead for all these years we still read about him in the press and his quips and funny situations are still very much alive. This factor is surely proof of the pudding – if one ever required such. He was certainly a thing apart.

Joe Beltrami

I first met Chic in the early 1970s at the house of the theatrical agent Ruth Tarko. Ruth lived in Cecil Street in Glasgow's west end, where Chic had a flat which he rented from her. On Friday evenings, around six, Ruth would host an informal drinks party and I would often encounter Chic there. I recall him asking me

if I was familiar with the American comedian Lenny Bruce. Chic very much admired the younger American comedians and I remember him saying, 'Nobody's doing that kind of stuff here.' Except, of course, on occasions, Chic!

Later, in the seventies, I had the good fortune to meet up with Chic in The Buxton Club in London. The Buxton was a late-night drinking club, much frequented by actors and musicians, whose shows often finished after the pubs had shut. Situated behind the Haymarket Theatre, The Buxton was rambling, noisy and shambolic, with a warren of rooms of various sizes stretched over several floors. Through these rooms wandered a clientele high on adrenalin and drink, a merry crowd. Around about two in the morning, I was drinking with a girl friend in one of the upper rooms in The Buxton. A bunch of people had just drifted off and we were alone, chatting quietly. Well, not quite alone; the other occupant of the room was a Golden Labrador, lying peacefully in the corner, observing the scene with drowsy contentment. Chic came in and started to chat to us. He had come from a recording of *The Eric Sykes Show* and was regaling us with tales of working with Eric and Hattie Jacques. From time to time, he would glance over at the corner where the Labrador lay, but said nothing about its presence. He continued telling us about a film he was working on in France, all the while darting glances at the dog. Eventually, as if he could contain himself no longer, he blurted out, 'Jesus Christ, the rats are big in here.' It was the perfect remark for the time and place and my girlfriend and I exploded with laughter. Chic continued with his story as if nothing untoward had occurred.

Another time, travelling on the shuttle between Edinburgh and Glasgow, I saw Chic, seated further up the same carriage and travelling with a small puppy. The puppy, though on a lead, was straining in all directions, overjoyed with the smells and treats on offer, and sniffing the carpet, the seats and fellow passengers. All this frantic activity was accompanied by yelps of delight and much tail-wagging. Chic spotted me in the carriage and declaimed, 'Hello, Johnny. How are you? Better than I am today, I think. I'm covered in confusion and embarrassment here. It's the dog. I don't know where he gets it from, but he has a very volatile personality. I must apologise.' To the dog: 'Down, dog! Down!' To me: 'You see, he just ignores me. Actually, it's

197

his birthday, He doesn't know it yet. We haven't told him. He's excited enough already!'

A sometimes-remarked-upon aspect of Chic's character was his 'carefulness' with money. I had reason to observe this when the train reached Glasgow Queen Street. In those days most bars in Scotland shut at two thirty in the afternoon. The train's arrival left a few minutes to spare before last orders. Chic said, 'This dog is holding me up. We'll miss the boozer. You run ahead and get the drinks in. I'll join you in a minute'

I acted with Chic on several occasions and invariably had a good time. The most memorable for me was working with him on the film *Scotch Myths* which was written and directed by Murray Grigor. An ensemble of actors played a variety of different roles in the film and, at one point, Chic was cast as a mad, ingratiating assistant to Sir Walter Scott, played by me. We were both ludicrously swathed in clashing tartans and plaids and Chic wore a bunnet which sported a large feather that dangled and flapped in front of his face. When it was in danger of obscuring his mouth Chic would blow on this feather and it would dance like a dervish, hither and thither, all over the place. Though it was very funny, indeed hilarious, Chic managed to maintain a straight face throughout. This heightened the humour, of course, and I could barely look at him for fear of bursting into paroxysms of mirth.

We were filming in a converted studio – a disused theatre in Edinburgh – and we managed to get through the first of our scenes, the naming of the tartans, without too much levity or difficulty. For me, however, it was touch and go. I had to steel myself not to react inappropriately to Chic's antics. The scene which depicted the arrival of George IV floored us both. The scene was based on a true incident which occurred when the king visited Edinburgh in 1822. The visit, full of pageantry and pomp and stage-managed by Scott, was meant to present to the people of Scotland a bloated and be-tartanned Hanoverian king as a worthy Jacobite replacement. Prior to official proceedings, it is said that Scott greeted George aboard the royal ship in Leith and that the pair of them had a dram together to mark the occasion. In his excitement, the Laird of Abbotsford asked the king if he could keep the crystal glass in which the toast had been drunk. The king agreed to this somewhat bizarre request and Scott put

the glass in his pocket. On the journey back to the Borders, he forgot about the presence of the glass, sat on it rather heavily, smashed it, and cut his bum (serves him right, one might say). In Murray's film, the Leith meeting takes place in a specially rigged bar, and the portly George IV is represented by a giant whisky bottle which Chic and I, still bedecked in tartan, are required to address in obsequious and reverent tones.

Scott's line goes something like this: 'In order that I might forever recall this momentous occasion I would ask His Majesty to allow me this honour – to keep the glass.'

I said to Chic that I thought it would be funny if, after I'd said the line, he were to look at me as if I had completely lost my marbles and then to repeat the line: 'Keep the glass?'

On 'action' we did this, and Chic burst out laughing when he came to the 'Keep the glass?' line. The surreality had got to him. Take after take was ruined by one or other of us being unable to complete his lines.

Chic was embarrassed. 'I'm famous for keeping a straight face,' he said, 'and here I am laughing. Very few people have heard me laugh. Don't you dare tell anyone I giggle like a girl guide.'

Murray had to empty the studio and eventually film Chic and me separately before he could get a useable, giggle-free take.

Chic loved wrong-footing people by giving them a response they didn't expect. He would invent things just to see how his hearers would process the information he'd given them. One day, in the canteen queue at the BBC, the checkout lady said to Chic, 'And how are you today, Mr Murray?'

'Call me Chic, please.'

'How are you today, Chic?'

'I'm sorry you asked that. I'm not too well, I'm afraid. The old war wound's playing up.'

I heard him drag out 'the old war wound' on several occasions.

We were in Oban once, in a packed souvenir shop; you couldn't move for tartan kilts, ties, bunnets, travelling rugs, etc. The shop was heaving with kitsch images of Scotland – Robert Burns and Highland stags – on mugs and calendars, ashtrays and tea-towels. We had a laugh or two about some of the wilder examples of the genre and bought some badly executed 'Scotch'

postcards. At the till Chic said to the owner: 'I'm afraid I've only got a ten pound note. It's ENGLISH! Is that acceptable?'

One often saw Chic carrying a couple of plastic bags. He used them as a substitute for carrying a briefcase. 'Who's going to mug you for a couple of plastic bags?' he reasoned.

Many people will remember that when he was arrested in a stationary car in Cecil Street and charged with putative drink-driving, Chic's plea was that he was using the car as an office. The students next door were having a party so noisy, he claimed, that he was forced to retreat to the car in the middle of the night to work on scripts. The case was widely reported in the papers. At the time Chic was appearing at the King's Theatre in Edinburgh. At one point in his act, his flow was interrupted by the loud wailing of a police car in the street. 'Listen,' said Chic to the audience, 'they're playing my tune!'   *Johnny Bett*

I was lucky enough to grow up in Scotland during a golden age of comedians, many of whom we would see in pantomime at the King's Theatre in Edinburgh. Stanley Baxter, Jimmy Logan and Rikki Fulton all seemed to have their own magic, and to think of them now is to smile. Chic Murray was always different, somehow unclassifiable, particularly if words like 'surreal' were not yet part of your vocabulary.

But I always treasured the oddness of his jokes, the mad logic, the deadpan delivery. It was only when I was writing the *Guardian* Diary many, many years later that I realised there was a whole universe of admirers of Chic, scattered across the world. When I slipped a couple of his jokes into the Diary, from New Zealand to Kenya, from Buenos Aires to Toronto, came e-mails and letters from his fans, all with their own jokes, their own memories, their own interpretations. As Chic might have said: 'It's a small world – but I wouldn't want to paint it.'

We all had our favourite jokes – the door in the nightie; the butcher and the steak – but we also knew that Chic Murray was always much, much more than a jokesmith. It was his private language, his refusal to conform. He was our philospher-king in a flat bunnet and we were privileged to have been present during his reign.

'There's many a joke told in Glasgow that they won't laugh at in London. You know why? They can't hear it.' But in fact

most of what Chic had to say travelled wonderfully well. Recount his story of his confrontation with a tight-fisted bed-and-breakfast landlady who asked him if he had a good memory for faces . . .

Chic: 'Yes, I do.'

Landlady: 'Good – there's no mirror in the bathroom' . . . and you can be fairly certain of a smile anywhere in the world.

There have been other great Scottish comedians since Chic, most notably Billy Connolly, who shared that magical ability to see life from sideways on and who has always paid tribute to Chic.

We have all seen the tea-towels on which are listed the great inventions and discoveries of the Scots, from television to the telephone, penicillin to golf, everything, in fact, apart from the wheel (still subject to an investigation at the Patent Office). Monumental accomplishments that we have generously shared with the world. What should, of course, be added to that list is the name of Chic Murray, the man who knew that the hardest work was to be done before breakfast: getting up.

Duncan Campbell

We were recording a TV show from the Octagon Theatre in Bolton and I couldn't find Chic anywhere (not an unusual occurrence – I often called him 'the Illusive Pimpernel'). I wanted to introduce him to another member of the cast, namely that wonderful character actor John Laurie from *Dad's Army*, who had only agreed to take part in the show because he so admired Chic and wanted to meet him.

I looked everywhere for Chic in and around the theatre. Eventually, giving up for the moment I went to the Gents. As I was washing my hands I could hear a faint mumble coming from behind the closed door of a cubicle. Putting my ears closer to the door I realized I had found him. To my even greater delight I had actually found him rehearsing his act; something he rarely admitted to, but of course had to do. His storytelling, delivered with style and confidence, leading his audiences into his bizarre world, often belied the many hours, days and sometimes weeks of writing and re-writing spent perfecting a routine which was truly unique.

Beneath the glamour and the glitz the reality was the comic genius who rehearsed in the toilet.

Ian Christie

My dad worshipped Chic Murray. He really did. He would have walked naked through snow to watch him. Chic had that level of loyal fans all over the place, and from all walks of life. I was too young to watch him live in the theatres, so only saw him on TV shows when he was invariably the best thing in them. I only 'got' Chic when I was older. He was, of course, a deeply sophisticated performer.

Many years later, at the BBC in Scotland, I got the chance to work with him and to watch him rehearse a few pieces for the camera. Suddenly, every crew member in every department of BBC Scotland found an urgent need to be in our studio, just to watch him work.

He had his own shorthand way of rehearsing, which was fascinating to watch, and, naturally, hilarious. Once the audience was there, suddenly the dry humour, the unhurried, glorious timing, slipped into gear and the result was simply sublime. He had a wonderful way of appearing to be surprised that anyone found what he was saying funny.

I cannot say I learned anything from him, other than that you could be loved by an audience without using any of the tricks that conventional comics used in those days to make an audience like them. He never made any attempt to ingratiate himself with an audience.

Chic was from the variety tradition. He could yodel wonderfully, could sing very well, as was expected of variety artists in those days. But that was where the music hall turn ended and something much more 'edgy' and unpredictable began. To say Chic was ahead of his time is hardly a revelation. But watching Eddie Izzard, another hilarious maverick, thirty years on, you are reminded just what a shock Chic must have been to all those ruffle-shirted patter merchants he would have shared stages with.

He once grabbed my arm as I was passing him in the Byres Road (I made him give it back), and told me I was a 'very funny boy'. My dad would have so loved that.

As I write this, I'm listening to Chic's routine about the woman with the huge nose. It still makes me laugh out loud, and I cannot count how many times I have listened to it.

We should have a Chic Murray Day. Tartan bunnets compulsory.

Robbie Coltrane

'"Hello," I said. I couldn't place her name. I knew her face so I said, "Oh, hello, dear." She had two antlers sticking out of her head.'

This witty wordplay may not leap immediately off the page, but if you heard it delivered on the stage by Chic Murray at an Edinburgh variety show, as I did in the 1950s, you would never forget it. In a cascade of puns, which my French wife Micheline says gets much closer to its true meaning as *jeu de mots*, or play of words, Chic played with the most ordinary words to reduce half the audience in fits of laughter and the other half in total despair. You either got it or you didn't. Chic Murray's brevity really was the soul of wit. His storytelling had all the logic of a shipwrecked dream. I thought then that he was the funniest man ever.

Sean Connery

Although I met Chic on several occasions, and of course felt a kindred spirit with him through our Scottish connections, I never ever, sadly, had the opportunity to work with him. I have some tapes at home which I look at now and again because they are always uplifting to see, and of course he has a style that is probably still contemporary to this day. In fact he was ahead of his time in a way that one could well see somebody dressed differently doing his material now at the Edinburgh Festival Fringe, and it wouldn't seem out of place. He was quirky, original, soft, sweet and of course, above all, very, very funny.

I still, because we have a house in East Lothian, pass through the Bruntsfield area, and can't do that without thinking of him because I know he had a hotel business somewhere up there on the way to Church Hill, the Braid Hills and Macsween the butchers!

I am very flattered to be asked to say a few words on his behalf and in his memory. He was a true original, a very funny, sweet and engaging man. I'm not sure at what stage he no longer worked with Maidie, but I remember when I first saw him Maidie was always slightly in front of him playing a musical instrument (am I correct?), or about to play a musical instrument. Chic with his amazing height would peer down on her in a rather suspicious, dubious way, and then later on I imagine he worked more or less singularly.

But I have great memories and the greatest respect . . . the

203

Palladium . . . the Edinburgh one, that is . . . in Fountainbridge . . . or was it Bread Street?   *Ronnie Corbett*

I must have been about ten or eleven, with a flickering black-and-white telly, and suddenly there was this big man with the slightly pretentious voice, Kelvinside, slightly upmarket, bettering yourself and that . . . that funny delicate walk and the bunnet. He was talking about objects fighting against each other. Now, as a kid growing up, putting language together, that's what woke me up! I thought, 'Who is this man?'

I am one of Chic Murray's greatest fans.   *Brian Cox*

I don't remember anyone quite like him. You could say he was unique; the timing, the material, and that wonderful face and suddenly the eyes would twinkle. He was a surrealist and he went his own way.

He was the maverick of the Scottish comedians; he was wonderful.   *Barry Cryer*

I remember Chic in Bangkok with enormous affection and perhaps mostly for the fact that in the film I was called Barbara and he called me Judith – a name I have never been known by, except when people were cross with me at school! Chic was totally unique to me because he could tell me a story at enormous length, of which I would probably only catch five words, but he would make me laugh until the tears poured down my face.

In Bangkok on days off I have a vivid picture of Chic lying in the hottest sun one can possibly imagine – in fact, during the filming he was known as the 'old leather bag'.

I was thrilled to have had the opportunity to know him and work with him.   *Judi Dench*

In the old days of variety hall theatres all the dressing rooms had loudspeakers and you could turn them on or off. The loudspeakers would enable you to hear the performers on the stage and if you were a comic you could listen very carefully to whatever comedian was on and check that they were using their own material. I first heard Chic Murray when I was topping the bill about 1958/59 and I had just had great success with

compering *Sunday Night at the London Palladium*. I heard this soft-spoken style, different from anyone else, and I thought, this man has warmth, and I watched him from the wings one night; such a clean comic. Of course, the Lord Chamberlain's office would send someone every Monday night, first house, to check for any rudeness. His timing – immaculate, completely different – and his vacant look sometimes made the line funnier. I thought he was wonderful.

Bruce Forsyth

Chic was the eccentric's eccentric. In the street he was just as likely to walk past you in an innovative trance as he was to hail you from the top of a bus. Coming face to face with you he would slip into performance mode and chat about ordinary things in that extraordinary way he had. Once he had discovered you were vulnerable to his lunacy you were a target for life. I certainly was. And he was merciless, on many occasions reducing me to a heaving mass of embarrassed hysteria. Yes, that was Chic. The word in French, of course, means skill, knack, smart or stylish. And that was Chic, too.

Rikki Fulton

He was one of the few Scottish comedians who was just as popular, if not more popular, down south as he was in Scotland. I mean, there's so few of them that actually make the transition. I would say it was only Chic Murray and Billy Connolly who bridged that gap.

To find a comic who can make the band laugh and make the audience laugh just as much is a great rarity – they call them 'dressing-room comics', the guys who make the pros laugh. Almost the last thing that Chic did on TV, I think, was in a show that I used to introduce every week called *Halls of Fame* for BBC Television and, I mean, it was a different routine he did when he actually got in front of the audience that night than he did at rehearsals.

Roy Hudd

A genuinely funny man; a master of dry, understated humour.

Peter Jeffrey

Chic Murray became one of the greatest comics our country has produced.

Jimmy Logan

I must be one of the few artists who knew Chic and Maidie in the early days of variety still around to tell the tale. As I remember it, Maidie was the star of the act. She taught him everything he needed to know to make a good solid living and he learned his trade. They blossomed as Chic Murray and Maidie, 'The Tall Droll with the Small Doll'. He became an alternative comedian before anyone knew what an alternative comedian was. He opened the gates for all to follow in the fullness of time. The man was a genius and Maidie wisely let him loose on the British public and he never looked back. To this day he is the only Scottish comic listed amongst the Les Dawsons, Tony Hancocks, etc. He broke the mould. His genius is folklore. Chic the young man, as a family man, loved his kids, Douglas and Annabelle. He and my late husband, Jack Milroy, went round all the toy shops in Edinburgh one Christmas to buy some new parts for his son's train set. When they arrived home to tea with Maidie and the family the wee boy had to watch his daddy play with the new piece of equipment – a big man with a delightful childish streak which Jack told me was quite lovable. Many years went by and both my late husband and Chic became 'stars' in their own right. Chic remained Big Chic!

We encountered him in a Blackpool hotel in the breakfast queue around eight thirty once (us on holiday and Chic working). Jack said, 'What are you doing here, Chic?'

Without breaking a smile, Chic said, 'I'm due to be flung off the North Pier at eleven o'clock,' and continued to choose a big breakfast. Follow that!

In every lifetime the 'sparkle dust' falls on a special person; it sprinkles large amounts of talent on the chosen one. Few are chosen; happily for us Chic Murray was.

Mary Lee Milroy

If you were describing Chic Murray to someone who'd never seen him, you would have to say you're either going to find the man one of the most excruciatingly funny people you've ever seen in your life, or you're going to wonder what all the fuss is about. I don't believe there's any middle ground with appreciating Chic. You either love him – he may be an acquired taste although from the first time I saw him I was 'his' for the rest of my life: he became one of my comic heroes instantly – or you will

not see the point of it, in which case, go back to your books or your ballet or your plays or your opera and please don't trouble me!

There's hardly a single routine of Chic Murray's that doesn't become an instant favourite as soon as I hear it. It sticks like comic glue to your mind. It attaches itself to you. It's the wandering inconsequential nonsense that fills the gaps between what are standard jokes from other comedians. That's what gives it its grace.

And what is also so interesting is that he was, himself, a graceful man. He was a big man, with big hands, big legs, big body and he stood there with that great dumpling of a face with hardly any expression. And everything was in the voice, those tiny unfinished sentences, that strange way of going off the subject, the rambling touch that Ronnie Corbett has made very much his own in more recent years. *Bob Monkhouse*

I first saw Chic on the telly sometime in the mid fifties. He and Maidie were on some sort of variety show and I remember my dad insisting that I sat down and watched them. Chic must have made a big impression on me because although I can't recall his patter (I was just a wee boy and we must have been among the first folk in the Gorbals to have a telly), in my mind's eye I can still clearly visualise Maidie singing and playing the accordion while Chic towered over her, warmly meeting her adoring glances then pulling faces as soon as she turned away from him. My parents were in stitches and I remember thinking Chic Murray was the funniest man in the world.

It was a major thrill for me when I worked with Chic for the first time on Bill Forsyth's film *Gregory's Girl*. I played a teacher at Gregory's school and Chic was the eccentric piano-playing headmaster. We had a scene together that sadly never made the final cut of the film, where the two of us are walking side by side along a corridor, discussing the possibilities of shuffling classes around due to an absentee staff member. I reassure Chic that I have the problem in hand and that he can rely on me to sort everything out to his satisfaction. He thanks me sincerely and starts to walk away. As soon as his back is turned, I start to pull faces and make 'V' signs to his retreating figure. Shades of his former variety act with Maidie . . .

Chic was a surrealist, in his own way as great as Dali or Magritte. The world was his canvas and its inhabitants were the raw materials he utilised in creating his eccentric masterpieces. An example: we were working together on Murray Grigor's film *Scotch Myths* and found ourselves standing on the jetty at Oban waiting for the camera crew to set up for our next scene at the far end of the pier. A couple of elderly American tourists stopped to gawp at the film camera and the lights. Like lambs to the slaughter they asked Chic if he knew what was going on. 'Terrible tragedy,' he sighed dramatically, glancing slyly in my direction.

'Oh yeah?' the Yanks chorused. 'Can you tell us what exactly happened?'

That was Chic's cue to start reeling them in like a couple of prime haddies. They hung on his every word as he explained how a tragic young couple, a local Romeo and Juliet, thwarted by their parent's opposition to their love, had plunged, hand in hand, off the end of the pier. I don't know whether the Yanks' mouths hanging open prompted the final piece of the tale in which the star-crossed lovers were inadvertently sucked into the gaping maw of a basking shark that just happened to be innocently hunting krill in the vicinity. I'm ashamed to say, from fear of being roped in as an eyewitness to the event, I quietly slipped away as, in full flow now, he began to describe the massive air-sea rescue search that even now was being despatched from Lossiemouth, to scour the inshore waters in the hope that the couple might, Jonah-like, have survived their ordeal in the beast's abdomen and be reunited with their grief-stricken, but now compassionate, parents . . .

It was on the same shoot, that I witnessed Chic become a supporting player himself in a bizarre situation that I don't think even his fertile imagination could have concocted. The two of us had been booked into a wee local hotel for the night, prior to filming the following morning at Fingal's Cave, on the island of Staffa. As we walked into the crowded hotel bar, we found ourselves in a scene from a cowboy picture. The place went suddenly silent as every head in the bar swivelled in Chic's direction. Time froze. Drinks remained halfway to lips in suspended animation. There was a long tense pause as Chic stood there, bunnet on head, suitcase in hand, eyeing the locals

eyeing him. The B-movie standoff was broken as a weather-beaten trawlerman in oilskins and gumboots rose slowly to his feet and in a louche drawl uncommon among fishing communities in the Western Isles, said, 'I was walking down the street. Well, I knew I was walking *down* the street because I could see the bottom of the street coming towards me.' Like the famous 'I'm Spartacus!' scene from the Kirk Douglas movie, that was the cue for every single one of the locals to stand up in turn and, in various approximations of their hero's deadpan delivery, perform their favourite Chic Murray one-liner.

'I bumped into the wife. I said, "Hello, dear." I often call her dear. She's got two horns sticking out of her head.'

'There was an awful clever wee thing about waist-height for opening the door. They called it a handle. I suppose if it had been lower they would have called it a footle . . .'

So it went on, Chic silently acknowledging his acolytes and rewarding their obeisances with a few gracious nods. I remember thinking it was unlikely I would ever again find myself in a more surreal scenario than standing next to Chic Murray in a Hebridean bar full of Chic Murray impersonators . . .

Years passed, and I had moved to London to see if I could make a splash in a bigger puddle. I hadn't seen Chic for a long time, so picture my surprise when, on a flying visit to Glasgow and queuing for a train ticket at Queen Street station, I became aware of a familiar voice from the direction of the information window on the far side of the ticket office. Sure enough, there was Chic, speaking in a rather loud and theatrical manner to a dazed-looking booking clerk. I heard him say something along the lines of, 'So, if I decide to make the return journey via, say, Lenzie, does that mean I would have to forego the possibility of securing a couchette in the observation car?'

The hapless clerk was doing his best to explain to an increasingly irritated Chic that there was no observation car on the 12:24 from Falkirk High, or indeed any other train this side of the Canadian Rockies. I left my queue and sidled over, hesitating shyly before interrupting with, 'Hello Chic. I —'

But that was as far as I got before he irately rounded on me. 'How dare you importune me in this manner,' he boomed. 'I have absolutely no intention of accompanying a total stranger to the gents' toilet. Now be off with you and ply your foul trade

with a fellow deviant who might welcome your sordid advances!'

I can't imagine what I must have looked like standing rooted to the spot, my face scarlet with embarrassment as everyone in the busy ticket office bore witness to my shame and humiliation. I have a vague memory of my mouth soundlessly opening and closing as a friendly arm slipped round my shoulder and a voice murmured quietly in my ear, 'Great to see you, wee man. 'Mon we'll away for a cup o' tea.'

Of course, Chic had clearly clocked me the minute I walked in the station. The entire pantomime with the booking clerk had been a carefully engineered sting to attract my attention and lure me into being an unpaid comic foil in his ongoing theatre of the absurd. When my breathing started to return to normal and my legs were steady enough to carry me away from the gawping crowd, the very small part of me that was still vaguely rational felt flattered that Chic considered me worthy of the effort.

We sat in a nearby café as Chic told me of films he was considering, tours he was planning, sketches he was writing and of the parts that, if I was interested, I could play in them. I think we both knew that the offer was notional rather than actual, but of course that wasn't really the point. The point was to let me know that he was still a busy and sought-after working comic. We sat together for about half an hour, polishing off our tea and sandwiches, exchanging in time-honoured theatrical tradition, some ripe anecdotes about the indiscretions of various well-known Scottish performers. No turn was left unstoned. As we were getting ready to depart, Chic decided to play out for my benefit one final little improvised sketch with our obsequious and rather over-familiar waiter. It went something like this:

WAITER: I hope you and your young companion enjoyed your tea, Mr Murray. I trust the service was to your satisfaction?
CHIC: Excellent, thank you. Tell me, would it be OK if I gave you a tip?
WAITER: A tip is always appreciated, Mr Murray.
CHIC: Oh good. [Grasping the waiter's eagerly outstretched palm in his and adopting a conspiratorial manner] Never tie your shoelaces in a revolving door!

Back out in the dreich Glasgow morning we went our separate ways with fond farewells and assurances that we would keep in touch more often. I had no way of knowing that was to be our final encounter until a few months later when I learned of his passing. There would be no more surreal scenarios or wonderful humiliations in store for me.

Now, whenever I bring Chic's memory to mind, as I do often, it's almost always accompanied by an image of a wee boy sitting entranced in front of the telly thinking Chic Murray was the funniest man in the world.

I still do.   *Alex Norton*

In the spring of 1977 I was invited to work with Chic in a couple of half-hour radio programmes called something like *Murray's Merry-Go-Round*. It was a wonderful chance to share the stage with a man I had admired since I was a boy and had got to know a little in his sojourns around the west end of Glasgow. I always seemed to bump into him at either Hillhead or Kelvinbridge underground station. He would mention his travels but it was never very clear where he was heading to or coming from. He would just immediately engage in free-range chat about virtually anything. In many ways the Glasgow underground was the perfect Chic Murray location: circular, seriously sensible but basically funny in an indefinable way. No surprise that it was the setting for some of his most reported anecdotes, like the legendary comment after asking the platform guard if there was a buffet on any of the trains. On being told that there was never, ever, at any time, a buffet on any train on the Glasgow underground, Chic replied, 'Oh well. We'll be starving by the time we get to Merkland Street'

Murray's Merry-Go-Round looked too good to miss. It also had what seemed to be the rock-solid asset of being recorded live on a Sunday night, not in a studio in Queen Margaret Drive, but in the cosy intimacy of the Greenock Arts Guild Theatre in the great man's home town. The programmes were to be a series of sketches written for and built around Chic with a small team of actors including myself. We would be the feeds and support, and with any luck we would become Sid James and Hattie Jacques to Chic's Hancock. I accepted without a second thought. Then I read the scripts. *Hancock's Half-Hour* could relax. Its classic

status would not be challenged by *Murray's Merry-Go-Round*.

On the night, the recording was opened by Chic doing the warm-up before the sketches began. He strolled on – and nobody could stroll like Chic – in his element in his home town, complete with bunnet, and instantly caught the audience in the palm of his hand. Everything was there: the doctor's waiting room, the adventures on the Euston sleeper and, of course, warm surreal memories of growing up in the streets nearby. The invited audience adored it and we watched spellbound from the wings as he left the stage to rapturous applause. Then, sadly, the green light went on and they started recording the terrible sketches with our desperate attempts to mug our way round the lame jokes and Chic stranded in the midst of us. Like a car crash, it felt like life was slowing down as we headed straight for casualty. If only they had just recorded the warm-up and dumped the sketches they would have saved time, money and reputations, and BBC Scotland would have had a hit show

I've often thought that that sort of misjudgement wasn't rare in Chic's career. It seemed that few people, certainly in Scotland, quite knew how to use his talent to the full. And that included Chic himself. Such a unique and individual comedy needed either a free reign to go wherever it led or a very special setting to show it off. Thankfully Bill Forsyth has left us just that with the headmaster in *Gregory's Girl*. The medium shot from behind, the delicate piano and the classic, 'Off you go, you small boys,' will remain forever.

I'm glad to say that Chic never held my terrible contribution to his career against me and in 1979, while I was in a long run at the Savoy Theatre in *Who's Life is it Anyway*, he would drop in regularly to say hello. I would get a call in my dressing room from a totally bemused stage-door keeper: 'There's a gentleman here asking if you're still married to that Cherokee woman and can he have his dog back?'

'Just tell Mr Murray I'll be right up and we'll go for a cup of tea'

He would wait under a sign reading 'Savoy Theatre Stage Door', surrounded by actors and stagehands coming and going and then ask me if I was working at the moment. I'd tell him I was in a show where I spent the entire time onstage paralysed from the neck down and asking for permission to die. He'd reply that he'd often felt like that at the Ayr Gaiety.

Although I played over 270 performances at the Savoy and Chic called in three or four times, as far as I know he never saw the show, but that didn't matter. He was there to spend an hour or so freewheeling about life in general before he set off to Euston to catch that sleeper north, and when Alex Norton, John Bett and myself did a benefit performance of John Byrne's *Writer's Cramp* to pay for the installation of the bar at the Tron Theatre, once again Chic didn't catch the show but volunteered to take the ticket out of the hat for the fundraising raffle. In the expectant hush, he produced the folded ticket and announced, in that much parodied voice: 'And the winning number is pink.' He then strolled off into the night.

There was nobody like him.   *Bill Paterson*

The 1970s were a good time to be a television dramatist. The spirit of the sixties was still around and nowhere was it more intoxicating than at BBC Pebble Mill under the gentle stewardship of the great producer, David Rose.

One day David asked me: 'Would you like to write a rock musical?' I hesitated before answering. A lifelong jazz fan, rock had always seemed to me an illegitimate offspring of the blues, whereby some smart white guys like Bill Haley and Elvis Presley ripped off the sound, but not the spirit, of the great black originals like Louis Jordan and Muddy Waters, did a slick marketing job and made millions of dollars. I still think that, as a matter of fact. David explained they had done some work with a young composer and keyboard player called Dave Greenslade, then, as now, a key member of a band called Colosseum. David thought we would work well together.

To be sure, rock musicals were all the rage. You couldn't move for them in the West End theatre and somewhere I still have a tape of a rock opera that was a big hit in Lithuania at that time. The composer (a far-out but brilliant Russian jazz pianist) wanted me to write an English libretto but I couldn't find a translator to tell me what the story was about.

I met Dave – sometimes called 'the quiet man of rock' – and we did indeed get on together. We still do. He had a shed at the bottom of his garden full of the latest musical gadgetry – fifty-seven varieties of keyboard, various percussion instruments,

some vibes and a synthesizer that would give you everything from the massed bagpipes of the Black Watch to the Vienna Boys' Choir.

I came up with a story of sorts. A young man called Benny, a plumber by trade, has done some work on a university campus and left a bag of spanners behind. He goes back to look for his spanners. He meets a wide variety of eccentric people, falls in love, wrecks a degree ceremony, then leaves. All in music and song, with a guest shot by Patrick Moore on a motorbike. You wouldn't get away with it today. I called it *Spanners Across the Campus* which was later changed to *Curriculee Curricula,* though I still prefer the original. One of the characters Benny meets is the boilerman. He looks after the boilers that heat the campus. He has one song – about being a boilerman. Our director, Alastair Reid, suggested we cast Chic Murray.

I was thrilled to bits. Over a long career I've managed to work with several comedians: Bill Maynard, Nat Jackley, the great Les Dawson, the legendary Sandy Powell, as well as the most famous straight man of them all, Jerry Desmonde. It would take too long to explain how all that happened, even supposing I could remember. But having Chic in the cast was very special. I've always described my work as falling into a category called 'gritty Northern surrealism' and he stepped into that universe as if he'd never lived in any other universe. Maybe he hadn't.

I can't remember much about the finished show. I don't have a copy on the shelf and haven't seen it since it was first transmitted, when it got what I've learned to call 'mixed' reviews, partly because some clown in BBC Publicity decided to bill it as an exercise in 'melody-rock' which seemed to me like a guaranteed way of putting people off, both those who liked rock and those who liked melody. I've been (by accident) to a Rolling Stones concert and, to be sure, melody had very little to do with what was going on.

I do remember an incident with Chic. I met him in a corridor at Pebble Mill. He'd just had a brief encounter with someone who – and it really was as simple as this – had responded to Chic's 'Good morning' with a 'Good afternoon' even though it was still morning. Chic's version of this non-conversation became a five-minute routine of extraordinary brilliance and wild fancies – a stunning performance for an audience of one.

There were no jokes, no funny lines as such, just Chic's take on the world that I found, and still find to this day, uniquely funny.

It's a quality difficult to define and impossible to explain, but as Louis Armstrong used to say of jazz: if you have to have it explained, you wouldn't understand anyway.   *Alan Plater*

Dear Chic Murray, wherever he is, will be laid back and smiling to himself at the absurdity of the afterlife and life as it was. If he's downstairs with Auld Nick with the whole place full of clergymen, pop singers and Tory politicians, he will, of course, be regaling them with subtle anecdotes about the wages of sin. If he has ended up in the other place along with God and all the Govanites and shipyard workers and jazz musicians and street bookies, Chic will also be in his element. Even if he is the only bloke in the place to have actually lived in Edinburgh! The big lad was quite simply the most original comic talent Britain has produced since Stan Laurel, and a magnificent character into the bargain.

Years ago, I was suffering from a very bad throat induced by the ravages of too many public meetings and too many fags. Chic came to see me on a Saturday night when friends and neighbours were in for a social chit-chat. He took me into the kitchen and treated me to a 'cure' for any sore throat, something he acquired from some old music-hall troupers. As I remember, it involved hot water, steam, and some tincture he had brought with him. Afterwards, Chic announced to everyone that I was forbidden to speak or smoke so he would amuse us for the rest of the evening. And so he did. Just think of it, one of our top entertainers was doing his stuff for the punters in my wee house in Clydebank.

That was Chic Murray – and wherever he is now, in heaven or in hell, the host, as always, will be the winner.

          Jimmy Reid

People don't realise what it means to be a comedian. A comedian is a man who says funny lines, but Chic, he was a natural and he didn't say funny lines, he said lines funny. You could try to have an ordinary conversation with him but halfway through you couldn't listen to him anymore, he was so funny the tears would come down your cheeks, and he didn't have to think of these things.

          Johnnie Riscoe

Chic was the master of deadpan comedy who timed the comic line to perfection. *Alex Salmond*

'Chic Murray' sounds great. I remember my dad saying, '"Chic Murray"; it's a great Glasgow name.' His material is left field without being 'I'm so close to Beckett'; none of that black tight stuff about it. Chic Murray has that Jack Benny chuck-away sort of thing without the American cool pizzazz but is very Scottish without doing shortbread-tin Scotland. *John Sessions*

There was Chic the comedian, Chic the observer of human foibles and failings, and then there was Chic the musician. Whether it was a yodel (he knew every yodelling variant, from Big Hans to Blue Grass), or the hilarious piano-playing sequence in *Gregory's Girl*, or simply a full-throated let-fly treatment of 'When You're Smiling', there came from his music-making an easy, unspoilt naturalness somewhere between simplicity and sophistication. There was a wonderful freedom about the way Chic, usually in close harmony with Maidie, managed to busk his way around a tune, never departing from the melody to any great extent but not imprisoning himself in it either. Just listen to the treatment of the song 'Ida', where he and Maidie are at it.

I never saw him performing live, but film clips are testament to how that lovely open-hearted vocal quality drew audiences to him. They loved him, I'm sure, as much for his musicianship as for his humour. Sometimes he would do a flourish, a bit of a cadenza, before the end of a number. No band to provide cover at this moment. Simply Chic, trilling away alone in the helden-tenor range. Brian Fahey and his BBC Scottish Radio Orchestra would finally invite him down to earth in the shape of the inevitable 'big ending'. For many singers this would be a mercy. But they would find Chic spot-on, in tune, at pitch.

People often wonder if naturally talented musical folk would have done better had they had full-time training. The question can't be answered with certainty. With some the talent is obviously embryonic, full of potential, and you sense the need for a strong, professional guiding hand. But with Chic the musicality is so strongly personified, so mature and ingrained, and also so much part of his unique indescribable humour. I'm thinking again of the headmaster's pawky pianism in *Gregory's*

Girl, wrists positioned just below the keyboard, rather awkwardly placed as he himself might have said. With this kind of genius nobody looks for perfection, for accuracy of execution such as he might have suffered at the hands of a musical finishing school. The remarkable thing is that, just as he was, we got both the accuracy and the genius.

Bob Simans

In 1984 I took part in *Rock Around The Clock* . . . a twelve-hour TV programme screened on BBC 2 as part of their music series, *Whistle Test*.

It was a marathon mix of live concerts, pop videos and interviews . . . and I hosted two gigs from Barrowland in Glasgow starring Aztec Camera and The Cure.

I was nervous. It was my first big telly. But things went well. The *Whistle Test* producers were pleased with my contribution and later hired me to do more work on the show.

The following week, I received a letter at the office. The envelope was stamped 'Holiday Inn, Liverpool'. I wondered why the hotel chain was contacting me. Had I forgotten to pay my room extras from a previous visit to a Holiday Inn . . . or was there a problem with a future reservation?

The handwritten address said: 'Billy Sloan, Pop Correspondent, Lemonade, Cola, American Cream Soda, Limeade, Daily Record, Anderston Quay, Glasgow G3 8DA.'

Puzzled, I ripped open the envelope and read a letter which said:

Billy,
Saw you on the telly on Saturday.
You were on before I could reach the switch.
Chic Murray

The maestro was in Liverpool playing legendary Scots football manager Bill Shankly in the stage play *You'll Never Walk Alone*. He'd clearly not shared the *Whistle Test* team's enthusiasm.

To say the letter is a prized possession is an understatement.

Billy Sloan

I never got to meet Chic Murray . . . that's a regret . . . just the wrong generation of show business . . . but God he made me laugh . . . and that takes a lot!!! Especially as a teenager, sitting

there watching this man in a tartan bunnet and overcoat who made funny, weird comments and observations on the absurdities of life. But his delivery was wonderful – that technique that looked as if he wasn't really trying, as if he had just wandered on to the stage!

At the time I was more into Marc Bolan, but the appearance of Chic Murray 'stopped the room' in our house and I loved the effect he had on my mum and dad. I loved that mixture of pride, understanding and laughter; the way my mum and dad's faces contorted as they laughed at him; the delay from hearing the gag to getting it was at times fantastic!

Culturally he was one of their own – our own; but not parochial . . . not just doing gags about being up a close in Barlanark which many of the mainstream Glasgow comics were doing at the time.

His humour was different – more universal and more absurd – but above all FUNNY.

He demonstrated that you could be observant, bright, intelligent . . . and funny.

The biggest compliment that one comic can bestow on another is to say that someone has funny bones: Chic Murray had a funny skeleton!

Him and Eric Morecambe are up there at the top of the tree and I am just so glad that he seems to have been recognised and appreciated by so many in comedy, though tragically never as recognised by the media at the time. Though that is nothing new with TV still run by metropolitan snobbery from the dominant south.

C'est la vie, eh? That's German by the way.

Thanks Chic for all you gave us as, especially the laughs. In this life they are like gold dust.   *Elaine C. Smith*

He died in 1985 but the people who remember him and carry on with him are the great comics of today. I can't really remember when I first knew about him; I feel I've *always* known about him. He was so professional.   *Timothy Spall*

I just have to think of Chic and I, you know, I feel better for just thinking about him. He was one of the all-time greats – a Scottish W.C. Fields.   *Eric Sykes*

All the comics used to go to the old variety theatres to see this man. We were in awe of him, he was so unique. He was the comedian, like Tommy Cooper, that made all the other comedians laugh – the comedian's comedian – he was so good at his job. His material was honed to perfection; it was such a thrill to have worked with him. Billy Connolly, who I adore, often reminisces about Chic; I roar with laughter.

I was privileged to have him on my TV show in 1984 and this was one of his last performances. He was wonderful. I wish he was here now so I could hear some of his patter and, yes, I would love him to do a bit of yodelling at the end of his act; such talent. *Jimmy Tarbuck*

I was having a cup of tea with Brian Cox in his Camden house about ten years ago. If memory serves, Brian was wearing a blue towelling dressing gown. Ergo, he was – how can I put this? – in relaxed mode. We had been discussing this and that (of which he knows a great deal). During a lull, I picked up a newspaper. A few minutes later Brian started giggling. He had picked up a paperback and was chuckling quietly to himself. I looked up from the paper (I'm quite versatile). He read me some of the stuff, adopting a slightly effete Greenock accent. It was immediately very funny and quite peculiar. Wedding guests with long noses, hotel bedrooms that lacked doors. I started laughing. He read some more. Soon we were both weeping hysterically. 'What is that?' I asked.

Brian looked at me in shock. 'Have you never heard of Chic Murray?'

Fast-forward a few years. Brian is now an International Movie Thesp and really very busy. We would have occasional long conversations over the internet. These would always degenerate into childish jokes and laughter (mine). And invariably I'd be fired up and saying things like, 'Brian, why don't you do *The Odd Couple* with Bill Paterson?'

'Simon, that's a very good idea.'

'With me directing!'

Long silence.

But on this occasion, I found myself saying, 'Brian, what about playing Chic Murray?'

'Simon, that's a very good idea, but Chic was tall. As a

midget that would be a bit of a stretch.'

'What about the radio? With me directing.' This time, no long silence. Brian was immediately up for it.

I pitched the idea to my loyal friend, radio producer Dirk Maggs. He loved the idea, especially with Brian attached, and took it to the BBC. They also loved it, bought it – and then presented the budget. There was no way we could do a drama on what they were offering. And so it became something simpler but arguably more in keeping with Chic's character – a lopsided celebration of a unique and adored man. During research I stayed with Chic's devoted daughter Annabelle ('Dad loved a big bowl of custard'), and met the indefatigable Maidie. I got to listen to and watch a lot of Chic archive, some of it pretty ropey because producers couldn't find the right vehicle for his talent. As anyone who was lucky enough to see Chic live knows, all he needed was a stage, a spotlight and a microphone. All kinds of people turned out to be fans, but with a passion and ardour that is quite rare. Billy Connolly, Timothy Spall, John Sessions, Bill Paterson, Barry Cryer and movie composer Patrick Doyle were among those queuing up to articulate what it was that tickled them. Often it was just a gesture or a look or a choice of word that ambushed them. Perhaps too they wanted to see Chic given his due. The tribute – with Brian narrating – went out on Radio 2 in August 2007. Gillian Reynolds of *The Daily Telegraph* called it 'a gem' and it was Radio 4's Pick of the Week.

To think it all started with a chuckle over a cup of tea. How very Chic.   *Simon Treves*

Chic Murray was one of the driest comedians I have ever known. His delivery was second to none. He was the Jack Benny of Scotland, a brilliant comedian and one of the most original talents to come out of Scotland. I mention him every night in my act and they all still adore him.

I stayed with him in digs in Manchester once in the early days; it was absolutely freezing. We sat eating our breakfasts, shivering in our overcoats. Chic eventually asked the landlady if she could open the window. The landlady with obvious surprise asked why and Chic, with perfect delivery, said, 'To let a little heat in . . .'   *Roy Walker*

I found him extremely funny.   *Terry Wogan*

THE CHIC MURRAY STORY

An excerpt from Chic Murray's obituary in The Scotsman, *30 January 1985*

Chic Murray possessed a wonderfully distinctive sense of humour which made him no less entertaining offstage than when he was performing in variety, cabaret, television and films. A tall, sturdy figure with a bunnet invariably topping off his imposing appearance, he was not a Scots comic in the conventional sense; but employed an accent that was hard to place and a style that was entirely his own. Some indication of the affection in which he was held by his colleagues in show business and broadcasting could be had from the tributes that were paid to him on hearing of his death. One of the warmest came from Alex Clark, a former secretary of Equity and a close friend of Chic Murray's. He said, 'He was always pleased to perform and was delighted with any success he had. It was the innocent pleasure which he clearly derived from giving pleasure to others that greatly impressed everyone with whom he worked.'

INDEX

A caricature of Chic and Maidie
performing their most famous song
at the Glasgow Empire

223

PAUSE
2 DRAWINGS.

(2)